P9-CLV-335

INTO THE BLAST FURNACE

COURTNEY PRATT and LARRY GAUDET

INTO THE
BLAST FURNACE

THE FORGING OF
A CEO'S CONSCIENCE

Random House Canada

Published in 2008 by Random House Canada, a division of Random House of Canada Limited. Distributed in Canada by Random House of Canada Limited.

Random House Canada and colophon are trademarks.

www.randomhouse.ca

Library and Archives Canada Cataloguing in Publication

Pratt, Courtney
Into the blast furnace : the forging of a CEO's conscience / Courtney Pratt and Larry Gaudet.

ISBN 978-0-307-35603-1

1. Pratt, Courtney. 2. Stelco Inc. 3. Chief executive officers—Canada—Biography. I. Gaudet, Larry II. Title.

HD38.2.P73 2008 338.7'669142092 C2007-906840-5

Text Design: Terri Nimmo

Printed and bound in the United States of America

10 9 8 7 6 5 4 3 2 1

To our families

Alexa
Brian, Kerri-Lynn, Sydney
Steve, Lisa, Cedar, Dawson

Alison, Jackson, Theo
The Smith and Gaudet clans

"I will live in the Past, the Present, and the Future. The Spirits of all Three shall strive within me. I will not shut out the lessons that they teach."

—Ebenezer Scrooge, from *A Christmas Carol* by Charles Dickens

CONTENTS

PRELUDE

TOO NICE A GUY

SEPTEMBER 2007

It's a blustery lakeside morning, threatening rain. From the upstairs family room in our townhouse, located in a suburb west of Toronto, I have views to the marina around the next cove, a five-minute walk along the pedestrian path that skirts Lake Ontario. The marina isn't a big operation, and is used mainly by recreational boaters. Surrounding it is persuasive evidence of gentrification: a hotel, shopping malls, condos, swatches of new parkland under which lie the remains of commercial life from generations past—the lost world of factories, shipping depots, stockyards. The jetty, constructed from boulders, slices out into the lake for perhaps three hundred metres, and my gaze tends to wander to where it ends. A tanker has been scuttled out there, parallel to the shoreline, and now functions as a sea wall. Up close, the vessel is probably a barnacled ruin, all rust and missing rivets. But from here it looks beautiful to me.

I've long been fascinated by industrial infrastructure: manufacturing plants, construction sites with soaring cranes and giant dump trucks, mining operations, oil rigs, harbours, electrical transmission towers. It's a cliché to say that men have a special attachment to machines, or to technology in general. But for much of my career, spanning more than thirty years in business, I've been at the helm of companies involved in heavy industrial activity. I know all too well that what looks benignly impressive from a distance feels different—more dangerous—once you're up close. But if you get past your awe (or fear) of large-scale mechanized activity, you realize these operations need people, and lots of them, to function effectively. When I stare admiringly at that tanker, I also see what's missing: the crew on deck or below, sweating in the boiler room and the cargo hold, everyone doing back-breaking labour, day in, day out.

This ship has a story to tell, or many stories. And while a good detective could likely dredge up old-timers who swabbed decks, coiled heavy ropes and set the rudder, before long only a few will be left to talk about what happened on those stormy nights on rough seas when the ship nearly went down. And while that's a shame, it's also reality. Stories die out if they're not shared, and the same goes for the insights that good stories offer. That's one reason why Larry Gaudet and I crafted this story about my tenure as the CEO of the steelmaker Stelco Inc., one of the great names from Canada's industrial heritage and the pride of Hamilton, Ontario, for nearly a century now. It's a story like no other in the history of Canadian business—a rollicking corporate soap opera, at times comic, but very nearly tragic. The resolution was in doubt until the very end, after playing out for two years in bold headlines in the media, where the reporting, on occasion, seemed to me a little less than informed or objective and more like character assassination, often directed at me.

When I joined Stelco in January 2004 after having served on its board of directors for nearly two years before that, my assignment was to help steer the revival of what had become an uncompetitive steel producer, struggling under high debts, including the $1.3 billion it owed to its employee pension plans. For two years or so, I was involved in making exceptionally difficult decisions that moved Stelco through a painful—and insanely protracted—process to emerge from the protection of the Canadian bankruptcy court into which we'd taken the company after years of losing money.

How to convey what that experience was like?

I was flipping TV channels one night a while back and found myself watching a show about a magician attempting to set a world record for holding his breath underwater, submerged in a glass tank with the cameras and lights on him, the crowd cheering. He intended to stay there—and remain alive—for something like eight or nine minutes. It was excruciating to watch. When it became clear that he was on the verge of unconsciousness and was inhaling water, his assistants went into the tank in scuba gear and pulled him out, just in time. All this was broadcast in prime time, a riveting spectacle, although also completely ridiculous, a manufactured crisis. But that's entertainment for you. The analogy to Stelco—and it's not perfect, I realize—is that we, as a company, were submerged underwater for the corporate equivalent of ten or maybe fifteen minutes, pretty much breathing water toward the end, floating face down in bankruptcy court and actually prevented from surfacing at times by those who put our survival at risk to serve their own needs.

None of this was produced for entertainment purposes, although there were certainly blockbuster costs. Our restructuring tallied $200 million plus in legal and consulting fees—money that would have been much better invested in making the company more competitive. But this was the price the company and its employees and shareholders paid for letting Stelco slide perilously close to ruin through years of losing money and of never resolving the fractious relations between management and the unions. Stelco's situation was far from unique, with dozens of steel companies in North America having already been through a major restructuring involving the courts. But Stelco was among the last holdouts to face the reality that it needed a total financial makeover to compete in a North American steel market increasingly subject to powerful global forces. And because restructuring had been delayed for so long, the disease of uncompetitiveness had progressed very deep, making our task much more difficult.

We stayed underwater until we fixed our finances. If we hadn't, in all likelihood a corpse—not a company—would have floated up. By the time we did come to the surface, we'd been in bankruptcy court for twenty-six months, an achievement one shouldn't be proud of. However, with so many cooks crowded into our restructuring kitchen—company executives, a battalion of lawyers, a Superior Court judge, court monitors, financial advisors, creditors, restructuring consultants, angry shareholders, hedge funds, government bureaucrats, union leaders and media commentators—it's a wonder we made it out at all.

The Stelco story, as I hope you'll come to agree, is rich with conflict and conflicted characters, including myself, and it has everything you'd want in terms of suspense and plot twists that brought out the best and the worst in the people involved. This is only one version of the Stelco story, my version, a snapshot through the lens of my memories and biases. It reflects my way of looking at the world, supported by the facts as I understood them to be, if not always how I wanted them to be. The stakes for Stelco and for me, as its CEO, had never been higher, and the consequences of failure would have been disastrous—liquidation, layoffs, economic catastrophe for Hamilton. It was the wildest, most challenging assignment of my professional life. And while this restructuring process unleashed plenty of rage and a few tears, the sound that lingers in my ears is the laughter of my colleagues—and pretty much everyone on all sides of the story—as we worked together, argued, negotiated and fought through long days and even longer nights to save the company from being scuttled.

Even when things were at their absolute worst, there was laughter—the most redemptive of all human sounds.

I hear Alexa in the next room on the phone, talking to our daughter-in-law about the new baby, an exchange between mother and grandmother about sleeping patterns, dietary quirks, teething. Our two sons are grown men, both fathers themselves, and by now I consider myself fairly fluent in on-demand parenting advice. But listening to my wife is always a tutorial on empathy in action.

In Alexa's voice are proven reserves of patience and wisdom shared without conveying that she always knows best. Still, after our thirty-nine years together, it never fails to amaze me how judicious she can be, how sensitive to the nuances in a conversation. As I eavesdrop for a minute, I hear that she listens at least as much as she talks, reacts as much as initiates and always responds on the basis that the quality of the ritual is as important as the advice dispensed.

In the midst of the restructuring, Alexa was diagnosed with cancer. There's not much I will divulge about that, out of respect for her privacy and mine. Anyone who has had a life-threatening illness understands the fear that metastasizes in you, and everyone close to you, through rounds of medical consultations, invasive surgery and the worries that come at night when the data you found on the Internet about mortality rates presents itself for sleepless contemplation. Alexa is in remission now, a full recovery, although the scars—in every sense—are fresh enough.

Her illness was one of many factors that affected how I made decisions that had consequences for thousands of other people at Stelco. And the fact that we were facing her illness probably affected those decisions for the better, if truth be told, even in those moments when all I could really focus on was her terrible confrontation with cancer.

You can choose not to learn from the hardest life experiences. Or you can absorb the blow and, if you're lucky, use it to humanize yourself—to focus your attention on the people who matter.

There's no such thing as work-life balance when a life could hang in the balance. On the day Alexa was in surgery for something like ten or eleven hours, I was as lost as I have ever been in my life, sometimes in the hospital coffee shop, other times wandering the streets of Toronto in a daze, occasionally responding to the BlackBerry on my hip that kept me informed of developments at Stelco as our restructuring careened out of control. At times the digital intrusion felt obscene, and it was, but let me tell you something else: a man flinging e-mails to his colleagues while his wife is on the operating table had better be making principled decisions on matters of substance only. He'd better be functioning with the fear of God in him, and with respect for those who are not in his position of responsibility and influence.

During that time I often felt like quitting and focusing all my attention on Alexa. I didn't quit. And I've had to ask myself why, given that I didn't need the Stelco job to support us. Without any doubt I could have walked away from Stelco. Someone would have replaced me and the restructuring would have gone on and things would have worked out. Only an egomaniac would suggest otherwise. But in the stress of the situation, Alexa and I agreed we could get through everything together, with me staying on at Stelco. This decision wasn't a pragmatic calculation to keep up appearances or prove what fantastic multi-taskers we are. It came out of the spirit of our bond and the deepest beliefs we share. I had taken the Stelco job because I believed I was in the best position to help the company through one of the most difficult chapters in its long history. And once I joined, I was committed. My integrity was on the line; I had to do the best I could, especially for the employees and pensioners who were counting on us. I had jobs and pensions to protect—many thousands of them.

There are moments when what you feel or experience or choose to do cannot be justified by logic. All arguments are defeated and all words pointless. All you can do is put one foot in front of the other, and keep walking.

During this difficult time, I needed to be the person my wife believed she had married all those years ago, someone who wouldn't throw up his hands in defeat when the world demanded more than he could or should give. Rationing your integrity—or conserving it—isn't always possible. It's not like making a choice about what kind of car or computer to buy.

Alexa isn't the type to belabour the costs of the sacrifices involved. She is courageous, an inspiration to me in a way I can't adequately describe within the pages of any book. When I reflect on the decisions we made together, I can see that neither of us complained to each other or to the world, and neither of us boasts today about the rewards, which in any case, like everything else in life, can be taken away in an instant. We both questioned the wisdom of my staying on at Stelco, if not once a day, then often enough. We persevered.

It didn't seem like there was a choice.

I'm too nice a guy—

How many times have I heard that line?

It has been spoken openly to my face by well-meaning colleagues intent on providing support in hard times. It has been relayed in hushed tones of pretend concern by the office gossips who emerge from the rumour flow with words from anonymous critics, of which there are always too many. Sometimes the message is carried by a complicated smile over lunch before the bill arrives, a weak handshake after a speech I've given, a cough at the end of the boardroom table while the vote is taken. It's a feeling I've had now and then after walking into a meeting and recognizing that the conversation I've just interrupted is all about how I'm not measuring up to a standard of brutality expected from a CEO.

Too nice to succeed in business. Too nice to be an effective CEO.

I'm not too nice to say that most of the people who think and say these things probably know less than they should about the recipe for success—not just in business, but in life itself.

The business world has its fair share of nasty characters. That's because business concerns itself with making money. Greed for financial gain can bring out a very visible form of ruthlessness. A flamboyant disregard for ethical behaviour, as I've seen—as we've all seen—can have ugly consequences when decisions are made to lay off thousands to create enough space on the balance sheet to justify obscene executive bonuses, or to generate even more obscene profits to reward speculators who invest in a company's shares hoping for a quick turnaround.

Let's leave greed aside for a minute—because we'll return to it soon enough in this tale. My point is, as someone who has had some success as the CEO or president of several multi-billion-dollar businesses, including Stelco, I have some trouble with those who say I'm too nice to succeed and yet miss the fact that I've been fairly successful in my career. Either I'm not nearly as nice as they say I am, or their definition of nice is superficial, or their understanding of leadership is seriously warped, which can be a consequence of inexperience in—or disappointment at—how the world actually works.

When you're required to make tough decisions to save or strengthen a business—or any organization, community or volunteer group, or, more intimately, a family—you can get pretty burned out under the strain and become cynical. It can be difficult to remain positive after you fire someone or break off a friendship or discipline someone for everyone's good. There are good and bad ways to make decisions, but there's no joy in closing a plant or a failing business unit, even if you're doing the right thing for the right reason—such as preserving the rest of the company and the jobs inside it. In these and other challenging circumstances, you can easily start to wonder whether you're still the good person you believed you were before things got sticky. Before you know it, you're wallowing in disgust at yourself and the world. You begin to think, hey, I'm not a nice guy any more. And neither, therefore, is anyone else.

It's an understandable response—but I mistrust it.

I have my strengths and weaknesses, the virtues and the vices of personality, including the blind spots in my psychology—the unknown unknowns, so to speak. But I do take some pride in being alert to the need to act responsibly when confronted with the ethical dilemmas that inevitably face everyone in business, where, to be frank, the smarter companies live and continue to make money and employ people while the dumber ones go broke and let their people go.

During our court-supervised restructuring, foremost in my mind, always, was protecting some six thousand jobs and upward of ten thousand retiree pensions that were on the line as we fought to stabilize this debt-ridden company. Even with that clarity of purpose this was no easy ride, and things I thought I knew I had to learn again. I experienced first-hand more than I wanted about how money talks—and indeed talks loudly and arrogantly—in shaping our world and our relationships to one another.

A year and a half after I left the job in the spring of 2006, I can say that when I look at myself in the mirror in the morning, my first reaction isn't disappointment. I did what I did for motives and goals I'll defend as long as I breathe, recognizing that outcomes can always be better—or simply different—and that my decisions made some people very angry, too, and took money out of their pockets. For me, the restructuring was a test that brought into focus the challenge in doing what our conscience tells us to do in times of crisis.

As the CEO of a large corporation, you cannot possibly know every employee among the thousands affected by your decisions. Yet you're accountable to them, and are managing as best you can complex forces that affect their livelihoods. You're accountable to shareholders, to the banks and bondholders who lend the company money, to the communities where the business operates and to governments. You're on the hook in so many ways, at the centre of a matrix of responsibility that can tear you apart if you don't have an appetite for complexity and, more importantly, if you're not anchored by empathy for those who don't work in the office next to you or belong to your club or go to the same fundraisers.

Empathy resides in each of us in different measures; we are not all gifted equally. But no matter how wonderfully empathetic you think you are on your better days, sometimes you have to work harder than you ever thought possible to maintain a human connection to people you'll never know—not really—as more than an input, a number on your cost analyses, in your business case. At the end of the day, though, you still need to answer the question: how can I do my job and remain human—true to my beliefs? And that work, in large measure, is a creative act. It is an act of moral imagination.

By the time Alexa gets off the phone, I'm dressed in my workout gear, ready for a jog. It looks like rain, but what the heck. I'm gone with a wave, my wife's voice silenced by the door closing behind me. If it rains, she wants me to come in the back door up through the garage, take off my muddy sneakers and put any wet clothing in the laundry before coming upstairs. Or else I'm dead.

I've always relied on exercise to help me gain a fresh perspective on things. It stops me from fretting about a problem and lets new thoughts flow to me. To that end, I've been trying to nail down how best I can summarize what the Stelco restructuring has taught me.

There is so much to say, and yet so much I'm not interested in saying. Scholarly articles will be written by and for lawyers about the precedents set in the courtroom that could affect how future bankruptcies are handled. There's probably a business reporter out there looking to persuade one of the main characters into a tell-all, score-settling account. I have zero interest in that. Economists and management thinkers may well write at length about Stelco as a case study in financial and industrial globalization, especially given that the company, after its successful exit from bankruptcy protection, was soon up for sale and later was bought by the American steel producer, U.S. Steel. But let me say here that I believe the deal is a very good one for Stelco, including for its employees and pensioners. Ownership may have transferred out of the country, but today this trend is evident worldwide, across the natural resources and commodities sector. Global conglomerates are buying what they can, where they can. And the nationality of a company—what does it mean any more? Is it about who owns the bonds and shares? Or where the jobs are? Or where the capital investments are made? Under the conditions of the Stelco sale, the workers and pensioners are better protected than they were beforehand. And as this story will chronicle, Stelco's fate came close to being much worse.

In theory, I have all the time in the world to contemplate what happened at Stelco. I don't have a full-time job at the moment, and it's taking some getting used to. I serve on some corporate boards. I do plenty of volunteering, something I've always done as an individual and as a CEO who believes companies need to have a strong community presence. I spend loads of wonderful time with the family, getting in the way of Alexa around the house and, more profitably, enjoying the freedom to visit our kids and their kids as a doting granddad. But what I'm most sensitive to right now is that I'm no longer deeply enmeshed in the human networks of the business world. I miss the people I worked with.

On my jog, I see all kinds of people on the path: teenagers on a date, an elderly woman walking a dog the size of a handbag, a guy who blows past me, clearly in shape for a triathlon. For an instant I try to imagine how they got here, what motivates them, where they're going. It sounds so simple: I'm interested in people and relationships. The human dimension in the story.

I make it back inside just as the rain begins to pour.

I cut it very close—but the best of life comes from calculated risk.

This book draws some inspiration from a comment attributed to the legendary business writer Tom Peters. To paraphrase him, if you're interested in relationships, in the human dimension of business, then maybe you should be reading more novels and fewer business books. This—from a guy who has sold millions of business books?

But I understand what he means. Relationship-building—as all competent business people know—is the essence of success in business. In everything.

The conventional wisdom is that novelists appreciate that the bones of every good story are the relationships that bring the human condition alive on the page. Novelists understand relationships and represent them through fully formed characters engaged in dramatic scenarios. There is a counterargument, naturally: novelists know very little about business culture and tend to view it superficially, as populated mainly by plutocrats who denude the pension plans, throw the workers into the streets and line their own pockets. Countless novels have presented business people as venal stereotypes, undeserving of sympathy. You might even say it's a grand tradition in the literary trade.

But what if the novelist and the business person came together in common cause? What if they brought the strengths of the novel into the world of business, and the experience of business people to the novel?

In telling my Stelco story, Larry Gaudet and I have relied on the techniques of the novelist to open up experiences that business journalism (at least in our opinion) doesn't normally allow. Much of what you'll read is reality as I recollect it, my truth turned into corporate memoir. I'm the main character, usually viewed from a third-person perspective, and sometimes viewed critically, too. It just felt like the right thing to do: to be described as others might see me. We changed the names of a few characters to protect the innocent, as they say. We also created a single composite character, blending into one person a couple of financiers I became acquainted with during the restructuring. The financier in this book is a comic figure, and greedy in a style I found callous. I suppose I could have named names here. I'm just not comfortable with that. The scenes involving this character describe events that really happened—let that be absolutely clear. As well, a few scenes from my domestic life with Alexa and conversations with my colleagues are reconstructions that we've often compressed for dramatic effect. It's the stuff of memoirs, based on real events and recollections, shaped to tell a story economically.

Between each of the main chapters there are conversations, or interludes, featuring me interacting with fictional characters, each of whom represents a dimension of my conscience as the Stelco CEO, in a variation on the technique used to great effect by Charles Dickens in *A Christmas Carol.* It's up to the reader to judge whether this fictionalizing works, but our goal is to literally humanize the CEO's conscience. And, in so doing, we have tried to bring to life the notion that ethical activity is really a principled act of the moral imagination. Which means what? To demonstrate conscience—for a CEO to operate ethically—he or she must be something of an adventurer of the mind, capable of travelling into the lives of those affected by executive decisions and hearing their voices, especially when they're not in the room. As you'll see, I considered myself accountable to a range of stakeholders, including the steelworker on the factory floor and the pensioner at home.

For the CEO of a large corporation to tell a story through the concerns of workers and retirees, and to give their voices a fair measure of prominence in the narrative mix—this seems to me a very exciting proposition. It offers a fresh way of looking at the challenge of leadership and reflects my belief that leaders need to be connected to viewpoints that can be distant from their own but are nonetheless valid.

I've learned in my life that truth best emerges in the cut and thrust of relationships. Truth takes shape when people genuinely listen to each other and, sometimes, shift their points of view because of that dialogue. I would also say that sometimes truth can only be understood as a conflict between differing points of view, or many points of view.

On that basis, let us begin the dialogue.

CHAPTER ONE

SCARY TERRITORY

DAY ONE

Courtney Pratt is behind the wheel as the Volvo sedan reverses away from the bungalow, the world still sunless, just enough light now to distinguish trees in the ravine behind this quiet suburban street. It feels colder out than the zero degrees suggested by the dashboard—a typical Toronto morning in early winter, which means it doesn't look like winter at all, the ground snowless, ice patches speckled in dead leaves and dog crap. He's been awake since a quarter to six, five minutes before the alarm was set to buzz. It drives Alexa nuts that he can usually do this six days out of seven. He's heading out for his first day on the job as the CEO of Stelco, dressed to the executive nines: dark suit, white shirt, brogues, a BlackBerry on his hip, a wool overcoat tossed into the back seat with his soft leather briefcase. His tie is a palette of Haida symbols: feathers, dorsal fins, bones and animal eyes. A totem pole on his chest.

On his street, hockey nets and basketball hoops are visible in a number of driveways, along with unlocked bikes, including one that lies in the browned grass of a front yard and another that leans against an SUV, damaging the paint job. Near the first intersection, Pratt sees a kid, maybe thirteen or fourteen, lugging a hockey bag through a yard toward a parked station wagon, his gait suggesting he's headed to the adolescent equivalent of recreational imprisonment without parole. His mother is a few steps ahead, her car keys in hand. The kid wears a toque pulled low on his forehead, a Leafs sweater down to his knees and construction boots so flagrantly untied, the tongues hanging over the toes, and evidently two sizes too big, that it's a wonder he hasn't tripped himself. The mother is saying something the kid isn't in any mind to hear yet in this journey to the inevitability of hockey practice, his gloveless hands bunched into his sleeves, a yawn on his face resentfully stifled when his mother turns to him after she unlocks the car. This domestic exchange makes Pratt smile.

As a boy, Pratt fell asleep on many winter nights, exhausted from the hours at the rink only two streets away from the duplex where he grew up in Montreal. He spent all his free time at that rink, after dinner, after homework, playing pickup games on ice made by human hands according to a simple recipe of subzero weather and a water hose, which produced overlapping, rarely blemish-free sheets—not like the outdoor rinks today, the ice manufactured by sophisticated refrigeration platforms and maintained to glistening uniformity by a Zamboni. In his youth, mothers didn't drive their sons to the rink or nag them to pack their face masks, jockstraps and cellphones. There *were* no face masks then, except for goalies, and it was still that way when he played at McGill. He played three years for a varsity squad that didn't win much, but they practised and competed and hit one other hard in that drafty arena where Pine Avenue starts climbing the mountain.

Comfortably settled above the seat warmers, Pratt fiddles with the radio in search of a traffic update as he enters the poshest area of the neighbourhood. To the northeast of downtown Toronto, the Bridle Path is characterized by properties sized to hobby-farm proportions for those who have arrived in life or who are in the process of arriving perhaps just a little too fast. It seems that every new home is either a faux French château or a Tudor monstrosity, mingling not so harmoniously, Pratt thinks, with a sprinkling of modernist bunkers whose roofs are barely visible above swales of designer landscaping. Pratt considers many of these houses to be the product of unbalanced egos. Then it occurs to him—and for the first time, too—that he enjoys visitors' reactions to his and Alexa's home when they realize that the single storey viewed from the street turns inside into two storeys that hang over the ravine slope, presenting views of a secluded back yard that blends seamlessly into forest. He loves the contrast between the modest exterior and the dramatic interior. He also likes to throw people for a loop. He and Alexa are only settling into their ravine sanctuary a year after buying it, and now they'll be moving yet again, something they've done many times for his career. His employment contract stipulates that he live closer to Hamilton. They've chosen Oakville, a twenty-minute drive to Stelco's steel mill.

He exits onto a boulevard that leads to the Don Valley Parkway, which cuts down through the city and is weirdly traffic-free when he merges onto it. Today is a lost day in the corporate calendar, a Friday sandwiched between the weekend and New Year's Day—the perfect opportunity for staff to orchestrate one more long weekend in the holiday season. But he expects that only a few people around head office will exercise that option. The steel mill is running flat out, a full set of shifts going, the place hopping, as it must. And corporate headquarters will contain a full cadre of senior managers today mainly because the new CEO is marking out territory for the first time. He feels bad about that. Why jump the gun? There will be plenty of overwork coming, the sacrifice of family time and holidays, given the financial crisis facing the company, the need to rethink everything and make serious changes or risk something drastic, like liquidation.

"Why the hell did you take this job?" a bewildered friend had asked him over drinks just before Christmas. "It's not like you need the money."

He replied, "Saving Stelco is essential to the country, to our manufacturing base, to the economy. It's a once-in-a-lifetime challenge. To give something back—there's an altruistic element. I just couldn't say no."

"There's no ego in this? Come on, Courtney."

His friend wasn't wrong. Pratt is in the national spotlight once more, and he's pleased by this condition of his employment, even though he would never let on to anyone that he is.

Southbound, he navigates the lazy curves of the road that flows with the contours of the ravines along the Don River.

Soon the road elevates and banks westbound onto the Gardiner, the expressway that cuts across downtown along the lakeshore, past the skyscrapers where he pursued his corporate career for many years. There he learned the management trade, distinguishing himself as an executive unafraid to bring new ideas into human resources and strategic planning, his initial areas of competence. By the time he moved on to join the Stelco board in 2002, he knew people who counted, the movers and shakers, the CEOs, the financiers on Bay Street and the politicians who made things happen. Today he's embedded in overlapping networks of influence because of his previous executive positions, board appointments, club memberships and volunteer work for big charities and hospitals during fundraising drives. He's learned to take money out of suit jackets and silk purses and move it to a cancer ward, a soup kitchen, a school where youngsters arrive on empty stomachs.

A commuter train slides past on his right.

To his left, Lake Ontario. Even in the sombre light, it's impressive, an inland sea. There's something about the relative emptiness of the highway and the lake view that reminds him that he's happy. He went out the door this morning in high gear, his mind a hungry sponge, ready for the multi-tasking madness required of a CEO of a large public company.

As he drives through the western outskirts of the city, it's now eight lanes of expressway traffic, a panorama of concrete and billboards, logos in the sky, a spaghetti of access ramps to the malls or other highways or a new subdivision. The highway is busier here, the vehicular mass moving above the speed limit. He scans his mirrors diligently, occasionally turning his head to check the blind spot that the car salesman said wasn't there but actually is, if you study these things, and he does.

He comes to a fork in the road.

Right takes him into downtown Hamilton to the corporate head office. It's the shorter route to work.

Left goes over the Skyway, a mammoth bridge high above Hamilton Bay, with the lake on the left and the Stelco steel mill and its docking facilities on the right. It's the longer way in.

Left, and up.

Sunlight emerges from a long rip in the clouds over the water, tinting the lake metallic grey. He glances over to the steel mill across the bay. It's all blue sky there, into which flames spurt from exhaust piping, the result of one process or another harnessing tremendous heat to produce steel, turning it from a burning liquid into slabs that are crunched and rolled into thin sheets the length of a football field. To some, no doubt, the Stelco complex is a nightmare vision, tentacles of steam-emitting pipes and struts, a giant lobster-monster from outer space. But Pratt sees a facility where some three thousand people earn a living, an industrial asset essential to the Hamilton economy. He never tires of contemplating the effort—hell, the miracle—involved in keeping these operations functioning productively, profitably and, most of all, safely.

The Hamilton mill—nearly a hundred years old, a symbol of Stelco's heritage as a Canadian industrial icon—is one of two manufacturing facilities in southern Ontario that make up the bulk of the company's operations. Hamilton produces about two million tonnes of steel a year in various forms—sheets, slabs and bars—that are transported to customers all around the Great Lakes and beyond to make cars, construction materials, appliances, highway culverts and other products. The other big operation is a two-hour drive from here on the shores of Lake Erie.

Coming off the Skyway, it's all heavy industry around him, not a single person on foot. Much of the land bordering the highway is given over to pyramids of coal, gravel, limestone and other raw materials. He exits onto an expressway that backs into the city through the industrial heart of Hamilton, a world of scrap yards, acres of mulched cars and ruined household appliances, along with manufacturing facilities—not just Stelco, but non-unionized Dofasco, the vastly more successful twin in the Hamilton steel family.

Stelco was born here, Pratt thinks, but could it also die here? The Hamilton mill needs plenty of investment to become competitive again. It has a high cost structure generally, and very high labour costs in particular, for the amount of steel it produces. It needs a big makeover: newer technology, newer processes and, most importantly, Pratt believes, a smaller, more effective workforce, freed from the bureaucratic culture that has taken root at Stelco over the years. And where's the money to accomplish all that, given the company's crushing debt load? In contrast, the Lake Erie mill is the most modern steelmaking facility in North America, its workforce about half the size of Hamilton's. As Pratt sees it, combining Hamilton and Lake Erie into an interdependent steel manufacturing system is critical to Stelco's future, the goal being to create much-needed economies of scale for the company. He also believes that raising cash to fix the company and lowering its cost structure will require selling off several smaller steel-related businesses and, in the process, getting rid of unprofitable product lines and dropping two thousand people from the payroll. Tough stuff.

Soon he's approaching downtown along a main drag that runs in the direction of Stelco headquarters, which are located on the top floors of a colossally bland office building. The elation he felt this morning subsides a bit. The building is so imposingly drab, so devoid of character that it almost disappears on him, giving nothing to the street except cold shadows and windswept alleys. It's also costing more money than Stelco can afford. One of his first orders of business, he thinks, should be to give up this space—pay the penalty to break the lease—and move the management group into the old headquarters next to the steel mill, a building that, while lacking in amenities, at least has some connection to Stelco's past. He needs to communicate the message that the company is serious about making changes and getting reconnected to the business on the ground floor, and he needs to do it fast.

As he parks in a public lot across the street, unable to drive into the parking lot below the building until he gets his corporate passcard, he reminds himself that he's walking into a bully's paradise at Stelco, with the occasional psychopath in the room, particularly when management and the union get together to negotiate collective agreements.

These encounters are often reduced to marathon pissing matches, an exercise in determining who's tougher, who blinks, who falls down first crying for Mama. Me or you? Stelco has a reputation as the poster child for horrible labour relations, with a legacy of bitter strikes going back decades, some legal, some not, often resolved by eleventh-hour deals, no one ever willing to give an inch. It's been a place where humiliating your opponent or even the people on your own team has often been done for sport, to get ahead or even just to fit in.

And the worst part, Pratt thinks, is that this approach has never resulted in a more competitive company, but quite the opposite.

Bullshit. Absolute bullshit. From the last century.

The elevator dispatches him on an executive floor at two minutes to eight. They're all waiting for him, which is clear from the furtive glances, the corridor buzz as he walks in. There are hands to shake and Happy New Year salutations. As he expected, lots of people are at work today simply because they knew he was coming. Nearing the end of the hellos, boisterous male laughter erupts from behind the closed doors of the boardroom. When Pratt checks in, he sees his chief operating officer, Colin Osborne, holding court with a contingent of external advisors from various law, investment banking and insolvency management firms.

"Oh, another consultant in a nice suit," Osborne says to Pratt, in a mock sarcastic voice, leaning back in his chair.

Forty at most, fairly tall, Osborne has the gangly presence of a guy who doesn't like to sit still for long. As Pratt walks toward him, Osborne clicks a ballpoint pen a bit manically, offering the room a hooded, playful glance.

"Well, Colin, I see you've taken your promotion seriously, it being entirely customary to greet your new CEO like this," Pratt says, walking behind Osborne to give him a friendly slap on the back.

"Happy New Year, Courtney. We have some serious financial engineering going on, which I don't get. I'm a mechanical engineer."

"Don't let this wiseass fool you," Pratt says to the room. "He was working from home on this all through the holidays."

Osborne has other jokes on his lips but stops himself. His humour has an edge better left disguised: genuine discomfort at having his Stelco world lanced by a bunch of outsiders earning big fees to tell him what he already knows, that the company is sucking more cash than it produces.

Pratt notices that Osborne is engaged in some internal war, but he's glad to see the tension blended with the upbeat cockiness. Osborne is ready for a fight. He's the best Stelco has to offer, the guy who won the medals at university and then spent nearly all his career here, rising through the ranks without, miraculously, getting blinkered by the culture. He's still open to new influences, still wanting to learn, on the cusp of being a CEO himself, his head full of schemes. About six months earlier, with the help of another board member, Pratt had convinced Osborne to stay at Stelco. It was dicey for a while because Osborne had accepted a job with another steel company, claiming he wanted out of the negative environment at Stelco, fed up with the war-zone mentality in the relations between management and the Hamilton union local in particular. Pratt told Osborne that the board wanted to overhaul Stelco's work culture. It's a process Pratt now wants to start by addressing head-on the complete lack of trust between management and the union. He wants to introduce modern management methods, the basics that all good companies have these days, like policies for treating employees as human beings with aspirations and integrity who respond better to the carrot not just the stick, rather than as prisoners who must be guarded, regimented, kept in line, controlled at all times.

He signals for Osborne to step into the corridor with him for a moment. "We have our hands full," Pratt says, after Osborne follows him out. "But the work you've been doing—it's a huge help to the company and to me personally."

Osborne takes in the compliment, the wisecracker in him momentarily caged. "Work? Before Christmas I thought we were in the steel business. But I've become an investment banker overnight."

"You'll get back to making steel, Colin."

"I've got operations guys crawling all over me with big plans to spend real money in the first half. Real money."

"We're going to have to look at that very prudently."

"Prudently?"

Marg Hutchison saves him from explaining with a tap on the shoulder. His new assistant speaks bluntly, long accustomed to thinking two steps ahead of men who believe they can solve the world's problems but who can't make a pot of coffee or use the photocopier without jamming it. She leads him through the morning, including the ritual of getting his ID photo taken for his passcard. He doesn't like the photo because of the frown. But what's he going to say to the guy behind the camera? That the new CEO needs a smile on his face? Pratt knows he'd freak him out. He thanks him politely by his first name, and gets moving again.

His office is nothing fancy, but it has great views of Hamilton Bay. Eagerly he sits down to get acquainted with his new computer. There are probably twenty or thirty urgent e-mails waiting by now, and he can't get too far behind on that front. And there are several websites he needs to surf for breaking news in the steel business.

The computer requires him to enter a security code each and every time he wants to use the Internet.

What the hell—

"The IT people made the decision," Marg Hutchison tells him.

"They did, did they? And this applies to everyone?"

"I think so."

"Can you ask them to take it off my computer?"

"Yes, Mr. Pratt."

"Call me Courtney, please."

"Fine, Mr. Courtney."

She laughs and he does too, which relaxes them both.

He takes pleasure in being approachable, a regular guy who can chat about the ball game with a secretary or maintenance guy, or have a sandwich in the cafeteria with a trucker or welder. Approachability is a means he has long employed to draw people into his world and to build their confidence. For Pratt, it's a proven way to make the people working for him more productive, which in turn makes him a better manager, the kind of leader you'd want to hire as a CEO. He has regrettably seen too many careers stall when otherwise talented, hard-working managers fail to help their people become better at their jobs, often because they believe themselves in competition with their subordinates.

At Stelco, he's under a microscope again, his behaviour a source of constant study by his managers, some looking for clues to help them adapt so that they can ensure their job stability in the new regime. Those who ape his management style and suddenly become the "people person" they never were he'll come to trust the least. He places a premium on honesty, or authenticity, or whatever the proper word is these days for when how you act on the job is, in essence, who you are, and not a superficial corporate persona bolted hypocritically over the real you.

In the boardroom, Pratt reviews his notes for a conference call. Then he contemplates the speakerphone. He has no idea how to operate it and is willing to bet there's someone on staff whose only real job is to operate the speakerphone and therefore has no intention of sharing that information with anyone else in the interests of job security. He considers himself adept at learning the quirks of new office technology, pridefully ignoring the manual, preferring to bumble along and learn by time-consuming experimentation. But the speakerphone looks to be something from centuries ago, a minor upgrade on the device that Alexander Graham Bell made the original call on. Something to break codes with in the war. This thing has knobs. He walks around the device, trying to decide whether to push buttons, call for help or rip it out of the wall.

His assistant returns just in time to make it work. Crisis averted.

It's just after two when he realizes he's hungry. He takes an elevator down to the food court below the building. He thinks maybe he'll pick up bottled water and a fruit salad at the deli. He also intends to check out the health club. He wants to keep in shape during the workaholic months that are coming. When he gets off the elevator, he experiences the only truly depressing moment of the day. The dark-tiled floor is greasy under his feet, and the tables are occupied by the most fragile and disenfranchised, many seniors—disabled seniors—hunched over franchise coffee. The indigent are there too, shifty-eyed and scared of everything.

Alexa calls him as the late-afternoon sunset bathes his office in a surreal glow. He tells her he'll be home before seven, maybe eight, an early night, although there are conference calls planned for the weekend and volumes of analytical work prepared for him on Stelco's competitive position that he has to get through. His first day at the office has been a pattern of orchestrated and random busyness. There were many phone calls, e-mails, reports to read, corridor chat with his COO, CFO and other executives. Everyone in the office was on high management alert, ready to get on board with the new CEO and take on new assignments. All this Pratt expected, and as the work day starts to wind down, he starts to feel comfortable in his bunker in the sky.

DAY THREE

Sunday morning. The phone.

"Courtney, I've got bad news," the PR guy says.

"What?"

"We've had a horrible accident at the mill. A fatality."

"Jesus Christ, no. No. What happened?"

"We don't know everything yet. But the investigation has started."

"Does he have a family? Wife and kids?"

"Yes."

His worst nightmare: the death of an employee.

He goes to the funeral home in Hamilton, where he extends his condolences to the man's widow and children. He sees a contingent from Stelco, co-workers and union leaders. There is a lot of awkward standing around. When the service begins, Pratt joins the mourners, his thoughts drifting. It irritates him when people refer to the steel business as low-tech, because the Stelco mills are full of new technology, even if Hamilton has fallen behind. But the coffin before him, he realizes, offers a rebuke to that irritation. A steel mill isn't a "clean room" by any means, a software lab where an accident will lose money, not take a life. No matter how obsessed a company is about safety—and safety has been an obsession of his wherever he's worked—a steel mill is still a dangerous place that can steal a life when even a small thing goes wrong.

WINTER FOG

In Toronto's financial district, Pratt walks into an afternoon surprise that lifts his spirits: fat snowflakes in the air, pixels of whiteness descending in slow motion, dusting his coat and smearing his glasses as he joins a swarm of pedestrians on a traffic-congested street. The first snowstorm of the year. He enters the ground-floor mall of the city's tallest office building, First Canadian Place, and exits onto King Street to face towers built of grids of black steel and glass. Midway across the pedestrian plaza he glances up into the falling snow to see a cloud bank hovering below the skyscraper rooflines. Watching a building disappear above you is an amazing sight, he thinks. He stops for a minute and lets a snowflake melt onto his hand. He changes his mind about the storm. It'll turn to rain soon. It's not nearly cold enough.

He steps into the high-ceilinged, glass-paned lobby of the TD tower, two minutes ahead of his next meeting. After a quick BlackBerry scroll, he looks up to see that fog has permeated the plaza. He thinks it's still snowing, but it's hard to tell now, given the garish streaks of condensation forming on the giant windows. When he gets off the elevator at the offices of McCarthy Tétrault, the firm that is Stelco's outside legal counsel, Pratt has a moment to admire the views. On a clear day he would be able to see across the lake to upstate New York, some fifty kilometres, and to Hamilton to the west and the Scarborough Bluffs to the east. Today the hefty slice of view available to him looks like what you'd see out of an airplane—blue skies streaked in faint brushstrokes of white cloud, the sun a yellow ball, and below him, a few floors down, the fog bank.

"Amazing, we get to work here," Mike Barrack says coming into the room, inviting Pratt to join him at the table.

Barrack is lanky, athletic, a man in his early fifties who wears a suit without looking taxidermied. He's a high-energy guy, not a watt wasted.

A sandwich tray sits between them.

"I had an office like this when I was downtown," Pratt says.

"Sandwich?"

"Thanks, but I've had lunch."

Pratt reaches for a chocolate chip cookie, breaks it in two and takes half for himself but leaves it untouched on his plate. He's not relaxed. He hasn't been clear with himself about why he needs to see Barrack, or what he hopes to accomplish in this meeting. Barrack is an ace litigator, the guy who thinks on his feet, the performance artist who lives (or dies) in front of the judge or jury, the crowd in the gallery, the media on the courtroom steps.

The conversation remains in get-to-know-you preliminaries, and Pratt wants it to stay there. He does know he needs to size Barrack up because of the important role the lawyer will necessarily play, as the company's advocate in the courtroom, should Stelco apply for protection under the Companies' Creditors Arrangement Act, commonly known as CCAA. This federal law enables financially troubled companies to restructure their financial affairs under the supervision of the courts. In its simplest incarnation, CCAA allows companies to avoid paying their creditors while seeking new financing or working out new terms of creditor repayment, which can include a reduction or forgiveness of some debts if a company can't pay them all back. The catch is that creditors have the right to vote on any refinancing plan, and they play a pivotal role in determining whether a company is allowed out of CCAA as a going concern or is declared bankrupt. Pratt, for all his corporate experience, has never managed a company in CCAA. And this worries him. Once inside CCAA, should that happen, Stelco's destiny becomes a matter of what judges and lawyers argue about in their black robes.

Barrack is chatting now about his son's progress at a golf academy, the kid's ability to drive the ball, which sometimes gets him into trouble. "He needs to understand shot selection if he wants to compete," he says. The talk about golf twigs with Pratt. He imagines Barrack coming from a world similar to his own, the middle of the bell curve of the vaguely WASP middle class, in Barrack's case perhaps in North Toronto, or small-town southern Ontario: a guy who had a decent start in life, then bettered that start on his own, drawn to the challenges and rewards of professional life.

"Did you play a lot of golf as a kid, Mike?" Pratt asks.

"Ah, no," Barracks says, and then volunteers, "We moved around a lot. My dad was a salesman when he was working, and there was a lot of moving around until he left. And then it was the basement days. Me and my mom, my younger brother. I guess I became a father even before I had kids."

"Where did your parents come from?"

"I'm Lebanese on my father's side. Irish-Canadian on my mother's."

"Barrack is a Lebanese name?"

"It may have been spelled differently at some point."

Barrack speaks with candour about his background and with efficiency. Clearly he has told this story before, but it is nonetheless forceful. Now Pratt gets an inkling of why people who know Barrack well say that he can win a case, decisively, in a thousand words or less in the closing argument, not with the ten thousand words the opposing lawyer uses in a losing cause. Barrack has moved on to talk about the law—a profession, he says, in which he sharpens his own sense of right and wrong every day. How did they get onto that? However they did, this talk impresses Pratt.

"CCAA decision time is approaching for us," Pratt says. "We're not ready to go to the board for a final decision. Another week or so. We are fine-tuning the estimates, and it's not a pretty picture of long-term solvency. You tell me what you need from us, and you'll get it."

"We'll have to see how well your solvency argument holds water."

"It will."

"We still have our work to do. We'll need to tear into it."

Barrack reaches for the half of the cookie that Pratt left on the tray. He doesn't bite into it either, but places it gently on a cloth napkin he's spread before him. "Courtney, you're not going to be offended by this, are you?"

"You'll have to explain what 'this' means, Mike."

"We have due diligence, too. We need to tear everything apart and put it back together. In our own way."

Pratt gives Barrack a look that says that he doesn't like his integrity or competence as a businessman being called into question.

"Courtney, from what I have seen, and heard, you're an honest guy," Barrack says. "But our story has to stand up to the abuse and scrutiny of the court. I have to answer not only to you, my client, but to the court, and to the lawyers on the other side. I've got my reputation—and the firm's—on the line. And a responsibility as a barrister."

"I realize that, but—"

"And I want to win when I go in there. Win."

Pratt leans back, arms crossed.

"Courtney, look, we have to get to know one another. It doesn't happen overnight."

Pratt shifts ground now, encouraging Barrack to tell him about the CCAA process from the legal end, and this goes on for about an hour. Barrack weighs every word, always leaving open an option for himself to reflect on what's being said in the here and now, to evaluate facts and perspectives and whether they'll stand up in court.

"And one more thing, Courtney," Barrack says, as if apologizing. "I would suggest you get used to the courtroom, if we go the CCAA route. You should plan to be there as much as you can."

"I'm interested in the process, but I have a company to run."

"The judge will appreciate your presence. And you will appreciate very much being on his good side. Trust me. This will help the cause."

"Every day?"

"As much as possible."

"Will I have to do anything?"

"If it's Justice Farley, and it likely will be—no, you won't have to do anything. But it doesn't mean Farley won't do something to you." Barrack is almost smirking.

"You're going to have to explain, Mike."

"Farley takes a proprietary view of what goes in the courtroom. It's possible that on a certain level he accepts that he represents the Crown. But at the level where it counts, Farley is the king of his courtroom. He's a character who will challenge the gallery from time to time, and, Lord, if someone's not paying attention—let alone dozes off—he'll stop things and conduct an inquisition right then and there."

It hasn't escaped Pratt that throughout this meeting Barrack has been evaluating him, probing for consistency. While there is chemistry here, Pratt feels on the defensive.

"Mike, what's it like, being up there, you know, day one on a big case, or making your opening statement?"

Barrack sits back for a second. Then he says, "I'm aware of the words coming out of my mouth, and of what's going on around me, what the judge may be thinking by how he twiddles his pen, how the other lawyer is reacting, even if he's barely in my peripheral vision, how my client feels and responds sitting behind me, and whether the bailiff is going to sleep. I can hear a pin drop, legs crossing, people yawning, shifting in their seats. I swear to you—this all affects the flow. You really feel you have eyes, not just in the back of your head, but on the side, too. And within the structured stress of the moment, there's always room for improvisation, doing the thing you hadn't planned on. And there's anticipation, too, being a step or two ahead of the conversation, ready to zig before your opponent zags. It's a weird zone to be in, but I love it."

As he finally munches on his half of the cookie, Pratt has no doubt that he wants Barrack on his side.

By the time he gets back to Hamilton, his equanimity has more or less returned, a process that has required emptying his mind of everything but the challenge of driving a slushy highway in cold rain. It's dark out when he walks onto the executive floor, a time of day that makes him think of coffee gone stale and pizza brought to the reception by the delivery guy who takes his credit card and couldn't care less if he's the CEO or an escaped murderer as long as he has a photo ID. He hears the distant hum of a vacuum cleaner from the night staffer whose pushcart can be seen at the end of the hallway.

As he passes the boardroom, he notices the PR guy, an external consultant, huddled over a laptop. Behind him, Colin Osborne and a crew of spreadsheet jockeys are poring over capital spending estimates.

"I don't want you guys working all night," Pratt says, a gentle reprimand that no one acknowledges. "Seriously, there's a point at which you stop being effective."

"And what point is that—*dawn?*" Osborne says, to general laughter.

Pratt affects a grim executive look. "If I hear you guys are here past five or six in the morning, I'm not going to be happy."

Some don't seem to be sure whether he's joking.

Pratt drops his briefcase and overcoat on a chair. He's fatigued, and shows it more than he knows he should, which dampens the spirit in the room for a minute. They all know he was in Toronto most of the day, and Toronto means long meetings with the lawyers and consultants about the possibility of CCAA. But he has nothing to report, not yet. All they can do tonight is crunch numbers, fine-tune arguments and keep weighing the alternatives to applying for CCAA protection. None of these arguments is appealing to him right now.

"Who's working the messages for the press release?" Pratt says, scrolling his BlackBerry for the e-mail that accumulated during his drive back.

"The draft is still coming together—but we have something," the PR guy says.

Pratt picks a hard copy of the release from a pile of printouts on the table. He reads it, pencil in hand, annotating nearly every sentence.

"This release, as written, is bound to cause some heart attacks and confusion out there," he finally says, looking up from the page. "There's no way we can even have the idea of 'downsizing' within a million miles of this announcement. First of all, I'm not even sure that's ever going to happen. It's just not a word that fits here."

"But Courtney, what you said—"

"I know what I said. The workforce is too large for the steel we produce. We all know that. But my feeling is that voluntary reductions should do the trick, given the aging of the workforce. Early retirement, not downsizing. But I'm not sure we say this now."

"What about saying we need to rightsize," the PR guy says.

"'Rightsize' is not a word I'm fond of," Pratt says.

"What about 'supersize'?" Osborne jokes. "We'll supersize the company, with fries, to be more globally competitive."

The PR guy: "If there isn't a severe crisis clearly expressed in this press release, it will raise questions about the validity of the action. There needs to be real conflict highlighted, the situation out of control."

"Out of control?" Pratt says sarcastically. "The fact is we can't continue to pile up huge losses and consume cash like it's candy. We're going broke fast. We need to reduce costs, improve productivity. We need to focus on key operations and products. And we need to become a lot more competitive. How out of control is that?"

Note-taking all around him.

"I like the positioning," the PR guy says.

Pratt continues. "There's not enough language in here on treating all stakeholders in a fair and responsible way. Put yourself in the shoes of the old lady in Hess Village living on her husband's Stelco pension. She's in her late seventies and her house is paid off, so fine. But when this news hits—if it hits, I mean, if that's the way we go—she'll hobble down to the bank every fourth Thursday, maybe her son or daughter will take her there in a cab, and she will be scared to death her pension cheque isn't going to be in her account. I don't want to have people like her scared."

Silence.

"I have issues with sending a screwed-up message to suppliers," Osborne says. "The minute we go into CCAA, our suppliers are going to become unpaid creditors. They'll go ballistic, totally non-linear. And we're still out there, even today, talking to them as if we have the means to pay. There's something not right about that."

"We haven't come to a decision, yet," Pratt says, "which puts us in a tough position right at this exact moment."

Osborne looks unconvinced.

"There will be money to pay suppliers—and employees," the PR guy says. "That's right in the press release."

Osborne gives Pratt a look, shaking his head, biting his pen. "That's true. But we're not going to pay them what we owe them. The payables. We can only pay them for services or products they provide *after* we go into CCAA. Who wants to work with a company that does that?"

Pratt is scribbling through this exchange, then stops. "Colin's right. There'll be nothing we can do once we go into CCAA. Suppliers we owe money to—they can't be paid. Our hands will be tied. We all have to understand that."

A chorus of gloom comes at him. "We're a big portion of many local businesses. What choice do they have? Some work is better than nothing."

"Suppliers will demand all cash terms."

"Some will stop working with us. It could shut things down in certain parts of the mill. I don't want to bet on who is going to do what."

Pratt knuckles the table to get the whole room's attention. "Let's keep in mind the bigger picture—the company's future— as we edit this release. I've been around the resource business a long time. Many times I've seen companies try to take the easy way out, and then pay for it. They think that if they wait long enough, rising commodity prices and a good exchange rate will save the day. This is an irresponsible route here. Stelco is in disastrous financial shape. A temporary price rise? That's only going to delay what we're contemplating right now."

Osborne is fidgeting, shedding sparks of suppressed discontent.

"What is it, Colin?"

"You really have to read between the lines of this release to understand what's going on. I don't see how this is going to provide a lot of comfort to the employees, never mind the pensioners or creditors. What exactly is the message, aside from saying we're going into CCAA?"

"It's a careful document, yes—it has to be," Pratt says. "We're a public company, and if we don't report to the market in a responsible and careful way, we create even more uncertainty."

"The union will drive a truck through this press release."

"Colin," Pratt says evenly, "it's a press release, required by securities law to advise the market. Words on paper. We are also going to have to go out there and talk to people—to our employees, the media, the market, the city of Hamilton. And talk to them in person, and take our lumps as they come. You and I and the whole Stelco team. We'll have to look them in the eye and tell them. And the sooner we act, the better our ability will be to preserve the cash we need, the easier it will be to fix our problems and emerge a stronger company and, very critically, attract the capital to invest in the business to make us goddamn competitive again."

"I like that last line, minus the 'goddamn,'" the PR guy says, tapping into his laptop.

"Yeah, well." Pratt feels like shit. He sees too much doubt, maybe even fear, in Osborne's face. And he can't blame him.

"Okay, guys," he says. "I've got a conference call in five."

Everyone assumes he wants them to leave. People get up.

"Where are you guys going?"

Stuttering.

"I'll take it in my office," he says. "Colin? You joining me?"

Pratt and Osborne leave the boardroom.

"I know what you're thinking," Pratt says as they walk toward his office.

"I'm not sure what I'm thinking."

"Look, we're not winding up the company—we're trying to save it. We're trying to get the means to rebuild Stelco, and get it off life support."

"Is that what I'm thinking? I thought I was thinking I was turning into a monster who eats widows and orphans with my cereal."

"We'll get back to making steel, Colin."

They take up positions on either side of Pratt's desk. "Who will be on the call?" Osborne says at the speakerphone.

"The chairman. He wants to know where we stand."

"Where do we stand? Where do *you* stand?"

"I don't know, not fully."

"You don't? Great. Very reassuring."

"I don't know any more than you do whether we can pull this off, or even if it is the right thing to do. We have the team to do it, and the opportunity, but a million things can go wrong. That I do know."

"But we're likely going to risk it, right?"

"I think the alternative is a dead company."

CONFIDENCE GAME

"I can't say for sure," Pratt says to the chairman of the board on the phone. "But it looks like we're running out of cash. Fast. And if that's the case, if we don't go into CCAA, we're dead. And not only that."

"Not only what?"

"We may have to do things I really don't like."

"Such as?"

"Cut pensions. Jobs gone, with no severance. Wind down operations, downsize. Shut things down. The human costs of all—"

"Can the team get this done?"

"I have a lot of confidence in the team. You have my word that we're doing our best."

MY WORD

On his drive home in the wee hours of the night, Pratt recalls the first, nice-to-meet-you meeting with the union guys before Christmas just after the announcement that he would be the new CEO. They had questions about whether he could be trusted, and bluntly requested that he tell them what was happening and keep them in the loop on the possibility or the timing of Stelco going into CCAA. He replays the conversation in his mind—not the actual words, but the intent, the distinctions he made that the union guys didn't want to hear.

I'll do what I can, he'd said.

What does that mean? they'd wanted to know.

Stelco's a public company, guys. Look, there's a matter of disclosure. What you reveal and when. There are legal limits. You can go to jail when you cross the line. It's illegal to give one stakeholder inside information and not the others. You know that.

Can we trust you, Courtney? Give us your word.

My word?

Later, as he climbs into bed, he wonders whether he was clear enough.

I was. Absolutely. How much clearer could I have been?

Lingering doubts carry him off to sleep.

GAME DAY

The dream starts off as it should: like a dream.

Pratt and a boyhood hero, Maurice "Rocket" Richard, are lacing up the skates beside an outdoor rink at night. Huge spotlights are strung tenuously above the ice, the snowbanks piled high above the boards.

Stepping onto the ice, the Rocket, the most revered hockey player in the history of the Montreal Canadiens, appears to be in his athletic prime—a figure from the early 1950s. Soon he's racing up and down the rink, stickhandling the puck, scoring into empty nets.

There is applause in Pratt's head but no crowd visible giving it.

Suddenly the dream version of Pratt, who is the same age as he really is now, is staggering alone through fields of ice, blinded by snow that whirls around him in a silent wind. He can't see—only hear—the Rocket skating, the blades etching the ice with each powerful stride. He's aware, somewhere in his interior world, that no matter how wild this scenario is, the truth of his life has followed him here: there's no way he'd ever be on the ice with the Rocket. He can't even lie to himself in a goddamm dream.

I am who I am, no matter how I remember it. The truth comes through, even when you're creating it.

The alarm jolts him awake, for once.

In a dazed state, he replays the dream before it's clawed away by the forces of daylight. As his feet touch the floor, the last thing he remembers is being on his knees, his frostbitten hands ploughing into snow to retrieve a puck that turns into a BlackBerry, a message in the voice mail from an elderly lady from Hamilton, inquiring about her Stelco pension and whether it's safe for another month.

By a quarter after seven that morning, Pratt is in the Stelco boardroom, seated at the centre of the long table next to the chairman, facing a roomful of board members.

"In summary," he says, then clears his throat. "First, is Stelco viable in its current form? It's extremely unlikely that we'll be able to operate past November. Even if we manage that, our uncompetitive position would eventually push us into insolvency—sooner rather than later.

"Second, are there alternatives? Yes, in theory. But we've tried some and they haven't worked. For example, we've asked the unions to come to the table and discuss concessions. That is a non-starter for them. The other obvious alternative is to keep operating until we do run out of cash. And, quite frankly, we have rejected that as irresponsible.

"Third, can we restructure successfully without creditor protection from the courts? This is the issue of the day. We don't believe so. We're running out of money and not attracting new capital. We are not cost competitive. We have financing in place to get us through the year with a healthy margin of error if we can use creditor protection to preserve our cash. That should give us the financial breathing room to negotiate with everyone affected, and create the necessary urgency to drive a resolution to our problems. This is a huge decision for all of us. I understand a lot more now than I did a month ago about how different our lives will be under CCAA. It's going to be very difficult, but it is the considered view of management and our advisors that we should seek creditor protection within CCAA while we still have enough liquidity left in the business to restructure. Our assessment is that waiting until we're totally broke to seek creditor protection would be irresponsible on our part.

"Are we ready to file for creditor protection? Is everything in place? The answer is that we are very well prepared. We are ready to file today at 10 a.m., with the board's approval, in front of Justice Farley."

The vote is taken, and is unanimous in favour.

"Our goal is to emerge from this process as a viable and competitive steel producer."

Colin Osborne says this to an empty room. His office, the door shut.

He has decided he can't sit there and pretend to be engaged in real management work while he's waiting for the briefing scheduled for eight-thirty with the two union leaders, Bill Ferguson from Lake Erie and Rolf Gerstenberger from Hamilton. Together they represent the vast majority of Stelco's unionized employees.

So he paces the office, walking in circles around his desk, pausing on each loop by the window, where he talks aloud to himself, voicing memorized lines from the final version of the "script." This script consists of answers, crafted by himself and others on the Stelco team, to questions likely to be raised by Ferguson and Gerstenberger once they learn the company is headed for CCAA.

He checks his watch twice, then stops himself from doing it again. On one loop he addresses the window up close, as if it's a real person only inches from his face. He fogs the glass. He has a momentary desire to draw a happy face—with the smile turned upside down.

"Our focus is on the future and on achieving a successful restructuring," he intones. He has enough self-possession to remind himself to whisper, so he won't be caught openly talking to the window if somebody walks in. "We have to fix our deteriorating cash position now or we won't preserve the money we need to restructure the company."

He decides that if he keeps this up, he'll have memorized every line. And then he'll sound like the kind of corporate clown the union guys have been complaining about for years: someone who doesn't know his own mind and can't think for himself.

"Guys, we have a serious situation. This morning, the Stelco board approved a decision to take the company into CCAA. I'm here to answer questions as best as I can. And to provide as much info as I can."

Better, much better. Sounds like me.

He'd prefer to leave the notes in his desk drawer. From experience he knows he'll be much more persuasive without them. But this is all new territory. Scary territory. And so he leaves the script on his desk in plain view.

Last night's meeting with his management team spooked him. All went well for the first five minutes after he distributed the draft press release, reminding his people that the decision wasn't firm until the board voted, and that this stuff should be treated as highly confidential, under strict embargo. He sat there and read along with them in the boardroom. He thought they'd then walk through the employee communications plan, the cascading of the message out to the workforce, with each manager calling his or her team together and relaying the story in person. But the meeting became a group meltdown, and he felt anger directed openly at him, as the messenger. Pratt had warned him he might get such a response and had advised him not to take it personally.

How else could he take it?

Some of the managers had been close to tears, wondering how their twenty-five- or thirty-year career with Stelco had overnight become this nightmare of instability and uncertainty. Some instantly aspired to vengeance, suggesting it was really time to screw the union, teach those bastards a lesson and get the company back on track—let's break them once and for all. At least two people approached him after the meeting, concerned only about themselves and the safety of their salaries and pensions, oblivious to their responsibility to carry the message out to the workforce and to reduce their workers' uncertainty where possible. Does it get more selfish than that? And, as Osborne channelled the outrage and disbelief around the table, doing his best to think on his feet and stick to the message, he had no confident reply when one of the purchasing managers said, as if speaking for everyone, "This is a complete disaster, Colin. We have a lot of folks, I mean, wow, the mom-and-pop companies, too, stretched to the absolute financial limit, paying them on a hundred days and hammering them on price, too. Are you telling me they're not gonna see a red cent?"

"We'll operate without interruption, serve our customers, deal with suppliers and pay our employees wages and salaries during the process."

What the hell else is there to say?

When the union leaders arrive, he walks to the lobby himself to bring them back to his office. Somehow it works out that he's on one side of his desk and they're on the other, which strikes him as pathetically typical. He launches into the core messages, not entirely liberated from rehearsed cadences.

Ferguson, the burly union leader from Lake Erie, doesn't seem too fussed. Osborne attributes his attitude to the plain fact that regardless of what happens to Stelco as a whole, the Lake Erie mill has a solid future, guaranteed, no matter who ends up owning it.

Osborne glances at Gerstenberger, the head of the Hamilton local. He's a middle-aged Marxist-Leninist with the demeanour of a bearded intellectual who never doubts that he's in possession of the only moral ideology in the room. Osborne is prepared for an outburst of proletarian rhetoric, but Gerstenberger is slumped, his head in his hands, totally sombre, only occasionally looking up at Osborne as the core messages are unveiled.

"At ten o'clock this morning, we'll be seeking the order from the court," Osborne says, turning his notes face down as if to re-establish credibility with these guys. "And I'd personally appreciate it if we could clamp down on this until then, keep the media blackout until it's official, so that we can tell our people without them hearing it on television or the radio first. I think we owe it to our people to keep the temperature down. As much as we can."

Osborne can't figure out whether Ferguson has taken in a thing, let alone agreed to anything, and Gerstenberger still has said nothing. Osborne is certain that Gerstenberger is truly at a loss as to how to respond—and he's obviously very upset, angry. This is Gerstenberger's first term as the president of the Hamilton local, and Osborne suspects that he's concluded the worst: that Hamilton, with its aging facilities and workforce, is the main target for concessions, for downsizing, salary cuts, the works.

Then the meeting is over and Osborne, once again alone in his office, isn't sure how it ended.

At one minute to ten, Mike Barrack, pulling a wheeled stack of document boxes, enters the high-ceilinged courtroom with its dark panelling and gallery of hard wooden seats, which offer a whiff of furniture polish mixed with the sweat of fifty years of squirming witnesses. Not long after he unpacks and settles in, he hears creaking behind him, the door opening to the judge's chambers, then feet shuffling along carpet.

"All rise," comes the announcement in the bailiff's deep West Indian voice.

Then Justice Farley, a compact barrel of a man in his mid-sixties, all eyebrows above a purposeful glare, strides through the door to the bench and, once seated, scans the courtroom for a good ten seconds, back and forth, twice, as if committing to memory the faces of all those before him—who he clearly expects will disappoint him with flaccid arguments that impose unwelcome burdens on the court's patience and its integrity.

Barrack loves this. This is his world.

He glances behind him: the gallery is half full now, not bad for a formality.

"Good morning, Your Honour," he says. "I am here with Mr. Gage and Mr. Hall representing Stelco. As you have seen from the materials, we are here seeking an initial order under the CCAA."

Pratt and the PR guy are huddled around the speakerphone, making calls to key players to give them a heads up.

"Who's up next?" Pratt says.

"The Premier's Office."

"Did you find out whether he's been briefed?"

"I think so. But the staff guys in the chain of command over there—who knows what they told him?"

"Are we speaking to the premier himself?"

"Yes."

The phone keeps ringing and ringing—

"Are they ever going to pick up?" the PR guy says.

Voice mail. It's an assistant to the assistant of some assistant.

Pratt hangs up. "Are you sure we have the right number?" he asks, scanning the list with the names and numbers for the courtesy calls they're making to politicians at different levels of government. He's not reading the list. Just looking at it, blind to the actual words, much in the way some people look at but don't read the menu when they first sit down in a restaurant.

The PR guy redials.

Ringing and ringing.

"How's it going with the cascade to our people?" Pratt asks.

"It's happening. But it's brutal, this is what I hear. There is some disbelief. Nothing violent, but people are upset."

A human voice. "The Premier's Office."

"Yes, hello, this is Courtney Pratt, from Stelco. We have a phone call arranged with—"

"The Premier will be with you shortly. May I put you on hold?"

He's on hold before he can say yes.

Pratt slumps into his office chair, relatively pleased with how things are going, although he knows this feeling isn't meant to last longer than the next ten seconds. The press conference in the boardroom went as planned. Messages were delivered and dutifully received by the media, and the interviews with the TV people had gone well.

"Hampton and Kormos are in the lobby," the PR guy says.

"Who?"

"Howard Hampton, the provincial NDP leader. Peter Kormos, the MPP from Welland. The bad boy. They're late for the press conference and apparently are disappointed the cameras are gone."

"Here to express solidarity with their union brothers and sisters?"

"What do we do with them?"

A crowd of Stelco executives soon forms in his office.

"You go talk to them."

"No, you go."

"What if we just hide here till they leave?" Laughter.

"They won't leave, trust me, without having their say."

"They'll finish each other's sentences."

"They will link arms, you watch. And sing protest songs."

"If the cameras were here, maybe."

"Let's not be mean-spirited. They're stakeholders, too. We don't want them against us."

"Politicians. Jesus Christ."

"There you go!"

"Guys, guys!"

"They're just doing their job."

"Enough," Pratt says into the executive babble. "I'll go talk to them."

Pratt invites the politicians into the boardroom and soon marvels at how they do, in fact, finish each other's sentences. He lets them talk and makes all the right noises in return. He answers questions, repeats core messages, absorbs the predictable banalities and delivers a few himself. When it's over, he feels he's done the right thing.

After the elevator doors close on the departing politicians, one of the security managers, a long-time Stelco veteran, steps toward him. He's a hefty man in his late fifties for whom this office job at headquarters is the cherished reward for a long career as a security guard, which involved years of night shifts patrolling the mill grounds and many days dealing with the usual incidents found in any sizable worker population—the theft of company property, sleeping or drinking on the job, smoking pot in the parking lot, sexual harassment.

"That was good," he says, "you talking to those guys like that."

Pratt doesn't understand the compliment, or whether it actually is one. The security manager sees the puzzled look on Pratt's face, then says, apologetically, "In the old days, around here, when those guys showed up like that, we would have just told them to fuck off, you know."

"So it's good thing, then, I talked to them?"

The security manager knows he's being teased. "Yeah. It's different."

The BlackBerry clangs, seconds before another boardroom meeting.

It's Pratt's son, calling from Vancouver.

"Hey, Steve, I'm on the run. What's up?"

"We're starting to see you on TV out here."

"Did I screw up? Come on, be honest—well, not too honest."

"It's not bad. No, it's good. Sometimes there's a vein that pops on your forehead. That's when you're mad—hey, I know the look."

"You're not downloading this stuff for that blog of yours."

"I was thinking I could link the CBC piece to the Christmas pictures, the one with you wrestling with our dog."

"Which one?"

"You and the dog are covered in torn wrapping paper, and you're wearing that sweater we got you, with the price tag still on it."

"Now, now. Be nice to your dad."

It's nearly eleven, too late for Pratt to go home. He and Alexa haven't yet found a place in Oakville and are still living in the ravine house in Toronto. Since he has a meeting at the Stelco mill early tomorrow morning, it's saner to check into a hotel in Hamilton. He wisely foresaw this eventuality and brought a change of clothing with him to work.

When he arrives at the hotel, he asks at the front desk about the possibility of ordering room service. As it's only four minutes before the kitchen closes, a long discussion ensues between him and the desk clerk.

Patience, he thinks. Patience. The kid's a rookie, and doesn't need a strip torn off him just because he's following the rules.

The negotiated settlement includes the last cheese plate on the premises and two bags of potato chips, plus the lukewarm beer available in what turns out to be the malfunctioning minibar in his room.

After settling in, he channel-surfs for news, and soon lands on a French channel out of Quebec, where the Stelco story is being served up by the anchorwoman. When the image zooms to footage of himself being interviewed, he experiences a moment of satisfaction that he was able to carry it off in French.

He's sitting on the bed, still in his suit.

He lucks into a feature on Stelco looping through a business news channel. He finds it weird to see different angles of himself, particularly his profile and the back of his head. It's not how he pictures himself. He chuckles when he thinks of the forehead vein, which isn't popping at all. He notices his jaw: clenched too tight, as if he's grinding his teeth. In some clips his voice really bugs him, attempting to stay modulated but sounding ragged, tired, up and down in pitch, trying too hard to give the impression of being calm, totally in control.

He calls Alexa. She tells him she spotted a stray eyebrow hair that she will tweeze out tomorrow whether he likes it or not.

Goodnight, Lex, sleep well.

At midnight he's drifting, a beer three-quarters full on the bedside table, the BlackBerry recharging in the corner. His documents are neatly arranged on the desk. He's put the remains of the demolished cheese plate outside the door because they asked him nicely if he would.

In his last seconds of consciousness, he's engrossed in a televised replay of a hockey game from the 1950s, the play-by-play flickering in grainy black and white. He thinks how much slower the action is compared to the modern game, the puck so easy to follow. Few players wear helmets; their pads are pretty thin under their jerseys. They look like real men, he thinks, not cyborgs, not football players on skates, hidden behind logos and protective gear. He remembers this game—or thinks he does. Actually, he remembers watching this classic game on TV not long ago. The heroes of his youth are on the screen, including the Rocket, who, after Pratt falls into a dreamless sleep, scores the game-winner from an impossible angle.

CONSCIENCE DIALOGUE

DONNY McCUNN, STEELWORKER

I'm lining up for lunch in the cafeteria at the Hamilton mill, which is a half-storey below grade in the old office building. It looks tired from decades of absorbing food odours and lunchtime gossip and being mopped down every day with detergents. In its cavernous kitchen, largely decommissioned, a short-order crew is churning out BLTs, omelettes and turkey dinners slathered in gravy the consistency of oil paint. Still, the cafeteria isn't an unpleasant place right now, bright in winter sunlight streaming in through windows that start chest-high and run to the ceiling, offering expansive views of the mill. I hope my management team gets used to this building, because this is where we're going to live as we fight through the CCAA battles ahead.

My perspective on the sunlight is obscured by a bearded, greying man, Donny McCunn, who's just ahead of me in the lineup at the self-serve counter. Donny's a little heavy through the middle, with forearms like stovepipes. This guy is all blue-collar, comfortable in an old leather jacket.

"You still got your Harley, Donny?"

"Ha. That's long gone for the minivan, but there's a '68 Firebird in the garage I've been restoring for, like, forever." He scrutinizes my tray. "You're eating like a bird, man."

A pre-made julienne salad. A yogurt. V8 juice. All wrapped. There's more plastic than food on my tray.

On his plate, a gargantuan helping of fish and chips. It's sort of an engineering achievement, his meal, the fries heaped over the fried filets that look as thick as fireplace starter logs. I'm not above eating fatty foods—my poison is smoked meat from Schwartz's in Montreal, where sides of kosher beef are cooked in chemicals that would freak out anyone concerned with healthy living. Where I take exception to Donny's meal is on practical terms: I'd be asleep all afternoon trying to digest it. After we each pay for our meals, we walk over to a table next to the windows.

"So how are things, Donny?"

"I'm in hock. The daughter's wedding. It'll be beans and wieners for years. Come to think of it, we might be doing that for a lot longer, the way things are going."

He's angry with me but has decided to deflect that anger into an extended squirting action with the ketchup on his fries. "Courtney, when my wife and I tied the knot, we had a keg of beer, a party down by the lake that cost less than a tank of gas. And the next day we got on the bike, took off north, stayed in motels. We went around Lake Superior, in early fall, a beautiful time of year . . ."

"I can relate to that—"

He interrupts the chit-chat. "You asked us to trust you, and this thing is a mess."

I pull the tab on the V8 juice and take a long slug.

I say, "I could no more tell you guys about our decision to go into CCAA than I could anyone else. Not before we made the decision."

"When you came to Stelco, you said creating trust with the steelworkers was important. You said openness was important."

I need to take this in, not overreact. "The mistrust has built up over many years at Stelco," I finally bring myself to say. "Everyone's got to take some responsibility."

"You met with the union before you were on the job, then six weeks later, kaboom, we go into bankruptcy. You turned my world upside down."

"In a fictional best-of-all-worlds, I would have sat down with key stakeholders before the CCAA filing to talk about the need to work together in a restructuring. But that's not possible with publicly traded companies."

"It might have been better if you'd said nothing at all about trust."

"Maybe that's what you're used to: nothing being said."

I can't totally blame him for feeling as he does. You do the right thing sometimes, and yet people still get hurt. You never get used to the paradoxes of management. I tear open the sad piece of plastic containing "diet Italian" salad dressing and squirt my iceberg greens.

"I really do not understand how you can feed yourself with that," Donny says.

Ah, an opening. A concession to the idea of civility.

"Let's go back to those meetings with the union when I was about to join the company," I say. "I always do this when I go into a new situation. I tell you about myself, my career, my family, my style of operation. And I ask you guys to do the same. My recollection was that I talked about the serious competitive issues Stelco faced. The possibility of CCAA was raised, and I said that this was not the preferred route but that the problems had to be solved."

"We're no closer to solving the problems."

"Let me finish the thought."

"Fair enough."

"You can't fault us for looking at all our options. That's only responsible. Truly—nobody wanted CCAA. Once I got on the job and it became clear we were heading toward CCAA, I didn't meet with the union leaders again—because if they had asked me about CCAA, I would have had to tell a half truth or to lie. That would have destroyed any chance at trust."

Donny jabs at the fish, as if momentarily bewildered by the task of cutting through inches of fried batter. It's my turn to keep things going.

"My arteries are clogging just looking at that."

He laughs, then looks away from me, squinting toward the windows. "Because of some rules somewhere in some stock exchange, you have to pick and choose when you're going to be open and trustful."

I look where he's looking a long second or two, the vast Stelco world outside the window. This mill is still working hard, or trying to, but it needs serious capital investment. "I'm not in the business of lying to myself or others. And if you can't see the value in creating trust, what's left to say? You go back to your conspiracy theories, I go back to my office and shut the door. And this company goes further in the tank."

"We're not pure," he says, shaking his head, "but we've been screwed over by twenty years of bad management. Everyone knows that. This used to be a great Canadian company. So when we talk about mistrust, let's not forget the roots."

He tells me more about his own roots. Thirty years ago, a year out of high school, Donny joined Stelco, just like his dad had before him. He was smart enough for university, but there'd been no encouragement. At the time, he'd been up to no good, delinquent out of boredom. After watching a few good buddies end up dead or in jail, he smartened up. His dad knew a foreman at the steel mill, and soon Donny was learning a trade as an industrial mechanic. Within a few years, he'd gotten married to his high-school sweetheart, bought a house, then raised a family, and now he proudly makes contributions to his retirement plan every February.

"It took a long time for Stelco to get into this mess," I say. "Given your history with the company, you know that already. You know that things can't change overnight. I can't be held to an unreasonable expectation of what it takes to change a culture which, if you're honest, is a poster child for bad blood between management and the union. And you can't walk away from some responsibility for that."

"You were on the board of directors. You're an experienced executive. Didn't you understand what you were walking into?" He's jacking me around, and enjoying it.

"I don't see you, Donny, as a negative person," I say, feeling myself redden. "Or many of the people here when I talk to them as individuals. But hardly anyone here has worked anywhere else. They've spent their whole working lives at Stelco. They don't know any other reality. What really strikes me here is the collective negativity."

"This is Hamilton, not Disneyland," he says with a shrug. "We've fought for every inch. Before you got here, and long before that, you'd think we were in a prison. Treated like prisoners, thieves. And so it becomes tit-for-tat."

"I appreciate that."

"So seeing the glass half empty, it's an occupational hazard."

He pulls out a newspaper clipping from his leather jacket. It's about the CCAA announcement. There's me in the picture, at a microphone in front of a crowd, a solemn look on my face, talking to the media. He drops it in front of me as if dispensing a dead rat. "My 'negative reaction,' as you call it," he says, as if winding up to some conclusion I won't like. "You should have seen it coming. I'm not gonna pretend I understand finances. But you took power away from Stelco—from management, the union—and gave it to lawyers and judges in Toronto. And those bondholders from New York. Look at that picture. I don't see many people like me in it, do you?"

I'm surrounded by other men in suits, lawyers, PR types, not a steelworker to be seen.

"You're right about how CCAA shifts control," I say, realizing I haven't touched my food either. "So why does a company decide to do this? The blunt answer: Because you're looking down the barrel of a gun. Stelco's financial performance has been horrible for years. Our major suppliers were putting us on shorter and shorter payment terms. And we had no indication at all from the unions that they were prepared to make any changes to help deal with the problem."

"So you put us into bankruptcy. Ace solution."

"CCAA is not bankruptcy—it's bankruptcy protection. It gives us breathing room so that we can work out a plan with affected parties to save the company. We chose to file for CCAA when, although we could still pay our bills, we were heading toward disaster. And the judge agreed with us."

"Fuck the judge. You brought him into this. To be honest with you, we think you want to use this process to trump the collective agreement."

"Bullshit!"

"Bullshit?"

"Look, CCAA allows the claims of creditors to be stayed. By that I mean that most of our financial obligations or debts to suppliers, lenders and bondholders are frozen until the company develops, in connection with all affected creditors, a plan that the court judges to be fair to all parties. In the United States, under Chapter 11, the judge can override a collective agreement. That is just not the case in Canada."

"Give me a little less boilerplate here, man."

"Do we want some changes to the collective agreement with the union? Yes. Do we think your agreement can or should be 'trumped'? No. Your members will have to vote to accept any changes. CCAA gives the union a significant role in coming up with the plan, if you are prepared to put something on the table to contribute to the solution."

"'Contribute to the solution,'" he says unhappily, checking his watch. "Look, I gotta get back on shift."

"Let me walk you back to the mill."

"Suit yourself."

We gather up our uneaten plates of food and drop the trays off near the waste bins. As we walk down the corridor, I'm aware of the eyes on us. Amazed looks. Donny picks up on that too.

"I'll hand it to you," he says. "Having lunch with the boss isn't something that went on around here before."

We walk up a flight of stairs.

"Let's step out here for a second," he says.

"It's freezing."

"I need a smoke."

We're in a nook between two wings of the building. Donny has the look of a hounded man, lighting up. We're both dancing on our toes to keep warm. It's well below zero.

"You sure you don't want one of these?"

I ignore the offer. "I know 'concessions' is a dirty word to you. But unions aren't the only ones in a tough spot. Creditors may not get a hundred cents on the dollar. Shareholders may be wiped out. But we're a sick, dying company at the moment—we're not Microsoft."

He puffs at me. "How many of us are you gonna fire?"

"The thing to remember is that the workforce—it's a fact—is fairly old. That's very good experience to have in the company. Still, we can accomplish the lion's share of workforce attrition through voluntary means—basically, people deciding on their own to retire."

"I'll let that pass, even though there's nothing humane about being sent home when someone else says you're surplus labour."

"We are trying to protect what existing workers like you

have earned. What is your due. The value of your sweat equity."

"Yeah."

"It's too fucking cold out here. I'm going in."

He looks at me as if he's never seen a man in a suit swear. He nods, almost willing to be impressed. While I wait inside the door for him to finish his cigarette, I reflect on things. Stelco is just one company, a small steel company by world standards, and uncompetitive. So what do we do? I respect Donny's position, but it saddens me that he doesn't accept that his pension really is at risk. Maybe he thinks Stelco is "too big to fail" and the government will step in. After all, this is Canada, not the US. In the US, many have lost their pensions because of those kinds of bets.

When he comes in from the cold, he brings an aura of smoke. We're soon moving again at a good clip.

"It doesn't matter what the roots of the problem are," I say. "But the way Stelco works today . . . it's regimented, bureaucratic, inefficient and costly. And so goddamm political. It's unwelcoming and alien to the new kids coming into the company. Surely you know that."

"Who do you blame?"

"Forget blame for a minute. Jesus."

"You're talking about getting into trench warfare here, Courtney. We know the mill and what works here. You don't."

I shake my head emphatically. "I'm not the enemy. We're trying to get a small steel company off life support, and to keep jobs alive. The entire North American steel industry has been restructured. New mills are opening all over the planet with a cost base much lower than ours."

"Every dollar spent on a lawyer is a dollar wasted."

"You guys don't admit there's even a problem."

We're in the coat room near the front entrance. He hands me a blue denim jacket, nearly as long as an overcoat. These coats are given to visitors for plant tours. Then he throws a hard hat at me. I install myself in the gear as we walk out into the cold, past the main gate, and get into a pickup truck that he drives over to the blast furnace. Donny manages a crew of mechanics over there. We're on his turf now, a thundering, hissing inferno. The blast furnace is the giant heart of this mill, veined in black tubing, sensors, all kinds of technology. We pause where the molten metal spits out at ground level into a channel, a river of liquid steel.

Donny and I look at each other, smiling. Two kids in a candy store.

Over the tremendous din, he shouts, "In the U.S. of A., you can pull a fast one on the worker. And government lets it happen. Union-Busting Central. Dog-eat-dog. Survival of the slickest. Sometimes the unions win. Often they get broken, or never formed. But believe me, workers are getting screwed. The standard of living goes down. Many people end up—after the downsizing—working as Wal-Mart greeters or cleaning toilets at Tim Hortons when they should be with their grandkids. No medicare, no health insurance. It's different in Canada. The government—they're behind us, they give a shit about labour laws."

There's something about two guys standing around in a steel mill—that invites a fraternal exchange of profanity.

My turn to shout. "The provincial government helped create the goddamn pension problem by letting the company slack off on its pension contributions going back a decade. With all due respect, you're carrying around a pretty selective view of what ensures worker protection. It's naive to ignore how much the US steel sector has come alive after being nearly dead. There are good jobs in their mills. A future. So there's plenty to learn from that experience from where I sit because, if you won't face the truth, I actually have to. Stelco is in the intensive care unit, no matter which view of the world you hold."

"The workers always get screwed."

I give him a look, as if the bitterness act isn't convincing.

"I can't hear a thing here," I say.

We navigate a complex route under steel ramps and around vibrating machinery. I love being in places like this, but, no question, doing this kind of work, year in and year out, creates a perspective on reality different from that of a guy with a big office in the sky.

Suddenly a door opens and we slide into a command centre, very high-tech, lots of computer screens. This looks like any computer room anywhere, but there's a fine grit over everything, the smell of grease, burning metal. Donny puts a kettle on then reaches for a jar of coffee.

"You may not like it, Donny, but those steel companies in the US are our competitors for the same customers and for the same investment capital. Almost all of them went through bankruptcy protection and came out of it with much lower costs than we have. And the same thing happened to a Canadian competitor, Algoma, which has been through CCAA twice! So if you want to stick your head in the sand . . ."

"Right out of some globalization handbook."

"I can relate to the fear—of being left behind, or thrown out of a job you've had for years. We're all struggling with those fears, at some level. But we can't let fear drive us to ignore the challenges we face."

"How do you value my thirty years in this mill?"

"We're trying to protect that value."

"Just like you're protecting shareholders! I've got a handful of Stelco shares in my RSP. They're worthless now."

"Shareholders are in a tough position. Absolutely."

The water comes to a boil. He's measuring coffee for his machine. He pauses, then nods at me.

"I'll have a cup, black."

He says, "Maybe you should spend more time in the plant talking with guys like me and my father, who is a pensioner."

"I've spent a lot of my career in unionized, heavy manufacturing companies. I know how hard you work for what you earn. Compared to most companies like this, your pensions are good. I also know that many pensioners, once they retire, do other work to make ends meet."

"It's one thing to look at our world from the executive office and say you understand it. And it's another to be in our shoes in the mill."

"Well, I'm here now."

He gives me something of a cynical look, but this time he's letting me know he's poking fun at himself.

Now is the moment. As gently as I can, I say, "I have never questioned unions, their role or their power. But I'm not going to apologize for the view that the board—which I represent in this process—is responsible for deciding what's in the company's best interests. It may be your sweat that's making steel on a daily basis, but that sweat's not covering your paycheque, or your pensions. And it hasn't been for a very long time."

He shakes his head, turning something over in his mind. "We're a strong union," he says. "We have options, too."

"You mean a strike? We don't think you have that right, and we'll fight it vigorously in the courts."

"We're just talking here, Courtney, one man to another, right?"

"Absolutely."

"You know we can bring this company to its knees if we have to."

I stand back, hand over my heart, as if flabbergasted, even though Donny gets the message that I'm not. "This company is already flat on its back! If we could only get it to its knees—that would be progress!"

He thinks for a long, quiet minute.

I'm as passionate as Donny is about the outcome here, believe me. But I can leave this job, as I have left others, and that works fine for me. But Donny? So much of his life is wrapped up in Stelco, the good and the bad of it. I can't match the depth of his emotion. I can try to step into his shoes, but I can never fill them. I actually see that as a strength here in a situation where change might come faster than he's ready for. I may not have the scars from thirty years of Stelco, but there are other scars that do just as well as I size up what needs to be done.

"I know how hard this has been on you and all the other employees and pensioners, and your families," I say.

Donny takes in this comment without a shrug this time, just a searching look directed at me. "This conversation isn't over, Courtney."

"You're right. And other stakeholders will join it."

"Stakeholders? I got a lot at stake here: my job, my pension, my whole goddamm working life. It's all at stake."

CHAPTER TWO

RESTRUCTURING BREAKDOWN

THE COMEBACK HEARING

Sitting in the courtroom, Pratt has nothing productive to do, no market assumptions to refine, no earnings estimates to sanity-check. His job is to symbolize executive engagement in the CCAA process, and to sit silently in the packed gallery that's separated by a railing—the actual bar in the court—from the swarm of black-gowned lawyers in last-minute preparations for the comeback hearing. This event, on the morning of February 13, the first courtroom encounter after the company's CCAA filing in the Superior Court of Ontario, is a judicial convention during which parties opposed to creditor protection for Stelco can make their case.

There must be twenty-five lawyers in the courtroom. Some jostle with papers while conferring in whispers with colleagues. Others do work on their BlackBerries and laptops or trade gossip with lawyers on the opposing side. Soon the area beyond the bar can't contain them all, and Pratt watches, completely fascinated, as they spill out from the centre of the room to the walls. Lawyers everywhere. Pratt half expects someone to pull on a huge white wig and start a chain reaction of wig-wearing.

Mike Barrack has achieved psychological apartness from all the futzing barristers—sitting at the front, perfectly still, not reading or doodling, a single file folder closed on the table in front of him. Others approach Barrack several times, but his posture, his aura of concentration, communicates that he wants to be left alone. (Later, Barrack will tell Pratt that it's typical for opposing lawyers to attempt to knock you off your game with idle chat. Anything for a competitive edge. He does it himself to other lawyers when he sees an opening.)

Pratt unholsters his BlackBerry, remembering that while he's permitted to send and receive e-mail from the courtroom, he cannot use the phone. An audible ringtone could result in him being asked to leave the courtroom, which would be embarrassing on his first day. He clicks off the ringer, then scrolls over to the calculator function.

He does the math.

Thirty lawyers here. At least one support lawyer back at the office for every lawyer in the courtroom. Let's say, sixty lawyers. Plus another forty consultants on retainer—some at two hundred dollars an hour, some at four hundred, some at eight hundred.

Say, four hundred per hour. On average.

One hundred times four hundred?

Forty thousand bucks an hour. Fifty thousand? Sixty thousand?

The volume rises as the courtroom gets even more crowded. The union has mobilized in several rows of the gallery, a boisterous bunch, mostly from Hamilton. Even though Pratt is still angry at the union for launching a court challenge to the company's decision to file for CCAA protection, he soon finds himself on his feet quipping amiably with the union guys, who are acting as if they're in the bleachers at a football game. This raucous spirit, Pratt thinks, is their strength, along with their absolute lack of respect for corporate authority—for authority of any stripe. It's also maybe a weakness at times. And then he thinks again, realizing that he has no idea—despite his advisors' reassurances—whether the union's challenge to the CCAA process has a realistic chance and could potentially scuttle the company's effort to restructure. What if the court sides with the union?

He arrived at the courthouse too early this morning, anxious about the hearing, eager to see the legendary Justice Farley on the bench and Barrack in live performance. He was told by a court officer to wait in the hall. When the doors opened and the crowd rolled in, he spent a fretful minute deciding how visible he should be. He thought sitting in the front row might provoke the judge, or perhaps, more practically, be an annoyance to Barrack and the other lawyers on the McCarthy Tétrault team who might not want their client hovering within earshot, as if ready to offer advice. The second row seemed a better choice: visible, but not aggressively so. Respectful. Still well within visual range of Justice Farley.

The bailiff, a tall, thin, grey-haired West Indian in his sixties, saunters into the courtroom from a door adjacent to the bench. "And how is Mr. Barrack?" he inquires in a rich baritone. "I hope Mr. Barrack is well prepared, because His Honour is perhaps not in the best mood today."

"Neville, as always, a pleasure," Barrack responds. "His Honour is allowed a private moment to reflect on the circus his court has become, but doubtless we can count on him to rise, again, to the challenge of judicial equanimity."

"Doubtless." Then the bailiff turns to the gallery. "All rise."

Farley enters the courtroom, the first time Pratt has laid eyes on him. Even in his black gown, the man gives off linebacker intensity, striding with his head tilted slightly downward as if readying to deflect an opponent's charge. The fierceness doesn't look like an act, but he strikes Pratt as a man who knows how to amplify his personality, his gestures.

Or does he, Pratt wonders, as Farley mumbles into the microphone. Pratt strains to hear him. The microphone is busted, and this is not at first apparent to the judge.

"We can't hear you!" shouts one of the union guys from the back.

Farley stops talking and searches the gallery for the culprit, the glare on his face soon turning to amusement.

Then he repeatedly taps the microphone. Tap. Pause. Tap. Longer pause. Tap. Tap. Pause. Tap.

Pause.

Farley stares at the microphone as if it's guilty of wilfully impeding the prosecution of justice. No one says anything.

"You'll have to speak to the attorney general about this," Farley finally says, to laughter. "In the meantime, if you can't hear me, raise your hand." The judge restarts—and a herd of hands shoots up in the gallery.

Farley begins again, his voice louder now, instructing the union lawyer to present the brief in opposition to the order of the court that granted Stelco creditor protection. It soon becomes apparent to Pratt that the lawyer, a labour relations specialist, not an insolvency lawyer like so many others gathered in the room, is getting on the judge's nerves.

"The three C's," the judge says impatiently during one of his frequent interruptions. "Cooperation, collaboration and common sense, I'd ask you to remember. This is what it takes."

The union's argument, as far as Pratt can determine through the lawyerly verbiage, is that Stelco management and its board of directors have acted prematurely, that there is sufficient cash in the company to restructure and, in addition, that the resort to CCAA would in practice function as a strategy for the company to ignore the collective labour agreement, and worse: serve as a prelude to asking for concessions from the workers.

Now it's Barrack's turn.

"Your Honour, I'll be as brief as I can be . . ."

Pratt finds himself engrossed by Barrack's presentation, the concise counter-arguments that incorporate the union lawyer's own words against him, everything building toward what Pratt hopefully assumes is an inescapable conclusion: that Stelco is hanging onto solvency by a thin financial thread.

Barrack argues that Stelco meets the test of insolvency, as defined under CCAA law, which deems a corporation insolvent if there is a reasonable expectation that it will run out of cash within a reasonable period of time for implementing a restructuring. Barrack cites the financial arguments in Stelco's forecasts, backed up by opinions from outside consultants, to make the case that the company expects to run out of money before the end of the year, given its projected revenues, operating costs, interest charges on debt and available loan facilities. As Barrack talks, the judge makes notes in grumpy silence. From time to time, Barrack slows the pace, restating arguments in different ways, as if repetition without nuance is a crime against the dignity of his profession. It's all over in about fifteen minutes. Barrack is, Pratt realizes, a monstrously effective fighter and, for an instant, his awe is mixed with a little fear: what if Barrack were on the other side?

After the hearing is over, Pratt walks over to Barrack, who is packing up his papers. "Hey, Mike!" Pratt says effusively. "Impressive."

"It was okay," Barrack replies opaquely. "I missed a few things."

Is this false modesty—or maybe the post-performance letdown?

"I appreciate what you've done," Pratt says, changing his tone. "You and your team. It's very good work."

Barrack pauses from arranging his papers. He seems to want to come out of his trance, and Pratt waits it out.

"Thanks, Courtney," he finally says.

"What are the odds of us getting the nod here? Seriously."

"We'll know soon enough—give it a week, or two."

"In the meantime?"

"We keep moving ahead. Or try to. The game is on."

THE GAME, THE PLAYERS, THE FEES

A bankruptcy court proceeding is the corporate equivalent of a tabloid scandal, the airing of dirty financial laundry, the publishing of photos from the crime scene where the business model died. When a company as big as Stelco seeks creditor protection to restructure its finances, it is a very public admission of failure. And such an admission angers those who believe that a large corporation—like a celebrity—should be profitably immortal, always flush, not given to rationalizing the process of reneging on its debts and screwing creditors as a consequence.

Here's how Pratt and his management team expect the restructuring to unfold:

Acting on the approval of the board of directors, they have taken the company into CCAA on the assumption that the unseemly reality of the court overseeing the company's financial affairs, along with the potential threat of liquidation, will encourage Stelco creditors to take concessions on debts owed to them. Unsecured creditors, including Stelco bondholders, will be encouraged to take less than a hundred cents on every dollar they're owed, maybe much less; or, alternatively, they might be invited to convert a portion of their debt into equity. Liquidation—should it occur—will leave them with a lot less than they might get in a negotiated solution achieved within CCAA. (The secured creditors—that is, the banks and other financial institutions that lent the company money and have collateral against their loans—will get paid regardless.) This concession-seeking strategy has been used in many CCAA events. And while these negotiations with creditors unfold, new investors will also be sought by management to provide new capital in the large sums needed to modernize the company and make it competitive again.

Management also sees a practical opportunity to use the threat of Stelco's liquidation to get the unions to fess up to the reality that the company is uncompetitive. This is partially the result, management believes, of an inflexible, too-rigid work culture that has developed over decades. To rein in high labour costs, management also wants to make changes to employee benefits programs. For instance, it wants to change employee pension plans, bringing in a two-tiered system whereby new unionized hires would not be entitled to the same level of benefits enjoyed by the existing workforce. The union will resist any concessions, management knows, and blame Stelco's problems on decades of management stupidity, arguing that this restructuring should not be carried out on the backs of workers. Still, management believes it has a chance to win some concessions in the name of competitiveness, hoping it won't have to ask for wage rollbacks or layoffs. But it will assert that Stelco has too many employees, and it expects to use voluntary early retirement packages to shrink the workforce, a strategy already in place.

Pratt believes management has a responsibility to use the CCAA process to extract concessions from *all* parties involved—to fairly balance the interests of all stakeholders. But what does "fair" mean? Fair to whom? Does it mean anything besides a savage process of forced compromises? A fair solution will indisputably involve a makeover of Stelco's finances and debts, and along the way someone will likely lose something of real value, the obvious victims on the front lines being the unsecured creditors and shareholders (who may see their shares made worthless in a new corporate financial structure). While a restructuring may be inevitable, there's nothing pretty about it: someone loses.

At this early stage in the game, nothing is being conceded by anybody. While it's accepted by all involved that Stelco is in trouble, no one can agree on the language to describe the problem or its severity, much less the means to address it. That isn't so unusual—it's still only a month or so into the restructuring. If recent history in corporate Canada is a guide, a restructuring for a company of Stelco's size and in its situation could take a year or so to complete. A few years back, Algoma Steel, a company of comparable size to Stelco, took eight months to restructure in CCAA. Air Canada, the country's largest airline, took seventeen. For Stelco, a year in CCAA seems likes a reasonable bet.

Every company that goes into CCAA collides soon enough with the fact that this process is ludicrously expensive, requiring the hands-on involvement of insolvency lawyers and other restructuring advisors. As the company is now subject to decisions made by a Superior Court judge, Stelco management has retained a provisional army of consultants to navigate the world of the courtroom and the intricacies of a CCAA restructuring.

Michael Barrack and his team of lawyers from McCarthy Tétrault are the advocates for Stelco inside the courtroom, which is now effectively a "boardroom" where major decisions affecting the company are made. Barrack's assignment, in the main, is to make submissions before the judge at every step along the way. This means—among many other things—eventually tabling a restructuring plan and the arguments in favour of it, fighting off challenges or counter-arguments from those opposed and generally functioning as the "face" of Stelco before the judge.

Hap Stephen, a partner in Stonecrest Capital, a small boutique firm that specializes in advising companies in CCAA, is retained in the capacity of chief restructuring officer. He'll be the point guy for Stelco in negotiations with those affected by the CCAA filing. The story on Stephen is that he's done it all: he's the CCAA veteran, the guy you hire to strategize but also to negotiate with bruising efficiency, arm-twisting creditors to take a haircut—to accept less than the hundred cents on every dollar owed to them, or maybe get nothing at all if the company liquidates. Stephen has been involved in some of the highest-profile CCAA battles of the past decade, including Air Canada, Algoma Steel and Eaton's.

CCAA is a very public process, often scrutinized closely by the media, who hope to report on lurid conflicts featuring a wild and unpredictable cast of characters. So Stelco will retain several public affairs specialists and communications advisors—a competency it doesn't have in spades inside the company. Management will need to communicate frequently not only with the media but also with employees, pensioners, the communities where Stelco has operations, governments and the investment community on its progress—or lack thereof—in restructuring its finances. It needs, basically, to generate reams of corporate messaging, some of it likely to be in reaction to arguments made public by the union, which disagrees with the CCAA approach to Stelco's problems. The communications strategy will soon come to include letters issued periodically to employees under Pratt's name. The letters will explain what's going on, as management sees it, and will argue for the company's plans to get out of CCAA.

The company must also pay for the services of a court monitor and his or her legal counsel. A court monitor is essentially a roving eye for the judge, an impartial observer accountable to the court. In practice, the monitor is a referee in all the messy negotiations outside the courtroom, a voice of pragmatism and experience in helping the different parties understand how CCAA works—and what will fly in Justice Farley's courtroom and what won't. Alex Morrison, a chartered accountant from Ernst & Young, is the court monitor for Stelco, backed up by his legal counsel, Bob Thornton of Thornton Grout Finnigan, a Toronto law firm that specializes in insolvencies.

Additionally, Stelco will hire financial advisors at various investment houses to create financing options and lead the search for new investors. Labour lawyers from Hicks Morley will be brought in, as they have been for years at Stelco at collective bargaining time, to help management negotiate with the unions. Consultants experienced at evaluating a company's prospects in the steel industry will also play a role in this restructuring, providing assessments to support the contention that Stelco is not competitive and to help Stelco develop new business strategies to compete more effectively in the future.

Finally, at great expense, Stelco will pick up the tab for all the legal help and other advisers required by the union, pensioners and creditors to represent them in the courtroom, where they will argue virulently against the company's plans. The Stelco board has decided that they want this process to be conducted fairly, with everyone well armed with competent lawyers and advisors (who tend to come at a high price), regardless of the fact that such extensive lawyerly intervention has the potential to slow the process to a crawl, as the various parties use the courtroom to file motions and argue before the judge to gain what they believe is their fair share of the economic value still left in Stelco.

In this restructuring, there will be a consultant at every turn, in every corner, for every person and every interest. But if Stelco is to live and fight again as a financially reborn company, it now must fork over large sums to the insolvency consulting culture in Canada on which it's now dependent. Keeping Stelco alive, employing people, contributing to the economy—these are goals whose worthiness few would dispute. But the price? The consultant army is taking money from the Stelco purse that the company could be using to invest in its future and pay back its debts, which it's not doing right now.

STAYED PAYABLES #1

The dinner meeting is in a restaurant in Hamilton. The hosts are three Stelco executives: Colin Osborne and two vice presidents. These men know the operations of the company inside out.

The guest is a supplier to the company, David Alvil, a senior executive of a large global corporation that's owed big money by Stelco.

"Gentleman, pay us our money or we'll remove our equipment from your mill forthwith," David Alvil says after drinks arrive. "Stelco, by our current estimates, is in arrears in the amount of 7.86 million Canadian dollars. We'll have that before I leave, or our equipment will be decommissioned from your facilities, starting this week."

David Alvil is British, his tone measured, his threat delivered from a well-groomed middle-aged face. He glances at the menu and puts it down instantly. Clearly, the nourishment on offer is an affront to a man of acquired good taste. Alvil is all spit and polish, as Colin Osborne sees him, a man experienced at stepping off an intercontinental flight with his wits intact, suit unwrinkled, tie firmly knotted, no time for small talk, certain his reputation has preceded him.

"Gentleman, are we in agreement?" Alvil asks.

"You gentlemen won't get a fucking piece of equipment past the gate," says one of the Stelco vice presidents, pleased to let his annoyance show. He's a man in his late fifties who has dealt with toughness before, but nothing nearly as tough as his own face in the mirror. "Nothing leaves unless we say it leaves."

The two go back and forth.

Osborne is taken aback, and he figures so is the other Stelco executive beside him, who is gulping Black Russians one after the other as the exchange gets increasingly hostile. Osborne expected civility at least until the appetizers arrived. So when Alvil just let it rip, he was distracted, blinking around the room, trying to get his eyes to adapt to the freaky medieval setting, the dim dungeon lighting, nearly every surface in the room draped in red velvet, weighed down by gold tassels, including the funny hats on the waiters.

"Are we ordering food?" he interrupts.

Alvil checks his watch. He looks like he's finding it an effort to treat Osborne, a much younger man, as an equal. "The salient matter," he says, as if speaking from a podium to a vast audience. "In Chapter 11, in America, companies can elect to pay suppliers who provide an essential service. Surely we can come to an arrangement. We get paid our money and Stelco can keep working with our equipment, which is in both our interests. Is it not?"

Over the next six minutes, during the foodless consumption of another round of drinks, the Stelco executives enlighten Alvil on the differences between creditor protection laws in Canada and in the United States. In Canada, there is no "essential service" provision that would allow Stelco to pay arrears to a single supplier, no matter how essential Alvil's equipment is to the operation of the mill.

Alvil leaves the restaurant before the food arrives.

"Let's get this straight," says the Black Russian guy during the meal. "Not only do we not have to pay them what we owe while in CCAA, the law says we can *force* them to keep working for us?"

"We have to pay the new bills, likely on cash terms, but the payables are stayed," Osborne says. "And that's all she wrote. We can take them to court if we want. And they will have to keep working with us."

"How fucked is that?"

"You're right," Osborne says, shaking his head. "The thing is, they have business all over the US with the steel companies, and they just thought this was another Chapter 11 filing. They knew the risk of us going into CCAA—they just didn't know Canadian law."

"Where's he going now?"

"To fire someone in his Canadian legal office, probably."

"The money is a drop in the bucket for these guys," says the Stelco guy who'd fought with Alvil. "Does he look like he's hurting to you?"

"Still," Osborne says. "We owe them money, big time."

HIS TEAM

After a half-day operating review led mainly by Osborne, a session devoted to the capital expenditure budget, Pratt is pleased by how well his management team is coming together under his leadership. Most are really putting in the effort, working insane hours on all fronts, supportive of their new CEO. There are holdouts, as he expected, a few executives who wear the psychological scars of their long Stelco experience as a trophy of manliness. They find Pratt's mantra of "respecting people" and "constructive dialogue" total bullshit, and see nothing wrong with top-down intimidation to keep order in the mills. Pratt isn't frankly too worried about them, as there are both subtle and obvious strategies available to an experienced CEO to marginalize or eliminate disruptive voices if he has the support of his board and of the majority of his executives (which he does, and he knows it). You put these guys in the penalty box, he thinks, in jobs where they can't hurt people, or you show them the door if that doesn't work, let them go with dignity, a severance package, a retirement dinner, the illusion that they left on their own—although, at the moment, in CCAA, Pratt's hands are tied, since he can't pay a severance package without sending it to the court to be scrutinized. There, any interested party—like a creditor—could object to an executive payout when the company isn't paying its bills. He'll have to manage for a while longer with a few negative voices around him. All in due course.

STAYED PAYABLES #2

She sends letter after handwritten letter. She leaves long, complicated and nearly incomprehensible phone messages about how the family business is about to go under, how they need the money Stelco owes them, how they have bills to pay and food to eat and medicine to buy. She tells them her husband is sick and they may have to mortgage their home again. She tells them she is not a teenager any more, and she tells them she will keep calling and calling. The messages and letters do keep coming and coming. She calls many Stelco executives.

Osborne has listened to some of the calls. He has read the letters, and he has read letters from dozens of other creditors, many confused, all angry. He has talked to the company's lawyers. She keeps calling and calling.

Her husband does not call.

Osborne talks to Pratt. "It's only—what?—maybe one hundred and fifty thousand bucks? Can't we do something? Anything."

"There's nothing we can do, legally," Pratt says.

"Nothing?"

"Nothing."

"This is real. This is Hamilton."

"There's nothing we can do inside CCAA. You know that."

"You're right. I do."

THE MULTIPLIER EFFECT

From the Stelco mill in the heart of Hamilton's industrial suburbs near the lake, Pratt drives downtown for his meeting with Mayor Larry Di Ianni, a courtesy call to update him on the CCAA situation. So far Di Ianni has been a positive voice, both on and off the record—consistently balanced, and expressing the hope that the situation can be resolved without an economic catastrophe for Hamilton.

It's a bright February afternoon, as snowless as it is in Toronto but authentically cold. Here and there people stamp their feet at bus stops, their breath exhaling as little grey puffs, evocative of car exhaust.

Before too long, gigantic white holding tanks loom before Pratt, containing industrial compounds he doesn't doubt are explosive, stabilized by engineered process and good technology—likely deathly toxic in gaseous form. He merges into an underpass cloudy in airborne grime. The route is fringed with access roads and train junctions that disappear into fenced yards canopied in massive cranes and other manufacturing infrastructure. Long conveyor belts flow in and out of buildings, and giant vehicles roll on knobby tires the size of humans.

He's overtaken on the left by a rampaging dump truck, the rear of the dumpster flapping against the chassis at ear-damaging decibels. The vehicle dispenses a trail of gravel that ricochets off the road toward Pratt's car. A mini-meteor shower. Miraculously, the projectiles don't hit the windshield, although he hears rattling in the undercarriage, pinging near the grill. He keeps driving through the street-level evidence of rugged economic activity, the blue-collar Hamilton spirit in action, the drivers who'll push you off the road—and swear at you as a matter of course if you come between them and a just-in-time delivery.

There are also symbols he cannot ignore of failure and lost dreams, images of rust-belt decay, like the largely vacant parking lot at the Stelco mill where he'd spent the morning at an operational review. He figures there were three or four hundred cars parked near the main office today, not several thousand like there would have been in the postwar heyday of the company. The fact is, Hamilton isn't succeeding nearly as well as it had in a previous era, when globalization meant shipping steel around Ontario and the Great Lakes to the car plants on both sides of the border and, in return, bringing up raw materials from the mines Stelco still owns in the US north country. Hamilton continues to have jobs, a community fabric and its pride; it hasn't become a shell of itself, like Detroit or Buffalo. Pratt realizes again how critically important Stelco jobs are to the stability of the city, to the employees and their families, and to the pensioners, the dependents on the company, some in their seventies and eighties now.

He has been asked, as well, to protect Stelco as a financial nutrient feeding a regional system of wealth creation, the tens of thousands of people in and around Hamilton who depend on the steel mill to keep directing money into the community.

The multiplier effect, he thinks. Great when you're growing—nasty when you're shrinking.

Hamilton City Hall is an eight-storey building, concrete rectangles latticed in foreboding grids of reflective windows. It doesn't look to Pratt the way a city hall should. It's too opaque, unwelcoming, like the headquarters of a UN agency in a small European city, or a bunker-like Soviet embassy spruced up with new windows in the spirit of glasnost. To Pratt's sensibility, the building lacks the soaring limestone *gravitas* of the older skyscrapers in the downtown.

"Come into my office, Courtney," the mayor says, in a hearty voice. He's a fair-sized man with a big bald head, a former high-school principal, a fact that Pratt mentions to get the conversation going.

"I was a teacher once, a long time ago," Pratt says. "And I worked in administration at a junior college in Montreal, too."

He spent a year teaching at a private boys' school, Lower Canada College, when he was fresh out of university, ready to change the world one math or English lesson at a time. There had been rewards in helping the youngsters learn and stay at their desks without killing each other or driving him to exhaustion. But there was much he wanted to explore about how the world worked, and he wasn't finding it in a classroom, no matter how idealistic he'd been going in.

"We know what you're up against, Courtney, it's no secret," the mayor says evenly. "Stelco has been in trouble for some time. But don't underestimate the pride Hamiltonians take in this company. Stelco is hugely important. Hamilton is the steel capital of Canada, and the steel industry has defined our community for generations."

"I didn't come here to preside over a funeral," Pratt says.

In the silence that follows this statement, the mayor seems to be waiting for more disclosure, to be taken into confidence. There is so little Pratt can say, yet. By the dictates of Canadian securities laws, he knows his words must remain mostly platitudinous right now, unless he's telling everyone the same thing, preceded by a news release or conference call. He's hoping his body language, which as far as he knows isn't regulated by any securities commission on the planet, conveys the message that Stelco is in a serious mess—and that he's well aware of what's on the line, and committed to fixing things up.

"Boy, it really hits home, how intense people are around here with respect to Stelco," Pratt says. "I've never felt on the hot spot before in quite the same way. It's like every set of eyes in Hamilton are on me. No offense, Mayor, but it's like being in a mining town . . . where there's nothing but you and your decisions stopping the town from flying apart."

The mayor laughs but keeps it coming, courteous but relentless, staying on message, rattling off his talking points. "Hamilton is facing serious financial challenges. For a decade now, Courtney, the downloading of costs from senior levels of government has forced municipalities into a very tight corner, and forced us to cut essential services. Both the federal and provincial government have taxing mechanisms that take away from cities like Hamilton and don't give enough back."

"I know these are difficult times."

"They are."

"I realize the importance of Stelco jobs."

"You know many local companies rely on Stelco business?"

They sit in silence for another moment, then bring the meeting to a close, offering the promise of openness to each other, moral support. There just isn't a lot to say right now.

"If I can be of any assistance, let me know," the mayor says.

"Thanks, Larry."

"I don't know how well you know Hamilton, but it's a city with many wonderful surprises. A proud city. Proud people."

"I see this every day at Stelco."

"Get to know us better. The city."

Once he's back in his car, before doing anything else, Pratt opens up his BlackBerry. It tells him that the operational review at the mill is still ongoing. He's needed there. He decides to drive back with a detour through downtown. It's an aimless drive, and he's not sure what he's looking for. But he heard the mayor: *Get to know us better.*

He makes a left turn where he thinks he should. The road starts to climb through a neighbourhood of small bungalows and brick row-housing, a charming but dilapidated area of town. Some of the side streets provide glimpses of Hamilton Bay on the left, including a dockland reclaimed as a park and marina, all part of the program to make Hamilton beautiful again. But Pratt has seen studies on street crime, poverty, the drug trade. So many residents in this neighbourhood and others like it—especially the most vulnerable, the elderly—are afraid to go out, not just at night but in daylight, too.

At a stop sign, Pratt admires an old brick farmhouse. What is poignant to him isn't just that this farmhouse has survived a century or more, but that it's maintained an aged dignity amid the franchise coffee shops, donair palaces, tire distribution outlets and discount furniture stores all around it. He realizes he's made a wrong turn, so he doubles back downtown, intending to leave the city by a route that goes through a warehouse district, featuring wide boulevards and block-long brick buildings from a bygone era when this town was really hopping with industry. Plenty of these buildings are vacant or vastly underutilized now, their parking lots yielding weeds and discarded fridges. Near the curb he sees a powder-blue Lincoln, which he thinks is abandoned, but it's not. There are two men in it. Just sitting there.

He steps on the gas, and within minutes he knows exactly where he is.

Hamilton, like a half dozen other small cities in Canada and the northern US, was once a proud regional power centre, a fiefdom of industry, the companies often locally managed no matter who owned the equity or the bonds. Then rampant globalization started to produce a different breed of conglomerate, which today has an increasing tendency to gut local representation in senior management and centralize many decisions in faraway places.

In the glory years, cities in this part of the continent such as Hamilton, Buffalo, Milwaukee, Rochester and Windsor didn't take crap from anybody and were wealthy enough to build tall buildings designed by famous architects, endow the local university and charities, hold a Santa Claus parade and send powerful politicians into the larger decision-making arenas to do the pork-barrelling. Hamilton in particular was energized, or refuelled, over many decades by many thousands of immigrants, most from Europe, who had gotten off trains or buses here because they were exhausted from travelling oceans and they knew a cousin or army buddy in a tenement and anyway they were down to their last thirty bucks from the fifty-seven they had when they arrived in Canada; many of them were monosyllabic in English, ready to let their names be anglicized, shortened to be understood by the foreman who determined who got a shift at the steel mill—and who didn't.

I won't preside over a funeral, he thinks. But it may mean living through a deadly circus all the same.

GOLDEN TULIP

When Farley's decision is faxed over by the lawyers to Stelco headquarters on the morning of March 22, 2004, some five weeks after the comeback hearing, photocopies are hurriedly produced for the small group of Stelco executives and restructuring consultants gathered in the boardroom—all except Pratt, who's on the phone with the chairman.

When he joins them a half hour later, everyone is heads down, reading, feverishly making notes. He's not sure what to expect from the decision, but he is definitely surprised to be handed about fifty handwritten pages of legal argumentation in a virtually illegible scrawl.

Before Pratt starts reading, he flips through the document. On many pages there are lengthy inserts, entire paragraphs of marginalia, some written sideways or up in the corners, the handwriting shrinking to fit the space available. Words and occasionally sentences are crossed out.

"I'm going blind reading this," someone says.

"It's all good stuff, though. He's agreeing with us."

"And doing so at exceptional length."

"Standard judge stuff. You cover the bases."

"Hey, anyone at page forty-two yet?"

That's where the paper used by Farley becomes hotel stationery: Golden Tulip Hotel, Dar es Salaam.

"Where is Dar es Salaam?"

"In Africa. Tanzania, I think."

"Where did Farley write this? On one of those lion-hunting—"

"It's called a safari."

"He works with developing nations, pro bono. He helps develop their justice systems, legal frameworks. Probably at a conference there."

"How do you take seriously a decision from the Golden Tulip?"

Pratt is oblivious, underlining passages as he reads.

> It seems to me that the CCAA test of insolvency advocated by Stelco . . . is a proper interpretation . . . a financially troubled corporation is insolvent if it is reasonably expected to run out of liquidity within reasonable proximity of time

> as compared with the time reasonably required to implement a restructuring.
>
> The status quo will lead to ruination of Stelco . . . in such situations, time is a precious commodity; it cannot be wasted . . . in the case of Stelco . . . it is in crisis and in need of restructuring—which restructuring, if it is insolvent, would best be accomplished within a CCAA proceeding.

BOARD MEETING

A day after Farley's decision is handed down, Pratt attends a hastily convened board meeting at Stelco offices.

"Thanks to all of you for being available on such short notice," Pratt says. "I have some good news. The judge rejected the union's arguments and basically ruled in our favour. So, theoretically, we should now be ready to move forward with the restructuring. The only problem is that the union has immediately launched an appeal of Farley's decision."

"What's the significance of that?" the chairman asks.

"We're not too sure yet. We haven't been able to move forward at all on any discussions with the union while this ruling was outstanding. Maybe they'll agree to start talking while we wait for the appeal to be decided. If they don't, then we're likely looking at another long delay before we get into negotiations. We'll just have to wait and see."

"Not very encouraging."

There is a general murmur of consensus.

Later in the meeting, Pratt makes reference to rising steel prices, noting that worldwide demand for steel, especially from China, is driving a market boom. He tells the board that the dynamics of the global steel market are changing so quickly that it's hard to predict what will happen next. "The Chinese are building the equivalent of the Canadian steel industry every year. And still global demand is outpacing supply. The price rise may only be temporary, but analysts are getting bullish. This is something we'll have to watch out for as it will impact our results."

PHONY WAR

Two months now into the restructuring, the union is still completely unwilling to accept the necessity of the CCAA process. This is a huge problem for Pratt and his team, one that's about to get a lot worse, effectively bringing the restructuring to a halt. And that's mainly because of one factor: soaring steel prices. Rising prices should be a very good thing for a financially strapped steel company. But, weirdly enough, they present a problem, too. High prices embolden the union to refuse to negotiate on the basis that Stelco is in financial trouble. The union argues that Stelco is not a nearly bankrupt company but a company on the verge of making a whole lot of money. As a result, the restructuring enters a period that might be called the "Phony War," featuring bluster by all participants, in the courtroom and in the media, objecting to one thing or another. What stands out most in Pratt's mind during this period is his inability to actually sit down and start negotiating with the union.

In April, the Hamilton union leader, Rolf Gerstenberger, is quoted in the media saying that a government bailout for Stelco using taxpayer money would be the "easy way out." This position strikes Pratt as hypocritically absurd, given that Gerstenberger, an avowed Marxist-Leninist, has often expressed the view that Canadian governments have not intervened enough to protect Canadian steel companies in trouble.

On April 29, the company releases a study it commissioned that claims that a liquidated Stelco would pretty much destroy Hamilton's economy, using the logic of the "multiplier effect" to peg the impact at 25,000 lost jobs and $1.9 billion a year in lost wages and benefits.

As June rolls around, however, nothing real is happening.

A flashpoint for concern is that the collective agreement for the Lake Erie workforce expires at the end of July. The union local there wants to negotiate one on one with the company. The company refuses, arguing that, in a CCAA restructuring—a crisis situation—it needs to negotiate on a broader basis, with all the stakeholders at the table at the same time. No one-off deals.

No one is talking productively to anyone.

A very big shoe drops in June when General Motors, one of Stelco's largest customers, decides to seek court approval to terminate its supply agreement unless it gets assurances that the Lake Erie local will, at a minimum, provide ninety days' notice before going on strike.

The GM ultimatum brings about minor progress: on June 23, the company and the Lake Erie local agree on a process for carrying out talks, which includes an agreement requiring the union to provide notice of ninety days before striking. This has taken four months to accomplish.

July is characterized by negotiating nothingness.

August brings a schism between the Hamilton and Lake Erie unions. Gerstenberger, sticking to his Marxist-Leninist guns, refuses to come to the table at all to negotiate with the "ruling clique and lending syndicate" that, in his view (as published later in a newsletter of the Communist Party of Canada), "seem to be calling the shots at Stelco using the federal CCAA law as a weapon to force anti-labour concessions and negate traditional labour law and human rights."

As the summer ends, steel prices are still very high. Nonetheless, the company holds firm to the position that Stelco needs a CCAA restructuring. The logic here is that an exit now would leave the company overwhelmed by overdue financial obligations and by legal action from angry creditors that would paralyze its ability to operate.

However, management's inability to forecast the rise in steel prices partially undermines its objective to be viewed as the arbiter of "fair" among the stakeholders. The unions in particular argue that management can't be trusted to do the right thing, given its bad forecasting. That steel prices have a tendency to fall, always, is beside the point. This time they've risen fast, which causes influential people—the unions, bondholders and shareholders—to claim that there's more value for them inside Stelco than management forecast when it sought CCAA protection. And that belief reduces the willingness of anyone to make compromises or join management at the negotiating table.

Meanwhile, rumours begin to circulate that stock speculators are sniffing around the situation, factoring in rising steel prices and its effect on the value of the company and its share price. Some speculators are rumoured to be aggregating large blocks of common shares, bought for next to nothing because, as a company in CCAA, Stelco's stock is practically worthless. The main reason they're doing that: to make big money.

Rising steel prices and, as a result, rising operating profits for Stelco effectively take away the threat of imminent liquidation, which is management's only real weapon, and encourage the unions to hold to their view that Stelco has no need for creditor protection.

When autumn arrives, the restructuring is at an impasse.

At this point, Pratt and his team decide to embark on a parallel process to recapitalize the company while the financial markets are favourable. If Stelco is ever going to become competitive, new money—big money—needs to be found. While that refinancing process gets going, in early October the Lake Erie union local issues a ninety-day notice of a potential strike, only a few days after agreeing to extend its non-strike agreement into late November. For Pratt and his team, this decision comes out of the blue.

Soon after, one of the subsidiaries that Stelco has already arranged to sell announces that its employees have also voted to strike, likely in protest against having been without a contract since the end of July.

And it gets worse. With steel in tight supply in the global market, General Motors and DaimlerChrysler—two of the company's largest customers—announce they will seek alternative sources of steel if the Lake Erie strike threat isn't revoked. Furthermore, GM decides that it now wants assurances from Stelco that it has obtained—or soon will obtain—the financial means to exit CCAA as a viable company.

When the company announces strong third-quarter earnings, the media and the union clamour that Stelco has no business being in CCAA.

It is all getting very complicated, and increasingly contentious. The one bright light for Pratt and his team?

In November 2004, the company receives (and the court approves) a $900-million refinancing plan from Deutsche Bank, working on behalf of a group of Stelco bondholders. Significantly, the plan doesn't require concessions from workers or pensioners. But neither is it designed to pay down Stelco's pension-funding deficit of $1.3 billion, an issue soon to become the rallying cry for the union, pensioners and, eventually, the Ontario government.

The plan is advertised by Stelco management as a "stalking horse"—something to be improved upon, an encouragement to other financiers to step in with better offers now that the table stakes are, well, on the table. Even so, Pratt and his advisors believe there's enough in the plan to give something back to everyone, including unsecured debtors—perhaps a combination of cash and new shares in the restructured company, with no concessions for workers and pensioners. It's a plan he thinks the union should be reasonably happy to support.

VANISHING ACT

Pratt soon discovers that he's dead wrong about the union's support for the Deutsche Bank plan. This happens during a bizarre lull in a meeting in a hotel conference room in Burlington, on the outskirts of Hamilton.

In a quiet rage, he watches ice melt in his water glass, wondering where the Lake Erie union leader, Bill Ferguson, and his guys have gone five minutes into the meeting to preview the plan. They just got up and left, claiming a need for a private powwow, abandoning Pratt and Hap Stephen, Stelco's chief restructuring officer.

"Where did they go?" Pratt asks.

"They said they'd be right back," says Stephen, a bearded, intense guy in his fifties.

A quarter hour passes, then a half hour. "This Houdini act is ridiculous," Pratt says.

"I could see something in Ferguson's face when we started talking about 'no concessions,'" Stephen says. "It's not what they expected."

"What did they expect?"

"I have no idea."

Pratt and Stephen are packing up when Ferguson comes back.

"Courtney, Hap," Ferguson says. "Thanks for your time. We like what we hear about the 'no concessions.'"

"Don't you want to hear more?" Pratt asks. "Hap's here to take you through the high points in the plan."

"Again, thanks for your time." Ferguson leaves.

Minutes later, Pratt and Stephen get into separate cars in

the parking lot. Stephen pulls out first and Pratt follows him.

Pratt calls him on the BlackBerry as the two cars wind along the lakeshore toward the highway. "I really don't get it," he says. "Something is going on."

"Clearly, someone else is pulling the strings."

HELEN REEVES

He can hear the heels from a distance, a clack-clacking which can only be her, moving at top speed and getting closer. He might as well put the phone down instead of dialling out again, because she'll wait him out, content to do e-mail or make calls outside his office on the various communications appliances in her handbag.

"Come in, Helen," Pratt says.

She enters with an armful of press releases and media backgrounders. A veteran public affairs executive in her forties, Reeves has an aura of energized unflappability. Pratt has a high regard for her unflinching attitude to the tough jobs. He's seen her more than once take down a bully with a sublime comment, the insult delivered as if providing a compliment, her smile tempered by a flickering darkness in her eyes.

Several months back Pratt hired her as a consultant to help with improving the company's portrayal in the media and its communications with the workforce. They have a previous history of working together that goes back nearly twenty years. As she settles into her chair across his desk, Pratt reflects on how far she has come in her career. She's all poise under pressure, calm, the best kind of PR advisor for him:

she doesn't want to spin him or the company. Instead, all she asks—no, demands—is that he stays true to what he believes is right.

"Well, Courtney, where do we begin?" she says, a half octave too sweet for his liking—an indication that she has zingers on her agenda.

"There are a dozen arrows in me. Take your pick."

She suggests issuing a press release immediately on his decision to decline 3 per cent of the equity in the company reserved for management—a wrinkle in the Deutsche Bank refinancing plan.

"We have no intention of taking that equity. People know that."

"How did the provision get there in the first place?"

"The Deutsche Bank guys. It was a surprise when I read it."

"Is it normal in this kind of situation?"

"Investors want management with skin in the game."

"And?"

"Anyway, I'm dead against it. Next." He's gruff now. Feigning impatience.

What he's really thinking about is their loyalty to each other. He'd seen something in the blur of a young woman who was everywhere at once at Royal Trust, possessed of talent and a work ethic that shone above her peers. He has teasingly suggested to her that back when he first met her she had spiked-up purple hair, which she denies, although she will say she was a fashion-crazy kid at the time. She's like family to him now.

We talk like human beings, he thinks. A precious thing in this mess.

RON BLOOM

"Who's coming to this?" Pratt asks, wearily fumbling with a briefing memo he should have read yesterday but didn't because of the review with the finance guys that went past midnight. It isn't necessary for Hap Stephen to respond, because as soon as they turn the corner in the lobby of the airport hotel, Pratt can see for himself that they're walking into a ritualized show of force from the union guys. The ballroom is kitted out with a seating arrangement done in a massive rectangle of tables, draped in heavy white fabric. Upward of thirty people are in the room.

"Who's on our side?" Pratt whispers.

"It's just us."

"Where are we—the Kremlin?"

"Say hello to the United Steelworkers. Now we know why Ferguson and his guys walked out on us in Burlington. Orders from Pittsburgh."

Pratt observes minute adjustments in gesture and demeanour to accommodate their arrival. The conversation drops off. Men start moving toward their seats. He can hear spoons tinkling in coffee cups, a laptop being rebooted, the doors to the ballroom closing, then the inevitable clearing of throats before they get down to business.

Pratt and Stephen exchange a glance, a microsecond of shared rage: they both want to tell these guys to fuck off, and then leave. But they wade into what, to Pratt, feels like a receiving line at a wedding where everyone knows the marriage is on the rocks even before the ceremony is over. They go around the room in a parade of cursory nods and hellos while shaking hands. The union group, maybe forty in number, includes executives from the international headquarters of the United Steelworkers in Pittsburgh, the guys from the Canadian executive and each of the Stelco locals—except for the all-important Hamilton local—and several lawyers.

When Pratt comes around to greeting Ron Bloom, the go-to guy from the United Steelworkers, a beanpole of a man, he wonders if Bloom is really going bald or if he is just one of those headshaver types. Pratt expects a gotcha smile from the man but gets only a feeble handshake and a cold look, as if Bloom couldn't give a damn whose body the hand is connected to. The one time he met Bloom before, in private soon after he accepted the Stelco job, the man was courteous and straightforward enough, as well as entertainingly profane. The message Pratt gets today is that Bloom is all business, and that he's not to presume anything.

When Pratt gets back to his chair, he considers the union team in its entirety: mostly hefty men in their late forties and fifties, all dressed casually. At the centre of everything, Bloom, the brainy high priest of worker solidarity, is composed in solitary thought, carefully making scratchpad notes. It appears to Pratt that the other members of the delegation are not his equals, but his bouncers.

The lack of any Canadian leadership—or real authority—on the union side pisses Pratt off.

While he unpacks his notes, he doesn't listen to whoever is reciting the agenda. He's upset for not having anticipated this ambush. Given all his experience in human resources and labour relations, he knows that union negotiators—like their management counterparts—engage in showy preliminary bullshit to show you how tough and united they are. Although Pratt finds the staginess tedious and way too predictable, he regrets having come undermanned. But this wasn't supposed to be a negotiating session, only a backroom briefing on the Deutsche Bank plan.

As Hap Stephen pitches the plan, Bloom frequently interrupts with challenging questions. The questions don't all come from Bloom but, as Pratt sees it, the others who do talk seem to emerge from his rhetorical orbit. Then Pratt and Bloom mix it up.

"Are you guys asking for concessions?" Bloom says, in reference to the company's intent to introduce two-tiered pensions at its Alta Steel subsidiary in Alberta, a manufacturer of steel bar that will join a list of subsidiaries that Stelco will eventually sell off as "non-core" assets.

The pension issue isn't on Pratt's agenda today. He came here to talk about the refinancing plan. But he takes the bait anyway—otherwise, as Bloom is showing little interest in the plan itself, there'd be little to talk about. "We're trying to bring the current employees at Alta Steel up to 'big steel' company pension levels," he says. "And they'll get big increases, even if the new guys will be getting less. If you call that a concession—which I don't—then I guess we are asking for concessions."

"Well, we consider that to be a concession."

The talk goes in circles, going nowhere.

As the meeting ends, Bloom thanks the Stelco team members for their time and tells them that a reaction to the plan will come in due course.

The next day the union issues a press release rejecting the plan on the grounds that the company is, unacceptably, asking for worker concessions and doesn't have any solution to the pension deficit.

GM WEEKEND

A quiet dinner at home, Friday night, late November, the domestic choreography unfolding between them with serene efficiency.

Pratt is assigned to shuck shrimps and rend chicken breasts from the bone, aided by a cold Moosehead, while Alexa does the brainwork on the meal, reminding him to clean the knives and cutting board right away after working with the raw meat, and to pour her a glass of red wine because he hasn't done so yet.

The new place in Oakville doesn't have a ravine behind it. But the two-storey bungalow, like the Bridle Path home, is deceptive from the street, modest on the outside with an expansive and high-ceilinged interior, especially the big family room with the fireplace and wood-toned accents you'd find in a ski chalet.

"I read something in the paper today you might be interested in," Alexa says. The casually upbeat tone—it doesn't fool him for a second.

"And this will improve my life—how?" he says, not looking up.

"This study said that if you live on four hours of sleep indefinitely, your mental response time slows, the equivalent of being on the tipsy side of things," she replies, opening the oven.

"Mental response time, slow," he says, then pauses. "I'd prefer to get there after one or two beers if I'm going down that route."

"You should try not to work so late, Courtney. So often."

She moves on to news from their sons—updates on their career moves, vacation plans. She has made her point without nagging. A slim, graceful woman, Alexa is rarely without a smile or kind word for people. She is a writer of heartfelt thank-you notes for the smallest acts of kindness shown to her, but she is no pushover, and in certain fields she is competitive. She owns a wicked tennis forehand. On the golf course, she has four holes-in-one, and he has exactly none. No one who knows her well, certainly not Pratt, would suggest she didn't know precisely what he was doing in the seven minutes between the time he said he was fetching the shrimp from the downstairs fridge and the time he returned. She's caught him before on the BlackBerry, scheduling into conference calls or replying to e-mail when he really should be doing something else.

He takes pleasure in the rituals and verbal shorthand developed in raising a family together.

"So what's the plan for the weekend?" she asks.

"Alexa." He's told her several times already: Stelco is the plan.

On Saturday morning, the wind is bracing, the grass in the back yard glazed in frost, the sun throwing off sharp angles of light, even though it's almost noon now. Pratt is slowly circling the pool, staring intently at the blue tarp stretched over it, pointlessly worried that there's a tiny gap somewhere into which his two-year-old granddaughter might fall, even though, with two hyper-vigilant grandparents and two hyper-vigilant parents, the chances of Cedar being alone outside by the pool are virtually nil. It takes two loops around the pool to convince him that safety is assured, unless his granddaughter arrives here in the exact shape of an envelope.

The tarp-covered pool, he thinks, could be redeployed as a kind of trampoline for Cedar when she gets bigger, but he'll say nothing of the sort to her parents, knowing that the idea will provoke fears in everyone. The tarp that could hold a hockey team.

There's nothing he can do today to resolve the conflict between his family and his professional life. On the digital pathways, his restructuring team has been conferring by e-mail and phone since before the sun came up, negotiating with Ron Bloom and other union executives in Canada and Pittsburgh. Unless the company can give GM reassurances by Monday morning that the Lake Erie union will revoke its strike threat, the car company will soon start sourcing steel elsewhere.

No one on Pratt's team is physically with one another, anywhere. It's a virtual collaboration, done from homes and cottages and on the move, in coffee shops, health clubs, malls. Everyone is tethered to work, regardless of where they are, and the quality of their weekend moments—as they walk around a pool, grocery shop with their spouses, get in a round of squash—is undermined by the venom leaking at everyone, electronically, from the negotiations, spearheaded by Hap Stephen going head to head with Ron Bloom.

Pratt pauses for a BlackBerry scroll, after neglecting to respond to the buzzing on his hip while inspecting the pool.

The e-mails are coming from many sources—Barrack, Stephen, Osborne, Reeves—everyone copied on everything.

> Bloom wants to tie every issue but the kitchen sink to give us the 90 days' strike notice we need. He wants . . . I don't know what he wants!
>
> I got off the phone with him. Nothing but obscenity. Gave it back.
>
> This is going nowhere.
>
> What can we give? Should we give?
>
> I don't know how we're going to get through this.
>
> We need two press releases in draft form. One if it goes well. One if it doesn't. Start with the doesn't.

Pratt is about to join the e-mail conversation by offering the standard (yet timely, he feels) let's-soldier-on-in-good-faith sermon, but he looks up when the door shuts harder than it should.

Alexa, hands on her hips, is wondering what he's up to.

"It's safe, the pool," he says as if making a profound discovery. There's understanding on her face, but also disappointment.

"What time are the kids getting here?" he asks.

"They land at five-fifteen. They're coming straight out."

He suddenly feels guilty.

"I need you to pick up some soy milk," she says.

"For the little one?"

"I'm not sure who for. They might all be off dairy by now."

She turns to go inside. He looks at the tarp. For a long minute, as he surveys the bright blue rubberized surface, he's tempted to stop off at the toy store and buy a gaggle of plastic yellow ducks and situate them on the tarp. Cedar would like that. But he dismisses the idea as a paranoia-creator for everyone. What if she wants to play with the ducks? And falls through the impossibly robust tarp?

Minutes later, driving to the mall, it's a struggle not to reach for the BlackBerry, which is buzzing enough to provide a near-constant hip massage. In the parking lot he catches up with the storyline.

Hap Stephen and Ron Bloom have made the fight personal. An e-mail brawl.

Pratt looks up. Cars on all sides. Directly in front of him, a young mother is loading an old Volvo from a full grocery cart, her two boys in the cart fighting with one another, the younger one in tears. Something in the woman's multitasking concentration, her ability to manage the kids, the heavy bags of groceries, reminds him of Alexa, of her constancy, how she remains even-keeled on pressure-cooker days.

His thumbs get to work.

> I'd like a look at both press releases tonight. Helen?
>
> Make sure we make it clear that we're going to the wall to get a deal. If this fails, I want people to know why.

> Hap, go as far as you need to. You know what has to happen.

For the first several minutes in the health food store, he's blindly walking the aisles, his mind elsewhere, fragmented into sectors of concern mapped precisely to the input of his restructuring advisors. Mentally, he stands between Stephen and Bloom, jumps into the message-shaping between Reeves and her writers, and he can hear the voices of all the lawyers in the background, the brilliant discordance among those who know when to disagree, when to harmonize and when to shrug at the nastiness, as if to say, look, we're only lawyers, not miracle workers.

"Soy what?" Pratt says to Alexa when he gets her on the phone.

"Soy milk."

He keeps her on the line as he walks around the store and asks two different staff members where the soy milk is.

"There are thirty different types of soy milk," he says to his wife, angry at the complexity in a genre of nutritional diversity that he used to take for granted, when milk was milk, not organic, not soy, not cow or goat, but pure milk, a cold white liquid, best taken with a chocolate chip cookie, not poured over muesli or used to chase supplements.

"The best-before date is what counts. But talk to someone."

"Talk to someone?"

"A service person. In the store."

Eventually, after fifteen fretful minutes of comparison shopping, he leaves with three different brands of soy milk, just to be on the safe side. One carton is fortified with vitamins that the teenaged girl behind the counter said were really, like, ace on the immune system. Another is non-fortified but has the word "organic" plastered all over it, and that must be good, he thinks. The third carton, his favourite, the one he suspects will meet with his son and daughter-in-law's disapproval, is a chocolate soy drink. He thinks, maybe I'll drink that.

Before he puts the car in gear, he scans incoming e-mail:

> Bloom keeps talking about a "nuclear option." I suppose he means a strike. What else could he mean? Beheadings?
>
> I've had it with Bloom. HAD IT. He keeps threatening to "crater" the company. And you just never know what he means. And he likes that. He likes that!!!!
>
> We're asking for civility—and they're holding us over a barrel.
>
> They don't see it our way. Which way do they see it?
>
> I gotta sign off for a few hours. I'm getting killed at home.
>
> My wife is going to crater me. CRATER.

On the way home, Pratt feels more stressed than usual. The outcome of this weekend in the life of this corporate restructuring—if it isn't good—could contribute to devastating outcomes for Stelco employees: layoffs, liquidation, collective pain for thousands. Losing GM's business—this is serious.

At dinner he excuses himself for a conference call. At midnight, everyone else in bed, he reads press releases. The following day is a blur of excuses around the house. If he could be in the moment with them, he would.

Mid-afternoon.

After reading an e-mail exchange between Stephen and Bloom that was forwarded on to him, he's certain there won't be an agreement. The nail in the coffin is the union's request for an all-night negotiating session with management.

On a Sunday night? No way we're going into that bullshit.

> I have to check out for a bit. I have things to do around the house. If something breaks, let me know.

Her hand is in his, small and warm. Grandfather and granddaughter, alone in the back yard, away from the tarped pool, at the back of the lot where Alexa wants to create a meditation garden next spring. Today the area is a corner of frozen mud where a sandbox had once been. He's being led by his granddaughter toward three squirrels that appear to be sharpening their teeth on the remains of a bird feeder abandoned by the previous owners. The squirrels respond to their approach by darting about. Cedar is burble-talking, pointing excitedly at the rodents. She breaks free from her grandfather and starts to run toward the bird feeder. The squirrels panic, skedaddling up a big oak, chirping madly as the girl picks up the bird feeder, behind which there's a mound of leaves. Pratt suspects that nuts—the squirrel's winter stash—are buried beneath the leaves. He wonders how the squirrels will respond to a violation of their food sanctuary. He's concerned that one of the agitated rodents will drop out of the tree—either by accident, or with plans to attack. He looks up. All three squirrels are manically jumping branches.

Once, in Toronto, on a jog along the ravine, he saw a squirrel fall out of a tree from maybe thirty metres or so, landing with a sickening thwack on the pavement. Pratt thought the animal was dead, and it was certainly unconscious for an instant, but when he nudged it with his foot, it took off like crazy and went up a tree. Scared the bejesus out of him.

He keeps moving, assessing the relationship of Cedar to the rampaging squirrels, putting into context the risk factors. The squirrels have descended down the tree trunk, gripping the bark near the base, all three upside down, possibly enraged by the little girl kicking through the leaves, goofing around with the bird feeder. His hip starts to vibrate. Incoming e-mail.

He keeps walking and is soon within hand-grasping distance again, putting himself between the squirrels and the little girl, picking her up and turning toward the house. He sees a raccoon, too, creeping along the border of the fence. Two raccoons.

"Who's looking at us from the window, over there?" Pratt says.

"Mummy."

"And who else?"

"Daddy."

"And?
"Gwanny."
"Now, let's wave at everybody. And say hello!"
"Hello, everybody!"

AUTHORIZATION (PHONE CALL)

"Helen—hi, it's Courtney."
"What's up?"
"It's all gone off the rails."
"Right."
"Get the press release out."

This is a very difficult situation for the Company and all its stakeholders. Contrary to the union's allegations, and as the public record clearly demonstrates, the Company had pursued every possible opportunity to engage the union in the meaningful discussions that could have provided our largest customer with the security it has requested for months. We have been prepared to meet right to the last minute in this matter. But as recently as last evening, the union made clear that it wanted to tie a large number of unrelated issues to the simple provision of security of supply GM required by this morning.

CONSCIENCE DIALOGUE

KAREN TURNBULL, PR CONSULTANT

I'm a half step behind Karen Turnbull on her morning run through the subzero November darkness. As a compulsive multi-tasker, she probably thinks there's nothing unusual in inviting me for a pre-dawn conversation on our PR strategy while she trains for her next marathon. I went along because, to be honest, I'm still not completely divorced from the athlete's ego I honed playing hockey at university way back when. I still have moments when I believe I can run at any speed I want. I'm loyal to the old notion that without aerobic pain there's no gain.

"I don't mind a pace like this, now and then, it's a good warm-up," Karen says after we've been running for about ten minutes.

"A pace like what?" I say, trying to speak normally as my breath comes faster and faster. I'm in decent shape—but this is hard work.

"A slow jog. When we're done, I'll crank it up."

"How much do you run?"

"Oh, I try to put in—what?—a hundred klics a week."

"Your feet must be a mess."

"Running through pain," she says. "Isn't that life?"

"Is it?" What a strange thing to say. She must be high on that endorphin rush that runners get.

"Well, there's always ibuprofen," she laughs, and picks up the pace.

Karen, in her mid-forties, advises large companies in times of crisis, helping her clients get their message out to the media and other stakeholders. She's a spin doctor, and very experienced in electing politicians, relying on the blackest of the propaganda arts in the service of partisan politics. She's a genius with negative advertising and other campaign strategies that demonize opponents in the court of public opinion.

I don't know that she'd agree with me, but Karen is what I'd call an ideologue, armoured not only with her helmet of blonde hair but the sound bites of moral certainty: she's always right, her enemies always wrong. Her success—and she's very successful—comes from rendering complex issues into black and white, as pro or con, as a competition between victors and losers, with no such thing as a middle ground.

I do not pick up the pace.

"So, Courtney, here you are, seven months later, and really nowhere in the process," she says, finally slowing down in order to stay even with me. "The union has the upper hand in the media, and they know it, too."

"That may be so."

"If you'd been more aggressive out of the gate, you wouldn't be in the weak position you're in right now."

"I think you're confusing media perception with reality. Yes, we're getting slammed, but I wouldn't say we, the company, are in a weak position relative to anyone. The lack of cooperation puts everyone—the union included—in a weak position if we don't come up with a deal."

She gives me a look, obviously unimpressed, and looks about to speed away from me, but fights that urge. "You want advice to win?" This is said in a singsong voice.

"I want to do the right thing."

"I have to be honest," she says. "In my experience, it's often men like you—in business, in politics, wherever—who boast about taking the high road but end up doing the dirtiest mudslinging. You start off squeamish, then comes the overreaction after not being truthful with yourself about the situation up front, naively assuming everybody is going to play by your rules. The monster comes out when you don't get your way."

"I'm not that guy, Karen."

"I'm not sure yet what kind of guy you are," she says plainly. "I would have the same goal as you do in this situation: to get a deal. But I'm getting the impression we don't have a similar view of the tactics."

"Maybe so."

"It's this simple to me," she says. "What happens in the media, whether you like it or not, has an effect on the power dynamics, and on who wins or loses. Maybe the judge isn't going to be totally swayed, but he's not immune to hits on his reputation in the press. And the big guys in government are, as you well know, highly sensitive to what makes the news. If the union beats you at the media war and makes the judge or government look bad, and also hurts your reputation as a capable CEO, you'll fail in your job and in your duty to protect the company's interests."

"What are you recommending, then?"

"You need to bring the union to its knees. Now. They're demonizing you. You need to get operational in taking them on."

"You want to ruin reputations? Get more confrontational?" I'm warmed up now.

"Now don't be naive," she says. "You get your core messages out . . . and, well, those core messages should include legitimate personal counterattacks. It's not as if they're not running your reputation through the mill. And Hamilton's your big opportunity. One of your Hamilton attackers is a known Communist, this Rolf character. You could rip his throat out just by replaying his own words. 'Ruling clique'? Come on! No one who reads a real newspaper or watches the tube likes an actual Communist for God's sake, not in Canada. Didn't we just watch the Russians and the Chinese drop the rhetoric over the past twenty years? They're more capitalist than we are! And they'd be taking a fairly hard line with the Rolfs of the world, no question. Very hard."

I try to interrupt, but she's not through with me yet.

"For another thing, you're the new CEO here, not deaf and blind and stupid from a lifetime of making steel. You walked in from the outside, clean as a whistle, kind of, although we'll have to downplay that you were a Stelco board member for nearly two years. I can see you quite easily making a very public case that the Hamilton union is holding a once proud company hostage—that it needs to be purged if not completely broken. This is Canada, after all. However, you will also have to fire a bunch of the old Stelco crowd around you now, in management. Wipe their names from the slate. Clean house publicly. So people *get* what you're doing."

"I'm not going there, Karen. You're also talking about waving a red flag in front of a bull. I mean that. We'd risk a strike at Hamilton with those tactics. Maybe a company-wide strike."

"Oh, we can hedge that. You just scare the crap out of the pensioners if you have to. Drive a wedge between them and the union. The pensioners need to understand that those Communist-led idiots in Hamilton are risking what they worked all their lives to build. You need to tell those pensioners that you've come into this place to clean up management, clean up the plant and clean it of the people who have turned Stelco into a loser and put their pensions at risk. And you need those pensioners, at a minimum, to become skeptical of the union, not, as they are doing now, supporting them."

I want to see how far she's willing to go with her strategically insane dirty pool, this propaganda jihad. "And Ron Bloom, the USW?"

"He's an American. He has a native understanding of how media confrontation—and coverage of any kind—works to his advantage. You could play Captain Canada here a bit more angrily. Get a bigger cape, Courtney. Suggest infiltration from Big American Labour, cry the crocodile tears. And this will set you up to play the Canadian card even more powerfully when the American bondholders get your head in a vice as the deal comes together, if it comes together. Because you're going to have to fight harder with them, that's for sure. That's one thought. But, with Bloom, I think you just ignore him in the public eye, except as a representative of Big American Labour."

I make a show of pondering her counsel, but I totally disagree with her. "You realize that any chance of building a better Stelco goes down the drain with that type of thinking. There's already a complete lack of trust between union and management. And you want to make it worse? The people in the Hamilton plant come into work every day and do a good job. As for scaring the pensioners, Karen, this is definitely a non-starter."

She kind of snorts at me. "Things need to get worse before they can get better, Courtney. And that may take a decade, a generation. Don't you see that? You must know that. Besides, who's to say you'll be invited to stick around after you get out of CCAA? That's not a sure thing. You're not a steel guy. So why not do the job you've been hired to do, which is get this company refinanced, and worry less about being a beacon of light for everyone."

"All these scenarios—where would they get us? As I listen to you, what's going through my mind is that it's probably better we 'lose' the media war. Or manage our losses and not try to 'win' something not worth winning. We don't need the public's vote, like politicians. We need a financial deal, as you say. I just don't see the ultimate benefit in making this situation worse."

"You'll get yourself fired, Courtney!" She's almost shouting at me.

Ironically, for someone whose passion had once been selling free-market capitalism as government policy, Karen takes a dim view of business executives, believing they don't understand the consequences of appearing indecisive in crises.

I see the giant wind turbine in the distance.

"You see that thing?" I say, pointing. "We put that there when I was CEO of Toronto Hydro. It was a PR move in a sense, of course, a token gesture in the spirit of promoting green power. That's the kind of spin doctoring I like: when we focus on the positive."

"But a token gesture all the same."

I won't respond to that.

"Courtney, you're too nice a guy to be involved in this." She doesn't mean to offend me. It might even be a compliment. But it pisses me off.

"I'm sure as hell not going to apologize for being nice," I say with more anger than I intend, which surprises her into silence.

We keep running, and I know now that it's up to me to get this conversation back on track, or else this interlude is wasted.

"Karen, hear me out on this. I don't think 'nice' needs to be a euphemism for 'weak.' Yes, we all decided to take the high road, and I still believe that's the right approach. Losing battles in the media, or in fact having my reputation put through the media wringer, isn't pleasant. They say I'm screwing shareholders. They say I don't know what I'm doing, taking a company into CCAA that doesn't belong there. They say I'm in the pocket—or will be—of American bondholders. It doesn't matter if my media critics, and I can think of a few, seem to be hand puppets to the views of the hedge-fund guys themselves. You read their columns and just wonder if they've ever seen a world outside their computer screens."

"For instance?"

"Why dignify these guys by talking about them too much? I'm saying that this kind of criticism, while personally upsetting, is much like those blackfly bites at the first of spring. After a while, you develop some kind of immunity. But it's nuts to spend too much time eradicating blackflies. You'll poison everything around you. That's what I really think."

"You're putting your job at risk."

"We're going to stay on the high road."

"You'd never make it in politics. End of story."

"Lots of folks have told me I'd make a good politician. But I tend to agree with you."

"At least accept that a key part of your job now is very public. Very political. You're no different than a politician in key respects. And if you're not getting results, you're failing. Right now, you're failing."

My turn to lapse into silence.

I simply refuse to admit that the media or "perception" war is a governing force that can shape our restructuring. We all get so worked up about these issues of perception because we live in a media-obsessed society, and so undue respect must be paid to those who watch and report on us, even when their journalistic laziness results in bad stories. I can't count the number of times that reports appeared in the national press in which liberties were taken with my reputation without so much as a phone call to get my viewpoint. I know those indignities are all in the job description, but to dignify them with further attention?

We're both picking up speed now: this much we agree on. There's a slight burning sensation around my knees and ankles, but that's never stopped me before. So I keep running. I'm sweating hard, and she's not.

"Look, I really do know the union guys are trouble for me," I concede. "They play their cards well. But they're one-dimensional. They don't worry about creditors or shareholders. They know I have to, and they're trying to make my job as tough as they can. All the same, I don't see myself going on an anti-union crusade. Even when they piss me off. They'd love us to get into the mud with them. They're good at it."

"I'd advise you to take some mud-wrestling lessons."

The closer we get to the wind turbine, the more I like it. It's a truly beautiful thing: a beacon for the promise of renewable energy, a positive message in the sky, whirling in the strong winds coming off the lake.

Before going to Stelco I spent just over two years at Toronto Hydro, helping the company get ready for what was promised by the government: a competitive marketplace for electricity distribution. The morning I announced my resignation, there was an awkward meeting with my management team—the news of my Stelco appointment had leaked to the media. There was disappointment on their faces, the sense conveyed to me, in not so many words, that I was deserting the ship. It made me feel terrible.

At Toronto Hydro I'd been on the hot seat in the summer of 2003 during the massive blackout that spanned much of the eastern seaboard. I did press conferences and media interviews one after another, trying to reassure the public—via the media—that all was being done to bring power back online. I know the influence of the media well, and respect it, even if I don't like it much right now. It's no fun being pilloried.

"I still think you need to hit back harder," Karen says, as if unsatisfied with my responses to her line of thinking.

Where did she learn to talk like this?

"Karen, you're from up north, originally?"

She gives me a suspicious glance. "I lived in Kirkland Lake until I was about fifteen."

"So, a mining company brat."

"How did you—oh, of course, you ran Noranda!"

"Your dad—what did he do?"

"He was a geologist for Kirkland Lake Gold. Looking for gold, always. He's living with us since Mom passed on. We had to take away his driver's licence last year. He's not doing so hot, frankly."

"Toronto's a long way from Kirkland Lake."

"Figure skating took me to Toronto. But not all little girls with big dreams make it to the Olympics."

But she's living a different dream: by all accounts, she's a supermom, with two kids in private school, a doctor for a husband, a big house in North Toronto, and a fair bit of community work in her schedule.

We're under the wind turbine now. It's hardly moving, the wind having died down completely.

I stop running.

She runs in place, staring at me as if I've lost my mind.

"Had enough so soon?"

I have, actually. There's a strain developing in one calf.

"Karen, your father. His pension, if he has one. If he'd been at Stelco, would you have wanted me to play hardball with him?"

That was below the belt.

Too nice a guy?

CHAPTER THREE

THE WATERING HOLE

OPENING THE KIMONO

As November flows into December, Pratt and his team start pitching the company, as planned, to different investor groups in the hopes of getting a better refinancing proposal than the Deutsche Bank "stalking horse." They appreciate now that if the union is going to support any plan, then that plan needs to contain a solution to the pension deficit. So, in the lingo of high finance, they open the kimono, and show a little more skin, to lure investors by talking up the intrinsic core value of the company, the strategic opportunity, contextualizing the problem of Stelco's lack of competitiveness, including a history of abysmal labour relations.

Day after day, Pratt and his team give presentations to groups, who are welcomed one after another into the company boardroom. They ruffle flip-chart decks, answer questions, have lunch brought in, don hard hats for plant tours. The investors come from steel companies in Europe, the United States and Asia, but also from private equity firms, the financial speculators—some in Canada, some not—that are evaluating a stake in a restructuring Stelco.

The pressure is mounting on Pratt. While he has more control here than in the courtroom or in labour negotiations, he's under scrutiny from all sides—the court, the unions, shareholders, pensioners, employees, the media. In the final days before the 2004 holiday break, however, he's a little more optimistic that they'll get the cash infusion they need. The presentations are going well. Some potential investors are more appealing than others, though. He's partial to the ones who view Stelco as a going concern, not as a divisible collection of assets that can be bought, rearranged or traded as if steelworkers were tiny plastic figures on a game board.

He urges his people to keep their game faces on. This enterprise in corporate survival requires discipline and putting your best foot forward, always. His people know this. They nod at him in the right way. They say and do the right things. They have hopes, too. They want Stelco to survive and they want to keep their jobs. Pratt himself hopes for a pivotal management role for himself in the Stelco turnaround, to carry on as the CEO. But, as the kimono is closed after each briefing, the coffee mugs and water bottles removed from the boardroom, he sometimes sees a shadow in the eyes of his colleagues, who know there's nothing dignified about inviting outsiders into your home when the "for sale" sign out front is there not by choice but necessity.

SOON, SOON

Rain. Days of it. Vancouver weather.

Pratt, seated in the cramped attic of his son and daughter-in-law's house, is e-mailing the afternoon away as preparations for Boxing Day dinner continue downstairs.

Laughter reaches him now and then and, once, a heart-breaking round of sobs from his granddaughter, who is overwhelmed by all the excitement of the past few days.

From time to time he looks up from his e-mailing to stare out the tiny gable window into the rain and fog and to tell himself he's a lucky man, surrounded by family for the holidays. Still, there's something not quite right about monsoon weather for Christmas.

The dog at his feet, panting hopefully, nudges a ball toward him.

Not now, Sandy.

Soon, soon.

NEW YEAR'S EVE

"Lex, with any luck, this thing will be over by spring."

"Let's hope."

"We're optimistic that good bids will come in. And when we're out of this, I can focus on running a steel company, not sitting in a courtroom."

"Our life can get back to normal. Wouldn't that be nice?"

"I really believe we're on track now, finally."

"Let's keep our fingers crossed."

DIAGNOSIS

In the new year, they're sitting together in the consultation room when the doctor walks in. "Well, it's cancer," he reports matter-of-factly, and then walks out again.

They sit there, stunned.

All that comes to him is the thought that the doctor walked in and walked out and they don't know what to do next.

Another doctor walks in. "Here's how we're going to deal with this."

BULLY

As January unfolds, Pratt finds himself wondering why he should keep working. What counts here? But Alexa wants him to stay on at Stelco. Or mostly she does. There are shared moments of doubt that float between them, nothing said, the wavering like a sudden breeze—here, then gone, just like that.

In the private language of their marriage, they talk in circles, providing reassurances on each loop through the arguments pro and con. Somehow the words keep coming, but it's not the words that matter to either of them, only the sound of their voices trying to harmonize, the message in the pauses and interruptions.

She tells him he made a commitment. They made a commitment.

He looks away, her courage too much to bear.

We'll get through this, she tells him.

He tells her, we'll get through this.

He thinks of the cancer as a bully, and bullies can be beaten.

He has fought a few bullies. There were unfinished battles that he's glad never went the distance or who knows what would have happened—like becoming a bully himself. You just never know until tested. You don't.

But he thinks he knows himself, and his wife.

We'll beat this, she says.

"THE SMARTEST GUY ON BAY STREET"

In January, a group of Stelco shareholders enter the restructuring battle and demand that their voices be heard. They're led by Toronto financial speculator Roland Keiper, the "Smartest Man on Bay Street," as he's been described in a national business magazine. Keiper, who has a reputation for buying into distressed companies and profiting on corporate takeovers and restructurings, has publicly expressed criticism of management and the board for putting Stelco into CCAA. He has also accumulated a big equity position in the company, giving him legitimate grounds to arrange a meeting with Pratt, Pratt's advisors and various members of Stelco's board of directors, including the chairman. One reason for the meeting is to enable Keiper to present his case that there's more financial value left in Stelco than was indicated in the management forecast that resulted in the decision to enter CCAA.

Keiper's negotiating position, however, is arguably very weak. In CCAA restructurings, the shareholders come last for consideration. That's because, to put it very simply, they have assumed the risks of ownership in anticipation of the rewards, a fundamental dynamic of capitalism. Stelco isn't in any condition—in management's forecast—to be handing out rewards, although in order to exit CCAA the company must restructure its financial obligations, or be declared bankrupt. What all this really means is that secured creditors get repaid first, because of the collateral they have against Stelco's assets. Unsecured creditors—such as suppliers or the holders of unsecured bonds—get paid next. Creditors have negotiating clout in part because the court allows them to vote on whether to accept any restructuring plan tabled by the company to exit CCAA. Furthermore, as Justice Farley has said in court on different occasions, the unionized steelworkers and the Ontario government each have "an effective veto"—if not a formal one—over decisions affecting Stelco's future. As it now stands, a whole lot of people need to be satisfied before shareholders get anything. In fact, in a CCAA restructuring, it's common for public companies to actually cancel their old shares and issue new ones to creditors or new investors who put up capital to get the company back on its feet.

So what card does Keiper have to play?

The fact is, shareholders are still the owners of the company and are ultimately responsible for selecting the company's board of directors, which means the board is likely to be open to hearing the views of someone who claims to own, or represent, some 35 per cent of the outstanding stock. As Keiper does.

What makes him—and speculators like him—a formidable voice is that he's a professional gambler with deep pockets, capable of making a big financial bet on Stelco by buying its shares cheap on the open market and then selling them after the turnaround when the stock has risen. But for that to happen, Keiper first has to persuade the board and others, including the judge, that there's value inside the company for shareholders beyond what's owed to others with stronger claims. He must demonstrate that Stelco's prospects and its asset base account for more wealth than is stated in management's forecast. And that's exactly his view.

A company's forecast is based partly on fact, but it's also speculative, an educated guess at how a company and its sector will perform in future. Ultimately, a forecast reflects the assumptions and biases of those doing the forecasting. The forecast, then, is Keiper's card, the one he's made himself, which shows how creditors can be paid in full with something left over for shareholders. He strongly believes there's no need whatsoever to cancel existing shares.

And that brings him to the meeting in the McCarthy Tétrault boardroom with the Stelco team. It's just like so many meetings in this restructuring: people with contrary views around a boardroom table. Keiper shows up with Michael Woollcombe, his legal counsel. Keiper looks to Pratt like a guy in his forties who has spent many years behind a computer screen, cranking out financial models and torturing balance sheets long into the night. He radiates intensity, but he seems oddly restrained as he reads from a prepared text. One sentence after another. One number after another. It occurs to Pratt that the only plausible reason why Keiper is reading from a prepared text is to discipline himself. He is known, according to Pratt's sources, as a guy whose brain never stops and whose mouth keeps going long after he's won an argument. The argument here flows from Keiper's confidence in strong steel prices and the quality of Stelco's operations. Keiper also suggests that Stelco's current share price is significantly undervalued relative to comparable steel companies.

As Pratt listens, he concedes that Keiper's work is based on sound logic if you buy his assumptions. But Keiper appears to give only minimal consideration to the effective veto of the union and the government that weigh so heavily on Pratt and team. The union expects a large payment toward the pension deficit, a perspective Pratt knows the government shares.

But voices like Keiper's must invade the dreams of all responsible CEOs in charge of publicly traded companies. And their nightmares, too. As the presentation comes to a close, Pratt is feeling uneasy. He's been on the receiving end before of the logic offered up by the Roland Keipers of the world. What do these guys want? When he asks bluntly what it is that Keiper and Woollcombe want, they tell him: seats on the board.

"We'll think about it and get back to you," the chairman says.

FORECASTING MADNESS

Stelco's forecast will continue to foment discontent—notably among shareholders—from now until the end of this restructuring. Pratt and his managers are under intense pressure to keep the forecast current, reflecting the rapid changes in a steel market that's in an unprecedented state of volatility, growth and consolidation driven by global conglomerates buying up steel companies like Stelco—or building new mills—all across the world. If they go looking for it, new data to update the forecast is available every minute in the working day, which is now genuinely twenty-four hours long: somewhere on the planet there's always an investor at a computer, or a stock market open.

Pratt finds corporate forecasting very frustrating, even with the analytical modelling tools and market data available to his team in so many forms. Every week brings a wild ride in steel prices and even wilder fluctuations in company valuations, which seem to go up or down by hundreds of millions. So many factors are out of his control, and out of the grip of any economist or chief financial officer.

For instance: there's the mobility and vastly expanded amounts of money flowing at greater and greater speeds across the industrialized world. There's money everywhere, moving where it wants, and when. The hedge funds in the West are searching for profits wherever they can be found. And now there's the newer money from rapidly industrializing countries on the rise: China, India and Russia, all keen on resource and metals investments, including upstream operations like steel mills. And all that money—this global pool of investment capability—is flowing everywhere in the form of digitally networked data. Every day many billions of dollars cross borders in transactions that can and often do have a big impact on national economies. And with that kind of money suddenly everywhere, coming from so many culturally and economically varied sources, Pratt has to wonder, what does "value" actually mean any more?

One investor's strategic need for the long term could just as easily be another's momentary trading opportunity. You have to ask, what does "value" mean to each player? What does it mean to the Chinese government, throwing billions at Western natural resource companies because it believes these assets could be strategically critical to its own long-term survival and prosperity? To stock traders slumped at many thousands of computer screens in a thousand North American buildings, buying in and out of stocks, based on this rumour or that, trying to make a dollar here or two dollars there? To an Indian or Russian or American billionaire whose motives nobody can figure out, apart from maybe to amass another billion or two?

The idea of value has assumed a metaphysical degree of subjectivity in global financial markets: "value" can mean almost anything, really, depending on who's throwing the cash around.

Information flow generally is the issue, Pratt realizes—its acceleration and expansion. Communications networks operate today at optical speeds, easily and affordably accessible not only to people employed in large corporations or investment houses, but to millions of day traders and rumour mongers and outright wackos everywhere, some working from basements and lofts and sailboats, others from skyscrapers and coffee shops. And within this constantly expanding mass of financial-system participants are many who are keen to inject their opinions, speculations, conspiracy theories and biases—as well as proper insights and hard data—into several million websites and blogs devoted to analyzing the global marketplace. The result? The vastly increased speed and fluid networking of the flow of information and misinformation—including the movements of money itself—has created a globalized dynamic that is driving economists and corporate forecasters absolutely nuts.

And yet forecasting must still be done, and done as well as it can be. This is what it means for a CEO like Pratt and his team to be accountable. They must stand behind their forecast, and give potential investors, suppliers, customers and employees the confidence that Stelco will soon be pointed in the right direction. When all is said and done, the forecast will be the basis of any plan the company puts forward in order to exit CCAA. But other stakeholders, including shareholders and creditors, will soon be flogging their own forecasts, based on different assumptions. The forecast, Pratt ruefully concludes, is also a forecast of more conflicts to come.

TOO BIG TO FAIL

When Pratt was a younger man, in the years before he made it into the senior executive ranks, he did not take into account that the work of a CEO would sometimes involve a daily exercise in reacting to unpleasant surprises. Today the MBA schools and countless business books proselytize about preparing the next generation of business leaders for the challenging dynamics of global commerce in the twenty-first century. That's all well and good, Pratt thinks, but how do such platitudes help me when every time I pick up the phone, someone's there punching me in the gut?

Jim Arnett, an advisor on the steel industry to the Ontario government, is the author of the next blow. He calls first—a courtesy to Pratt—before he sends the formal letter to Stelco and releases it to the media. His message is that the restructuring must include a fair and reasonable downpayment on the $1.3 billion owed by Stelco to its pension plans. He doesn't make explicit what the government would consider to be "fair and reasonable." While Arnett emphasizes that the government will be flexible in helping Stelco through its difficulties, Pratt hears the subtext: the government will throw its weight around if it must.

Several years back, the province came to the assistance of another failing steel company, Algoma Steel, which was at the end of its financial rope, on the verge of being whacked into bankruptcy by a judge's gavel. The government put many millions into Algoma Steel to protect pensions and help the company survive. It doesn't want to do that again.

But, Pratt wonders, what does the government want? Though Stelco is in pretty bad shape, it's not seconds away from being pronounced dead, as Algoma Steel was. Stelco has sufficient funds to work through a long restructuring, if need be. To Pratt, it looks like the government wants to improve its position at the expense of a vulnerable company in a vulnerable state, and to lower any future risk of taxpayers having to fund Stelco pensions. Which annoys him, since the provincial government, of course, is part of the reason why there is a huge pension deficit in the first place: a classic example of institutional amnesia.

When a leftist government came to power in Ontario in the early 1990s, led by NDP premier Bob Rae, it passed legislation that gave the very largest corporations in the province more flexibility in how they funded pension plans. The legislation—nicknamed the 5.1 election—made it possible for these corporations to select between two kinds of math in determining how much money went into their plans each year.

The first math determines a company's pension payments based on being a "going concern"—the assumption that it will carry on business forever. The second math determines payments based on the company being "wound up" tomorrow and thus immediately on the hook for the total amount owing to its pensioners. The 5.1 election allowed some very large companies in Ontario to ignore the so-called second math based on the brave premise that they were assumed to be "too big to fail"—deemed viable until the end of human economic time. If you're too big to fail, you don't need to worry about your pension plans being funded on a wind-up basis as long as you keep making payments as a going concern.

Stelco, classified as too big to fail, elected to use the 5.1 election—not a brilliant idea, in retrospect. But as any student of commercial history knows, the idea that some companies are too big to fail is hogwash. And when big companies fail, it's a big failure.

The 5.1 concept seemed like a bizarre step for the NDP, a government elected with the strong support of unions. What the province did was cut the corporate managers of large Ontario-based companies serious slack in funding employee pension plans. At the time, however, the provincial economy was in recession. The NDP feared for the financial health of many large companies, including the auto companies. Some had multi-billion-dollar pension funding obligations, a heavy financial load projected to get heavier as the baby-boom generation neared retirement.

However, the 5.1 regulation didn't die in better economic times or when a right-wing government came to power for two full terms. And so, over the years, Stelco created that $1.3-billion pension deficit. And now, a Liberal government, with Arnett as its messenger, has decided that enough is enough. In the letter that follows his call, Arnett writes, "I have been instructed to advise you that upon emergence from CCAA, Stelco will not be entitled to the benefit of Section 5.1."

Another unpleasant irony for Pratt: even though Stelco has funded its pension in an entirely legal way over the past decade or so, it has now been made the solitary scapegoat for bad public policy—this at a time when the company is trying to raise new capital with new investors. How will investors react now that the government has just completely gutted the company's forecast because no one knows what a "fair and reasonable" pension contribution actually is? Why would a smart investor step into a situation so uncertain?

After he gets off the phone with Arnett and the letter lands, Pratt e-mails his team:

> We need a conference call asap. I just received a letter from the Prov signed by Jim Arnett. The

> Prov doesn't think we have made it clear to bidders their bids need a pension solution. So they're saying publicly that the 5.1 election is dead after we come out of CCAA. I'm not sure why they felt they had to do this, but it could have a chilling effect on bidders. It could seriously jeopardize—not only our ability to raise money, but also shrink the envelope we have available to invest in the business with the money we do raise.

In the days after Arnett's letter arrived, Pratt figures out, with the help of the company's actuarial consultants, that if the 5.1 provision were no longer open to Stelco, the company's total annual cash payments to its four main pension plans would rise from about $64 million a year to more than $353 million in order to eliminate the deficit over a five-year period.

These are payments Stelco cannot afford. If the company has to make them, Pratt believes, they'd have to jump right back into CCAA.

Will the government really play that card?

BOARD APPOINTMENT

On February 18, 2005, Stelco announces that Roland Keiper and Michael Woollcombe have joined the company's board of directors.

LOSING MORAL GROUND

As shareholders and government officials put something of a squeeze on Stelco, the Superior Court of Ontario, via court monitor Alex Morrison, voices its displeasure at recent developments. Morrison, in his early forties, is the court-appointed officer from Ernst & Young who helps to ensure that the CCAA process moves along in a fashion that treats all stakeholders fairly. Pratt sees in Morrison qualities he admires: a likably shy manner, nothing bullying about him, yet very solid. He gets things done like a tank, climbing obstacles or driving through them.

"You have real issues now," Morrison says quietly to Pratt at a Starbucks near the courtroom. "Putting those guys on the board, whether it's the right or wrong thing to do, you're compromising the company's role as the 'honest broker' among the different stakeholders."

Pratt shakes his head. "These guys are *big* shareholders, Alex. The pressure to put them on the board—we got calls from many big shareholders who support Keiper. And the board is of the view that we cannot ignore the fact that shareholders, in fact, elect the board."

"Precisely: they're shareholders," Morrison continues. "*Activist* shareholders. With an agenda. Whether or not they elect the board is beside the point. The perception of the board in the court and with the media and other stakeholders as the entity that fairly balances everyone's interests—it's taking a hit. You're losing moral ground here. These guys want shareholders to be in the driver's seat by coming on the board. The perception now is that they're going to have undue influence on the exit plan. I'm not sure how the judge is going to respond. Not well, I think."

"Alex, is it really that bad?"

Morrison nods toward the entrance. "Ask Bob."

As if on cue, Bob Thornton walks in from the cold. The legal counsel to the court monitor is a naturally comic presence, with his head of blond hair still winning the fight against the grey and with a gaze perpetually in search of a punch line. But today Thornton is dead serious, even ashen.

"So, Bob," Pratt says.

"I understand why you guys did this, but there are going to be consequences," he says in a strained voice. "The judge is likely to be apoplectic over the government stepping into his courtroom over the pension payment. And now you guys seem to have tilted things unfairly toward shareholders."

The men hunch silently above steaming coffee mugs.

Pratt stares out the window. It's a peculiar February day. It had been nearly impossible to assess a proper clothes-layering strategy before he left the house. Too cold in the wind and shadows to go without a coat, and too hot to be wearing one in the sunshine or sitting under a ceiling vent that is blasting heat at your forehead.

A homeless-looking man drags a soiled hockey bag past the window.

Frustration surges at Pratt from another blind spot in his mood. He should be out at the mill. There are operational decisions in the business that need to be made. But here he is downtown, being scolded over coffee.

"Where do we go from here?" Pratt says, beleaguered. "I wake up each morning and it's a variation on the same story.

The same disaster, coming at me in different ways. No progress. More of the same, every day."

Morrison and Thornton exchange looks.

"Remember *Groundhog Day?*" Thornton says, mustering a wide grin.

"Bob, have you lost your mind?" Pratt says, smiling. He knows the movie well enough: a cynical but ultimately lovable TV newscaster played by Bill Murray is snowed in overnight in a small city in upstate New York where he'd gone to do a news story, and somehow ends up in a time-warped reality: he wakes up in the same hotel, on the same day, day after day, destined to repeat that day, possibly forever.

"I know this feels like your personal Groundhog Day," Thornton says. "The same day over and over until—"

"Until what?" Pratt interrupts. "Until we can't afford to pay you guys any more?"

Hearty chuckles all around.

"I think you guys have some trouble ahead here—but it's not fatal," Thornton says. "You now have to be extra-vigilant in ensuring the board stays above reproach. And you're going to have to deal with the judge on this. There could be setbacks. And we won't know for sure until Farley actually responds."

Pratt feels his anger resurface, but he tries to stay even-keeled. "The huge problem we face, Bob, is that there are no goddamn deadlines here! And that's what we need to make this work: deadlines. We're adrift. I can't get the unions to sit down because they think high steel prices means lots more dough for them. The creditors are dancing around us with their proposals. The government's into this now. And the shareholders, too. And if we do everything that everyone wants, Stelco will remain a basket case. And we'll be back in CCAA right after we get out. Groundhog Day is right. They're all grinding us into the ground."

"The message of the movie is a little more complicated," Thornton says. "You're destined to live out the same day over and over without meaningful progress until you have a therapeutic moment of self-learning that translates into love and respect for your adversaries and their loved ones, and of course the feeling has to be completely mutual."

"When do you expect that to happen, Bob?"

"When our fees are paid, actually." A laughing fit from Thornton, high-pitched, unhinging just about everyone in all corners of the room, including Pratt.

SAFETY

It's past midnight and Colin Osborne is in his study at home, a cup of coffee gone cold on his desk. His wife has long since gone to bed.

Dinner was pizza ordered in and eaten standing in the kitchen. Then he spent the evening reviewing operational reports, marvelling at what he has concluded is a statistically meaningful improvement in productivity—and safety performance—since the CCAA process began.

More steel? Fewer on-the-job injuries?

The only thing that makes sense to him is that some employees have awakened to the reality of Stelco's being on life support and have decided to pull their weight, and maybe someone else's weight too.

GROUNDHOG DAY (REPRISE)

On February 25, in a decision by Justice Farley, the court removes Keiper and Woollcombe from the Stelco board of directors, basically saying that the board had acted improperly in appointing them in the first place. Keiper and Woollcombe immediately appeal Farley's decision.

On March 1, the company announces that none of the bid-refinancing proposals it has received from prospective investors is satisfactory, and that the board has decided, as a consequence, to pursue new financing alternatives in the capital markets, a strategy that will require the court's approval. A month later, Stelco receives court approval to go forth to find some combination of debt and equity financing.

On March 31, the Ontario Superior Court of Justice overrules Farley, allowing Keiper and Woollcombe to rejoin the Stelco board, stating that Farley had overstepped his legal bounds in denying the board the right to elect new board members.

In light of these events, what is Pratt's frame of mind?

SUNDAY AFTERNOON AT THE PRATTS'

Alexa is knitting a sweater, an intricately beautiful thing that she knows will be too small for her granddaughter within weeks of Cedar's putting it on for the first time.

Pratt's fingers are BlackBerry busy.

They sit across from one another next to the fireplace, a modest fire aglow, just enough to make things cozy. A roast in the oven, an uncorked bottle of red wine on the counter. When they occasionally look up from their work, they see each other, but also the fact of the days finally getting longer.

Then.

"These fuckers are driving me crazy," he shouts, after reading an incoming e-mail.

"Which fuckers are we talking about this time?" she asks.

Without looking up, stifling a laugh, he says, "All of them."

DRIVING TO THE HOSPITAL

"This guy is one of the best," he says.

"I'm sure he is."

"You're not supposed to eat anything before the operation—what, after midnight? Did you eat anything? Or drink something?"

"Courtney."

"Okay."

"The kids are going to be there."

"Okay."

"Make sure they don't worry too much. Take them out for a bite."

He nods. "Do you—"

"Courtney?"

"Nothing."

"What?"

"Honestly, nothing."

"There's a steak defrosting in the fridge."

"Okay."

TRICAP ENTERS THE PICTURE

Ron Bloom is phoning Pratt, who takes the call in his car. "I'm giving you a heads-up, Courtney."

"For what, Ron?"

"We've got our own financing deal together to get the company out of CCAA. With some people you know well. The Brascan guys."

"You mean Tricap?"

A Stelco board meeting, hastily convened. "We need more time to analyze this deal," Pratt says. "Hopefully, it'll stay private. Because once it's out into the public . . ."

The United Steelworkers immediately issues a press release, widely reported in the media, extolling the virtues of its financing arrangement with Tricap, an investment fund that had earlier declined to participate in the process orchestrated by the Stelco board.

The so-called Tricap deal includes a $500-million payment into the pension plan and a severe haircut for creditors. The immediate reaction of the salaried Stelco employees and pensioners is very positive.

Hap Stephen says in an interview that the deal between Tricap and the United Steelworkers is "dead in the water" because it will be rejected out of hand by the creditors.

The media war escalates.

TOP GUN?

On occasion, Pratt, is invited to respond to serious questions posed by newspaper editors, TV anchors and radio talk-show hosts.

Is Stelco an example of Canada's growing inability to maintain its manufacturing base in the global economy? What does this situation say about the changing relationship between global private equity and national economic development? What are your views on the safety net in a post-industrial dynamic?

Questions, always questions . . .

Now and then he has been cornered by strangers who want to talk to a real, live CEO—at cocktail parties, in ballrooms at charity fundraisers, in the corridors of the health club or the airport. He has given speeches to university students, non-profit groups and industry associations. Everyone wants to know how battles are fought in the corporate arena. Everyone wants to know how decisions are made.

When he reflects on his experiences so far as Stelco CEO, the memories that stand out the most—the incidents that will eventually give this experience some redemptive definition—are those that have little to do with decision-making in the narrow sense of the term: the machinations of himself and his colleagues that eventually and sometimes messily lead to yes, no or maybe, not now, maybe tomorrow or next quarter or maybe never. Decisions can never be divorced from the background noise, the laughter in marginal encounters, a practical joke here, a sly remark there, the comic scenarios that flare up before and after meetings, not just within them. After this is over, he thinks, he'll forget the bile spewed, the crises in every moment, and remember the cast of characters, their stories and personal quirks and foibles, the anecdotes given birth by pure folly, the lampshade moments, the shtick of those just trying to get a laugh to break the tension or just because guys like to compete hard to see who can get the biggest laughs.

How is the battle fought? What's it like being a CEO during a restructuring negotiation?

Like a fighter pilot, preparing for hours, days and years at a time—then ten seconds of combat. Kill or be killed, in a sense.

A dogfight every day—but no, it's more than that. Imagine a half dozen war planes in the sky at once, everyone shooting at each other. And when you shoot the bad guy down, he comes back tomorrow.

How's that for fun?

He loves the fighter-pilot analogy, knowing that it's only that: in corporate life there are no actual detonations, no airborne blood, no death, no pain caused by actual physical harm. No heart failure in that final second before the missile shatters everything. Only simulated violence, as much as it feels very real right now. Psychological games, designed to injure—to get leverage.

A big decision in a situation like this, he knows, is never a clear victory after a straightforward test of arms. It's a more complicated ordeal, a series of engagements—some held in murky waters, some fought out in the open, some that can never be acknowledged without violating confidences. It's a situation in which no one knows for certain who their allies are or should be, or whether, in fact, there is or should be an enemy at all. A decision can often be the outcome of conflicting forces interacting in a way no one fully understands or foresees, in which people blindly grope toward a consensus that, at the outset, they can't imagine ever accepting. A decision can be where you go only after all other alternatives are exhausted.

CONSPIRACY THEORIES

Stelco advisors sit in a boardroom, speculating, as Pratt listens. Sometimes, when the tension gets too much and everything looks hopeless, the only recourse is to conspiracy theory.

"You gotta believe Bloom was working the government hard. I can see him, preying on the fears at Queen's Park, telling them that unless they step in and kick our ass over the 5.1 election, some guys in New York are gonna buy the company with lunch money, shut Hamilton down and sell the Lake Erie mill for ten times what they paid for the entire company. And leave the taxpayer on the hook for billions in pension debts."

"That's paranoid."

"Bloom brings it out in me."

"The government is the government—the organizational attention span of fruit flies."

"The Tricap deal. That's Bloom. Pure malevolent genius."

"That deal is dead. Creditors will reject it."

"But what's Bloom's next move?"

"It's all about making moves. Causing chaos. Drama. Unhelpful."

"Of course. But you'd think someone would have given us a heads-up. Hell, Tricap never even bothered to come into our bidding process. Why? Were they already talking to Bloom?"

"An interesting thought. I mean, if that's the case, we're talking about a seriously major strategy to fuck with us. From the beginning? I find that hard to believe."

"You can bet the Canadian unions were doing nothing more than carrying Bloom's laptop into the meetings. If they were even invited to the meetings."

Pratt listens, thinking that the truth has never felt more elusive.

FIRST-QUARTER EARNINGS RELEASE (PARAPHRASED)

> "Stelco continues to benefit from robust market conditions and steel prices during the first quarter," said CEO Courtney Pratt on Stelco's recent financial performance, including record net earnings of $49 million. "I hope that all our stakeholders will take advantage of our positive performance to work toward our shared goal of a viable and competitive Stelco, rather than let this opportunity pass." The Company said that although a significant increase in operating earnings is expected for 2005 as a whole, given the

current dynamics of global steel markets and the effect on steel prices, the markets had become more difficult to predict.

AT THE WATERING HOLE

Pratt is channel-surfing late one evening at home, after another bruising day on the job without meaningful progress. He is pressing the TV remote for no other reason than that there's a button under his thumb that doesn't fight back. A sweet reversal of roles, he thinks, in his relationship to the media. He's still angry about what happened last fall. A business columnist for a national newspaper went on a sustained jihad, devoting a snarky column to Stelco pretty much once a week for more than a month, calling into question his and the board's decision-making, suggesting that the recourse to CCAA was a crime against the rights of shareholders, a power play by Pratt to secure his position as CEO. The columns stopped only after Pratt, fed up by the exaggerations, detailed the journalistic abuses against his reputation in a lengthy letter sent to the columnist, a point-by-point rebuttal.

Click, click, click.

Sometimes he pauses for a minute or so in his channel-surfing, letting a scenario materialize on the screen, but he doesn't have the appetite for story right now. He's happy with fragments, soundless clips one after another. It amazes him how many infomercials there are between channels 1 and 40, the places in the TV pecking order where you expect network entertainment, not pitches for zirconium-studded jean jackets, abdominal-firming exercise machines, the bracelet made from copper with magical healing powers, capable of curing arthritis, allergies, stress. Right now he could use some magical healing powers from the metal business he's in. But there's no 1-800 number on the screen providing an instant fix for an ailing steel company.

Click, click, click.

Alexa is in bed, asleep before he got home.

They got it all, they say. The cancer. They think. But there are always rogue cells, attaching invisibly to an essential part of you. He can't think about that, and won't.

Compartmentalize, then click. One channel after another.

A young Paul Newman on the screen. A prison movie. He doesn't need the soundtrack, and he knows the great line that is coming up. *What we have here is a failure to communicate—*

He thinks the Stelco story could make a good prison movic. The union guys, he's long ago concluded, weren't expecting the new CEO to be someone who wanted to be their partner, a cooperative colleague bound by mutual commitment to fix the company. They really did expect a warden, and, as far as he can tell, they'd be more comfortable dealing with one: a top-down guy who rules with an iron fist and dispenses favours to those who crawl on broken glass to kiss his feet, but who is also wise enough to let the prisoners police their own on the steel-mill floor.

That doesn't cut it any more.

The union guys say they like him, in private. In public? They tear him a new one every time a reporter's within earshot. Is that just business?

He knows they wouldn't fall to their knees grief-stricken if he stumbled into the goddamn blast furnace. Some would help him fail for no reason they would consciously acknowledge, not even to themselves. He's seen organizational destructiveness before, the repressed spitefulness and deception permeating the ranks, the bureaucratic subterfuge in every process and department, the nodding assent from the egos in the office and on the plant floor who have no intention of changing their ways, regardless of the incentive or the threat.

Click, click.

Donald Trump doing reality TV: *You're fired.*

Trump makes him think he's from another planet, another era, although he accepts that appearing competent before the TV cameras is something required in his job these days.

You're fired, Courtney.

Fine by me.

Click, click.

As a Stelco board member, Pratt led the executive search committee, which turned up good candidates after the last CEO left the company. But the uncertainty around Stelco's future had the preferred candidates hesitant, flip-floppy. Tentative employment contracts started to get complicated, clause-heavy. And so the board came to him. Pratt had successfully lived the realities of unionized industrial companies. He understood people and people problems. He appreciated the magnitude and context of Stelco's challenges as well as anyone, given that he was an insider himself, on the board. And what was Stelco but a unionized industrial company whose problem mainly related to people?

A failure to communicate indeed.

A nature program on the TV screen, black-and-white, a rerun from the sixties or early seventies, tops. Africa. Or some place like Africa. A parched savannah. Drama by the watering hole, which appears to have shrunk to a muddy puddle. Lions and zebras are skin-and-bones. Others animals hide here and there—boar, maybe a hyena. Animals make furtive efforts to drink at the watering hole. There's a skeleton under a tree.

He turns the sound up, then down. He knows the story.

The story is water: the battle for survival around a shrinking common resource.

He clicks away, does a channel run up into the hundreds, then starts to click back in search of the program again. He can't find it.

He reaches for his BlackBerry to send himself an e-mail. He doesn't want to forget the parable. He'll use it at some point.

> The watering hole. What happens in nature when it starts to dry up. The fight for scarce resources. Everyone lives on less. Adapt collectively or die. But what happens if you have some temporary overflow? High steel prices creating temporary financial overflow. What happens then? Not only do people think they should not live on less or what they needed before. They want more to drink. Greed. Believe they're entitled to it. Greed. The issue is: what happens when the watering hole starts to shrink again?

STALEMATE

In mid-April 2005, the Stelco restructuring is a study in stalemated complexity and uncertainty created by a variety of backroom negotiations that have the effect, Pratt believes, of further polarizing stakeholders.

No one is prepared to make concessions. Everyone is trying to improve their position. Incredibly, some want to emerge from CCAA with more than they went in with. In a sense, they're imagining that the watering hole is larger than it was before it began to shrink.

The government has joined the process through its heavy-handed intervention, apparently intent on fixing the Stelco pension situation once and for all.

The activist shareholders represented by Keiper and Woollcombe are now on the board—invited there by Pratt and other board members, removed by Farley, and allowed back on by the Ontario Superior Court. The court monitor believes this development undermines the board's—and by direct implication, Pratt's—strategy to be (and be viewed as) the honest broker among the competing stakeholder interests. Pratt feels torn apart by the paradoxes of trying to treat everyone fairly. No matter what he does, someone is offended and comes down hard, unwilling to give an inch but, instead, demanding a yard or two.

Ron Bloom has usurped the role of the Canadian unions, forcefully establishing himself as the deal-making voice for Stelco workers and pensioners by lining up a financing arrangement with Tricap. It's troubling that the company's efforts to raise capital on its own have not been successful yet.

In late spring 2005, Pratt and his advisors make one more move of note: they serve notice to all stakeholders that they intend to table their own restructuring financing plan, one which will have a better chance of winning creditor approval than the Tricap plan. On May 18, after days of discussions with the government, the union and others, the company agrees to a process for kick-starting the stalled restructuring—a process that will come to be known as "the mediation."

CONSCIENCE DIALOGUE

G. DAVID CARTER, LAWYER

Naked men sit all around us, gossiping, shaving, reading the paper, doing e-mail, watching CNN on wall-mounted TV sets.

Some guys openly scratch certain appendages of the body, or adjust their positioning once the boxers are pulled back on.

I know this locker room well from the years I worked in Toronto. It's a men's club for the Establishment, where the sweat and steam-room fog and sound of squash balls being whacked mingle with serious money.

We're towelling off, David Carter and I, after long showers.

He smoked me on the squash court. I'm not over it, no matter how jovial the jock patter between us. The recreationally summoned anger is ebbing. But not totally—the bastard loved torturing me, and I know he invited me here to inflict another kind of pain: his views on Stelco's corporate governance situation and other legal issues in our restructuring.

David is soon dressed in an olive linen suit, matched to a fairly bright pink shirt—the image of metrosexual refinement, I guess. He's tall and rakishly boyish for a man approaching sixty. I'll bet his dramatic mane of dark hair is treated by a colourist who charges as much an hour as he does, in his capacity as a senior partner at a blue-chip legal practice.

"Great tie," I say as he knots it up. "The colour—it's what? Chartreuse?"

"We haven't seen much of you here lately," he says, ignoring my provocation. "From reading the papers, you can't be having fun."

"It's a tough period. It's all fighting, not my preferred style."

He nods as if mystified, which annoys me. "David, the money we're spending on lawyers and advisors. They're making a killing on us. And—"

"You're getting killed, I know," he interrupts. "The system is far from perfect. It has many faults. Many. One of which is the expense of legal guns for hire. And, of course, the costs don't become apparent until you get into CCAA. You go in wanting a quick end, and it's never quick. But we are not the problem, Courtney. Perhaps we're a symptom of it. Or the consequence. But lawyers didn't put Stelco into the financial hole. We're just profiting from that."

"You said it."

"Do you want to go back in time to when clan leaders and feudal barons adjudicated these matters? You would have been forced to accept arbitration without the rule of law. And some of those who reneged on their debts found their heads on pikes rather than being discharged of their financial obligations by a forgiving court. Come on, show some perspective. This is civilized, no matter how expensive it is."

He has a point. But it's amazing how fast he moved on from the money it's costing us to a philosophical riff on the rule of law. I didn't write those laws. Lawyers did. And who benefits most from this? I take a deep breath and try to leave the beating he just handed me on the squash court behind. I'm here because I want his perspective on all the criticism we've gotten for putting an activist shareholder on the Stelco board.

"I like your tie, as well," he says. "But I believe aboriginal patterns were probably more in fashion last year." He winks at me. Even off the court, we're still competing.

"You used to be seen as this 'good guy'—what a reversal," he continues.

"Be careful about what you read in the papers. We should be able to work our way out of this."

He signals for us to start moving toward the bar. I don't like his silence as we navigate the corridors through the weight room and past the squash courts.

"Is your house in your wife's name?" he asks casually.

"What?"

"Your director's liability insurance is up to date?"

"Hold on."

"Because you're in a helluva mess now."

He strides toward the bar and takes a stool.

I feel sweat breaking out on me again.

"David, I don't like where you're going."

"I'm sure what happened is that your boardroom suddenly got a lot more interesting when you let the shareholders join the party."

"The dynamics are—well, they're intense. We've got a strong group of directors. Dedicated. The demands on their time, their minds, their patience—it's been overwhelming. We've met countless times since we went into CCAA. And let me tell you, the spectre of lawsuits haunts all of us. It could hang over us for years. This eats at people, especially if they think their personal assets are at a risk."

"That's why guys like me get paid big bucks. To make sure you do things right. The trouble is, too many of our clients—in my experience—don't take what we say seriously enough. Look at Conrad Black."

"Let's not."

"All sides these days are investing in very clever lawyers. And if you're not exceptionally careful, these lawyers will find a way to nail you."

David excels in the intimate meritocracy of the boardroom, providing legal counsel to CEOs and their bosses, the members of the board. In that rarefied world, his counsel is valued to corporations under attack. His bag of tricks goes as deep as the deep pockets that pay him. He owns a red sports car, an Italian number, and covers two alimony payments. He dates a woman less than half his age, apparently.

"It's exhausting being on the board," I say. "We have to overthink everything, with our lawyers. It's measure not once or twice, but four and five times, then cut. And if we cut wrong . . . the consequences could really hurt the company and board members personally. It all feels unfair, this legal preoccupation. And, frankly, it makes it tough to find, never mind keep, good directors. Who wants to take risks like we're taking?"

"That's why you need lawyers you have absolute trust in."

"Luckily, that's what we've got. And the bills to prove it."

He gives me a smile that says he's not the enemy. "As I see it, you brought the shareholders onto the board and pissed off everyone else, including the judge. You've put out a plan no one likes. And you've got the USW and Tricap scoring points in the media with a ridiculous plan that the creditors are going to reject out of hand, not to mention the shareholders. And now you're going into a mediation process that will have you isolated and exposed, with a mediator whose goal will be to 'get a deal' at all costs. All this is happening on your watch."

"Let's get a bite," I say, heading off toward the dining room, although I feel like walking out the door and getting on a plane to nowhere.

Once we're seated near the windows, with a spectacular view of the city from ten storeys up, I try to regain my poise. We're a million cultural miles from the steel mills of Hamilton and Lake Erie. From the dining room I can see City Hall, the courthouse, Bay Street. The nearest a steelworker would normally get to these places is producing the steel beams in these buildings. This is where I live now many days.

"I wonder how I got into this business," he says while scanning the menu. "It truly puzzles me some days. How I got from A to B."

He decides to divulge an aspect of his personal story, which seems like a genuine effort to put me at ease. He succeeds, I'll admit, with an articulate display of—of what? Self-criticism, I think.

Thirty-five years ago, his dilemma was choosing between corporate law and environmental advocacy. In his hippie days, as he tells me with comic aplomb, he was a legal mind trapped in the idealism of a counterculture activist. He loved being at the helm of a speedboat on the high seas, tormenting the whalers, or chaining himself to giant trees in old-growth forest. He was adept at a microphone on the jailhouse steps, and he seduced (or so he baldly hints) a fair number of eco-groupies over cheap wine and pasta at the communal farm. But when his comrades started talking about bombs, going underground, taking up the class struggle and overthrowing the Man and the System, his legal mind rebelled. It's one thing to fight injustices within the bounds of democratic dissent, he reasoned—quite another to become a murderous idiot.

Anonymously, he snitched out an incompetent Maoist group planning a bomb run on a bank known to finance logging companies.

"So here I am, Courtney, doing the hand-holding for the Man."

I laugh at that, uneasily. I've always felt a commitment to doing good in the community. My parents knocked that into my head early. I've always done volunteer work, and still do, lots of it. But I never had the torch-carrying ego to be at the head of any progressive ideological pack. If that's a failing, fine. But I've also never had reversals like David's. I didn't go from being a self-styled world-saver to a cynical corporate mercenary . . . which, I think, is how he sees himself.

We're near the same age. We do similar kinds of work. Both of us have seen power in action. But as I listen to him talk, he definitely seems more cynical about it than I do. And maybe that's why he's so good at what he does. He sees the darker angles in people and in difficult situations . . . he sees, I guess, what I wish didn't exist.

"David, we're in a very tough situation," I say trying to get back on track here. "We're the ones—the company, the board—caught in the middle. We can't choose sides. We're the only ones with a legal obligation to get to a deal that will be seen by the court as fair to all stakeholders. We have to engineer a deal that all the stakeholders with real or effective vetoes will accept. And you know how far apart all the parties are?"

"With Roland Keiper on your board?" Eye-rolling.

"I agree. It's problematic. Everyone's kicking us over that one with the exception of the shareholders, obviously. I'm doing my best to adapt, but in a principled way. Trying to regain the high ground as the honest broker here . . ."

"You'll never get a deal."

Anger quickens in me. "And you guys will keep making a killing. I'm not questioning the integrity of our lawyers. They're indispensable. But we're paying for everyone's lawyers, now, on all sides. It may be the right thing for the company to do. Boy, oh, boy, though, it creates some awful dynamics."

"Yes, but can I remind you of something fundamental here?"

I nod.

"Advocacy is the heart of the issue. Lawyers have an obligation to get the best deal for their clients. We don't exist to solve *your* problem, as the CEO of Stelco. That's how the system works: advocacy. Representing your client. And through the company's largesse in this process, suddenly everyone's a client with an army of advocates."

"David," I say, "you were a serious environmentalist way back when. Surely you understand the need for collective action for the greater good?"

"Who are you—my daughter? She's gone vegan, totally. And timed it, I might add, for when I did some advisory work for the burger people. The greater good? Courtney, that's true, but only to the extent that it produces the best result for my client. This kind of law isn't social work. It's not a group-hug system. It's based on checks and balances, a fight between competing viewpoints. Or are you the only person on the planet who hasn't lost years watching *Law and Order?*"

"A fight? It's a barroom brawl. Impossible to referee."

"And you have hopes for the mediation?"

"I do."

"You're dreaming. Everyone smells blood. Someone else's blood. This is only going to get worse before it gets better."

I order a steak. Rare, with a plate of fries.

We're at the point in our meal together where we really don't know what to say to one another. We're not good friends, and I'm not as fluent as David is at releasing the backstory of my life—unless I really want to get to know somebody. But I forge ahead anyway.

"What does the 'G' at the front of your name stand for?"

He laughs. "Well, it's not on my birth certificate."

"It's not?"

"And it's not short for anything pompous, like Graydon or Garfield. I know it sounds odd, but when I got started in the legal world, I just added it. As a lark. My first wife thought I did it to make myself sound more important. But it's not true. I thought I was being funny. And maybe I was uncomfortable with trying to be so serious and grown up. And then the 'G' just stuck. It became part of me, my identity."

"No kidding." I honestly don't know what to think.

David searches my face.

I'm good at the bluff some days. Now I just look back. Blank.

He takes my response well. Or so I think.

"Never mind, Courtney."

"What do you mean?"

"You must know what we're talking about."

Now I'm really confused.

"I'm talking about identity. How we create it, make it real. It's something of an act of faith, but also a conscious act. We don't get to be the power players we are without being very conscious of our image."

"And to you, that means we're faking something. So I'm faking?"

"On the contrary. You're very well constructed. You say the right things and do them. You walk the talk."

I'm following him, more or less.

"Anyway," he says, then drains his glass of red. "You can be as well constructed and ethical as you like. And sometimes . . ."

I want to ask for the bill. But our meals haven't arrived yet.

"Courtney," he says, in a fierce undertone. He wants my attention.

"Yeah."

"The pretence of civility is absolutely essential here."

"But what? There's a 'but' in your voice, David."

"As well-intended as you are, I wonder if you haven't misjudged the intent—the spirit—of good corporate governance."

"How so?"

"While you guys waved the rule book, or hid behind it, your board got compromised. You've weakened your hand, trying to do the right thing. How strange."

CHAPTER FOUR

THE MEDIATION

MISSION IMPOSSIBLE

They exude an aura of purpose, three businessmen in forward motion, in control of the sidewalk. They pause to squint into the cloudless sky when they walk out of the shadows, the sunlight ricocheting from concrete and pavement. It's humid and hot already in the financial district, but tranquil in the way of big cities on summer mornings before the smog and noise of rush hour. They start walking again, conscious of the silence between them as each performs the mental equivalent of snapping on armour. There's an accident in front of them, a bashed-up passenger bus, attended by emergency vehicles and personnel equipped with high-tech gear. It's a ruined whale of a vehicle, evidently in the aftermath of collisions involving speed, exploding fuels, metal barriers, utility poles, shattering glass, bodies. Around the scene is the eerie nimbus of video lighting.

Mike Barrack, in the middle of the threesome, turns to Pratt, on his right. "You know what to expect—Adams will use every tool to get a deal," he says with the sly deference of an experienced advisor offering a gentle warning. "He'll get to you by being unpredictable, drawing you in, personally. He's good at that."

Pratt nods several times in quick succession.

They're closing in on the wreckage now, entering the din of men and women speaking in acronyms. It's hard not to rubberneck. Pratt stops abruptly and turns his back on the carnage to face his colleagues, partially blocking their view of the street. The BlackBerry on his belt chimes, a hokey musical ringtone. It sounds like a bad joke made at an inappropriate time. He doesn't answer it but shakes his head once, as if knocking loose a thought. "This process is more out of control than I want to admit," he says.

"We're going to be fine—it's not the first time we've been around the block," Hap Stephen responds, craning away from Pratt to look at the disaster scene. His way of bolstering collective team confidence is to keep it short and to make nothing of the fact that in his many years of consulting experience he's never seen a restructuring process so screwed up.

Pratt looks skyward, exasperated.

"It's amazing what they can do," Stephen says neutrally. "It all looks so real. Talk all you want about computer graphics, but sometimes you just have to blow things up to tell a story on the big screen."

They start walking again. It occurs to Pratt that there will be people involved in the mediation against whom he now bears grudges. Whom he wouldn't mind choking. But his appetite for macho confrontation—the top-dog bullshit—is a fleeting psychological craving. It's the junk-food approach to management, he thinks. Fills the gut fast, but how healthy is it? Where does it get you in the end?

They negotiate a path through fake cops, fake victims covered in fake blood, tractor trailers, sound booms, lighting towers, cabling. "They've really gone to some trouble here," Pratt says.

"What really gets me is when they have to dirty up the streets to turn Toronto into an American city," Barrack says.

To see these suited men amid the cinematic fakery is to see children given a reprieve from homework by a magician's act. But while the three men's minds are entertained, their feet keep moving.

"Don't kid yourself," Stephen says. "Maybe fifteen years ago Toronto didn't have graffiti on the mailboxes, garbage in the streets. We do now."

"What's up with this?" Pratt says as they enter the hotel just across the street. It's another disaster zone. There is scaffolding everywhere, and the noise and dust of a sustained crime against the mainstream dignity of the edifice. "Are they filming here, too?"

"A renovation," Barrack says matter-of-factly.

"Looks like a bomb hit it," Stephen adds.

Barrack tugs absently at his sleeve, then sweeps his lapels clean of imaginary dust specks. He too has moved to a new psychic zone, cleansed of any coaching urges.

Pratt is multi-tasking, checking e-mail on the BlackBerry. Several crises are in progress back at Stelco offices, as they always are, relayed to him as hand-wringing scenarios of imminent doom that can be avoided only by the CEO's immediate, heavy-handed intervention—which is rarely true, but these e-mails are a staple of his daily information diet.

In the bowels of the building, a jackhammer delivers a monstrous jolt that vibrates through the floor, a body-rattling surprise. A shower of dust, gypsum in the air. A workman bashing through a wall with a big mallet.

Here we are, he thinks, the scene of a real accident.

THE ADAMS FAMILY

The conference room is the definition of blandness. It's one among many millions of similar rooms in good hotels the world over: a high-ceilinged box lit by overhead halogens, with indestructible broadloom and partition walls that pull back to create larger spaces. Today the room is outfitted in a horseshoe configuration of long banquet tables draped in pleated white bunting. Here there is no distraction from architectural splendour or compelling views of the outside world to delude the participants that they are here for any other reason than to get inside each other's heads, isolate weakness and angles of leverage and discredit any views of the restructuring alien to their own.

Pratt and his advisors adhere to the standard entry protocols in these formal corporate dramas, which require hearty greetings with those well known to them and more reserved exchanges with those they don't know or dislike with a relish they'd be reluctant to admit. There's diplomatic chit-chat by the coffee station as people plunder heaping plates of pastries.

In the first few minutes, Pratt's team also addresses the matter of where to sit—the artful task of staying together without appearing too paranoid of who they could end up with. All their moves appear natural, inevitable, and since everyone's more or less playing by the same rules, the horseshoe fills up without many awkward moments.

As Pratt pointlessly rearranges documents in front of him to keep his hands busy, he surveys the room, visualizing the vectors of disagreement, like an air traffic controller on a bad-weather day. Problems have been landing non-stop on his watch, and more problems stacked upon problems are circling overhead, demanding attention all at once. As much as he wants to walk away from the scenario, there's too much at stake, the well-being of too many people, including those creating the problems.

When he imagines the days ahead, the expected collisions of ego and self-interest disguised as high-and-mighty principle, he can't picture the Hollywood ending—the handshakes at the press conference, the ceremonial compliments paid to him in the media by his adversaries after the backroom bruising and foul-mouthed epithets uttered between bites of stale room-service sandwiches. But he prides himself on the practical wisdom of expecting the best, not the worst, and so he attempts to clear his mind of negative speculation. He glances at the combatants within visual range, the people who need to start speaking to each other with more respect and willingness to compromise.

There are now upward of fifty people in the room, almost all men. There's representation from the unions, creditors, government, salaried employees, pensioners and company management, each party accompanied by advisors, mostly lawyers. All are gathered for this professional mediation of—as yet—an undetermined duration. Most would admit to being clueless about how it will all unfold.

Standing behind the apex of the horseshoe is the mediator, George Adams, a diminutive, energetic man, in a huddle with Alex Morrison and Bob Thornton. He is making gestures with a capped whiteboard marker and Thornton flinches from one of the wilder jabs, as if concerned about the possibility of being physically annotated. Adams is legendary in the mediation business as a whiteboard wizard. Just when he appears to be actively searching for a writing surface on which to inflict red ink, Adams reverses course and takes a seat, facing the group. At first he leans forward, hunched on his elbows with the unspeaking seriousness of a politician contemplating a prepared statement at a press conference, but Adams isn't a stay-on-script character. Clearing his throat, he gingerly pushes his notes aside as if they're toxic. He intends for his audience to appreciate that it's not about the notes, the formalities. It's the brain, the experience, the ability to think on your feet and connect person to person in taking complete control of the room. He smiles, as if sharing a joke with himself, then leans back for a long, chin-rubbing minute.

"You guys have been at this for—what?—eighteen months, right," he finally says. "In bankruptcy court? And no deal. Look, I'm not going to be the saviour here." His tone manages to be both sympathetic and brutally instructive. "You're going to do that, if anyone is. I can lead horses to drink. I can facilitate till the cows come home, and if there's a deal to be made, we'll make it. But if there's no deal to be made, just say the word and I'll be gone. We've all got better things to do."

He pauses, staring into space as if the enormity of the challenge remains bewildering to him, something he hasn't seen before.

Then he carries on, reinforcing just how experienced he is and how he'll do whatever the hell he likes to bring people together and get the job done on an agenda and timetable of his choosing. While Adams meanders through the peaks and valleys of restatement, Pratt listens attentively; he's searching for clues, no matter how small, to prepare for what lies ahead, but feeling well out of his comfort zone now. Pratt's been an advocate of mediation, but he now realizes that he's sitting around a table with a group who all have licence to provoke, insult and cajole him to say or do things that he'd probably rather not. In the interests of getting a deal, he must allow himself to be backed into corners, taken for a ride, challenged to step outside, into the parking lot, let's settle this like men, you leave your guys inside and I'll do the same, got that, Pratt?

As he contemplates the situation, he discreetly checks out the other guys. First the bondholders, including a gaggle of hedge-fund guys, the financiers who, Pratt figures, bought their Stelco bonds or other creditor debt at a massive discount. He knows the breakthrough—the first gesture at compromise—isn't going to come from them, not on this go-around. That's a problem, because they hold big cards. Today their contingent is mostly devoid of senior partners, and is represented by the youngsters in sharp suits, one with spiked-out hair. The B team, Pratt thinks. This means they don't have authority to horse-trade, only instructions to repeat the same old story, which is that they won't have their bonds forcibly converted to equity by the Tricap plan developed with the union, no fucking way is that happening. This conversation is over—that's what one hedge-fund guy actually said on a conference call last week. Over. The thickest Jersey accent: *Ohh-vah.*

When did I start taking crap from twenty-eight-year-olds?

Pratt rests his gaze on the government crew. He decides to reserve judgment on their value here. They're stakeholders, true, but they sent the process careening in new directions when they threatened to revoke the 5.1 regulation on Stelco and demanded that any restructuring plan be acceptable to them. Fine, Pratt thinks, use your veto. But to publicly convey the impression that crimes against God and nature have been committed by the company? Nuts.

Adams's voice breaks in on his reverie. "You might be wondering how this all works. To make this as simple as possible, it's something like shuttle diplomacy. I'll be Henry Kissinger. You guys are the delegations clutching for dear life onto completely unreasonable points of view that are dead in the water without making serious compromises, but unwilling to remotely concede anything at all at this point. Right? This is where you are. Where we are. There'll be meetings that go on for too long. Meetings that go on all night. More often than not, I'll be trapped in very small rooms with one side or another, trying to figure out why the hell you can't take even the smallest steps forward. So be prepared for lots of sitting around. For frustration. Boredom is built into this process, and so is the desire to speculate about the ten ways the other guy is trying to screw you over by telling me lies and poisoning my ability to work. Bottom line: this isn't a train station. There isn't a schedule, and there won't be one. So don't expect the train to leave on time. It's been sitting in the terminal for eighteen months—so we have to be reasonable."

He sits back, twiddling his whiteboard marker.

There is evidently time now for questions from the horseshoe. A few eager hand-raisers—a teacher's pet or two—belabour the obvious, inquiring about minor points of protocol and voicing their high expectations for the outcome. Adams, still in performance mode, is indulgent enough but impatient to get on with things.

Pratt turns to his left. He gets the I-told-you-so look from Barrack, who knows the Adams routine from prior experience and hasn't taken any notes, his laptop still in sleep mode.

Hap Stephen, to Pratt's right, appears visibly, even aggressively, nonplussed, wrapped in a complicated silence, a solemn display of skepticism. He leans toward Pratt and whispers, "Okay, so when will Bloom start his slouching?"

Pratt stifles a laugh—but it's a question on his mind, too. He considers the composition of the union team in the room. In the middle of that group sits Ron Bloom, flown in from Pittsburgh by the parent union for the duration. Pratt and Bloom earlier exchanged polite nods when their glances settled on each other. But Pratt couldn't resist a little slouching himself, a sarcastic act of mimicry, his chin tucked, enabling him to stare at Bloom over glasses that he'd let slide down his nose, openly conveying bemusement. He thinks: okay, Bloom, when will you really get into the slouching, making yourself part of that chair, legs akimbo, hands folded over your chest, the taunting voice, playing good cop, bad cop, every kind of cop, whatever it takes to press my buttons?

It gets under Pratt's skin that he can't figure Bloom out, except to be wary of him and his vast experience from so many steel-company restructurings south of the border. Bloom left behind a career as a New York investment banker to join the union, probably for a whole lot less money. How do you deal with someone who makes a career change like that?

The questioning from around the horseshoe dies out. But it still isn't clear what happens next. Someone states the obvious: "Who goes first?"

"We'll get to that," Adams say. "When I need you, I'll call you."

And then it's over. The first anticlimax. Class dismissed.

NOWHERE LAND

There's very little that's dramatically compelling in observing a corporate executive enduring hours of unproductive boredom in a hotel room when he'd rather be at work, actually doing his job at the helm of a large company. For Pratt, the hours keep passing in the windowless breakout room, waiting for George Adams to call. He bullshits with his advisors, repeating the same old clichés about what it's gonna take to do this deal, soon running out of meaningful things to say, eventually being reduced to commentary about various sporting playoff cycles just now reaching their televised crescendo.

It's a test of patience for Pratt, who spends far too much time quaffing bottled water and fruitlessly scrutinizing the room-service menu for anything that might be called heart-friendly food. There's a suggestion not seriously voiced by someone to wander down to Queen Street, have a patio beer (or two), enjoy the carnival scenery, the bohemian poses, and observe how people walk around virtually naked in downtown Toronto in the summer. But no one goes anywhere, under the assumption that Adams will call any minute to announce a compromise from the other side, triggering more compromises, triggering a deal.

The call doesn't come.

The Stelco team had been the first group summoned, minutes after the opening session. They regurgitated positions they'd outlined to Adams in the various sessions that had led up to the mediation. Again they went through the rationale of the middle ground they would like to occupy by developing a new restructuring plan to bridge the vast differences—especially on the pension issue—between the union and government on the one hand, and the bondholders and shareholders on the other. It was a cautious exchange, with Adams making a show of testing Pratt's willingness to compromise, and Pratt indicating that he would, should others do the same.

There was minimal whiteboarding.

After the session, Pratt had a quiet moment of crisis. While he and fifty others are trapped in a downtown hotel, talking *about* each other but not *to* each other enough, the billable hours are ticking off for the advisors. A small fortune.

Who's paying for that? We are. The company.

He thought about the blast furnaces at the Hamilton and Lake Erie mills, spewing out tons of molten iron by the hour, running flat out to pay for this mediation and the many thousands of billable hours in the eighteen months leading up to it . . . thousands of workers in those mills, gritting it out in the fire and brimstone, at the controls of heavy equipment, stomping through long shifts in work boots and hard hats, making steel in the deafening clamour, in the oven heat. What the hell would *they* make of this?

Hours pass. A call from Adams doesn't come.

While Pratt is confident in his operational people at the mills, he feels that there's something unbecoming about a CEO sitting around in a hotel room debating whether he should order the garden salad and fruit plate or splurge on the triple-decker chicken club, on brown, no mayo, hold the fries. In these undignified tests of executive endurance, he realizes that it's important to eat right, or at least to restrict the damage. It would have been a good idea to have packed gear for a workout in the hotel gym, but the union guys would gossip about a CEO more concerned with burning calories than making steel.

Hours more pass. The call still doesn't come.

In this negotiating void, there is nonetheless information flow. The news that comes to Pratt does so in whispers and at unofficial moments, in the chatter of advisors hopping between rooms, during "accidental" meetings in hallways. It's like a political convention operating on no deadlines or scheduled vote, a corporate existential zone where the rules of productivity just don't apply.

As the first day turns into evening, it becomes clear that there'll be no breakthrough. Long past midnight, people are advised to go home, get some sleep and return early the next morning.

Unbeknownst to everyone, George Adams keeps going, pulling an all-nighter with his advisors to assemble a "straw man": a compromise position intended to be acceptable—or reasonably so—to all parties.

REMEDIES

This restructuring has become much more complex and contentious than Pratt ever anticipated. However, the remedies open to Stelco are familiar territory to those who live beyond their means. At root, CCAA is about getting out of a financial jam with your creditors. In the Adams mediation, the company and its stakeholders are struggling to find some combination of the following alternatives to get to a deal:

- You can get on a more flexible repayment schedule with your lenders, buying some time by paying back your debts over a longer period while still operating as a business; this is known as "extending maturities." These arrangements could also include deferring or lowering your interest charges for a while, or even for a long while, depending on how dire your situation is.

- You can say, look, I'll never be able to pay all this money back to you, not in this lifetime, so let's agree that I'll repay you 80 per cent or 50 per cent on the dollar, or even less, depending. The idea is to get creditors to agree that they'll take a portion of what's owed them. If they do accept less, you know they're doing so because you've proven to be a poor financial risk, and possibly a bankruptcy candidate, meaning that they may get nothing at all if they don't accept less now than they're actually owed.

- You can convert all or some of the money you owe into equity that you give to creditors, and, presto, debt evaporates from your balance sheet (and so do interest charges). In this scenario, creditors become owners of your business. The risk that creditors take here, in an established public company, is that the value of common shares is often linked to competence in producing profits. Stelco has not been sustainably profitable in years.

- You can raise cash by selling off assets, much like people who sell their cars when they have trouble making the payments, and then use the money to pay down debts. This is always a risky endeavour when done in a crisis. A smart buyer who knows you're pressed for cash will dangle a token amount at you—a firesale price—knowing you're desperate.

- You can do some combination of all of the above.

- Or you can declare bankruptcy, and let the court sell off your remaining assets. This is the worst-case scenario, always.

STRAW MAN

Day two. The whiteboard in Adams's breakout room is covered, as the straw man is presented separately to each of the parties.

At his session, Pratt feels a tiny flush of vindication: the straw man proposal, to his thinking, is a thoughtful compromise, not too far off his own team's position. But soon there are ugly reports from the other breakout rooms. Although Pratt has no direct knowledge of the conversations going on all around him, apparently hours are spent providing George Adams with denunciations of the straw man.

The day unfolds as a series of pseudo-encounters: bluffs, threats and disavowals communicated between groups, mainly by proxies, in hallway whispers that may or may not violate confidences. There are cryptic conversations after which no one will admit to remembering what was said. There is no deal, not yet, not even the remotest possibility of one.

At one point Pratt, unable to sit still, meanders by himself over to Adams's conference room. He hears shouting behind closed doors, a litany of curses from men to whom creative swearing is a core business competency . . . scumbag this, cocksucker that, parasite this, those fucking fuckers, we've fucking had it, we're gonna go nuclear, the nuclear option, those fuckers are gonna regret it.

Must be the union guys, Pratt thinks, amused. Bill Ferguson? Bloom himself? Hard to say. So many voices. Some are complaining about the bondholders. Then Pratt hears his own name orphaned in a sustained sequence of "fucks" and "bastards." He doesn't find this upsetting at all, given his own rough use of the language lately. He'd be more worried if they were talking about him in lovey-dovey terms, which would only mean they'd be lying, and likely planning another leak to the media that would seem to have no other purpose than to question his motives, tarnish his reputation. Then he hears something about the "nuclear option." Yes, it is the union guys in there after all.

On the phone to Stephen, he says, "This nuclear option thing . . ."

"Who knows what it means."

"Do they mean a strike?"

"They're never clear."

Another walk-by of the conference room produces an image of Adams alone, during a break in the meetings, scanning a newspaper while wolfing down a sandwich that he hasn't bothered to fully remove from its plastic wrapping. He's framed by the whiteboard, its whiteness scrawled over with multi-coloured, multi-symbol corporate graffiti that probably makes sense—if it makes sense—only to the person wielding the markers. Adams is pensively engaged in his reading, but it has occurred to Pratt that he might just be ignoring everyone and anyone who presumes to intrude. Pratt moves past the open door.

On the phone later, to Barrack. "I don't get this at all."

Barrack, fresh from a series of hallway confabs, makes it clear that Adams has sidelined everyone from the negotiation—including Pratt's team—except for the union and the bondholders, the main adversaries.

"So we're bystanders?" Pratt says.

"In the bleachers."

GHOSTLY IMAGES

As the afternoon wanes without news on whether the mediator Adams is making progress, there's agreement between Pratt and Stephen that, in this age of mobile phones, they should be able to leave the premises for a decent meal nearby. In the event of a summons from Adams, they can easily get back in minutes. Barrack says he's going home for a while but will join them later, or sooner if the situation demands it.

Once outside, they confront the heat, the June afternoon having melted into dusk, the evening light an alluring swirl of violet and orange, the psychedelic effect of smog filtering through a dying sun. The sultry weather is an assault on the wisdom of wearing a suit and tie.

The restaurant is around the corner, a landmark institution near the stock exchange, popular among investment bankers and traders, especially at bonus time. It's known mainly for its impressively vertical food, served by attractive young women in tight formal livery who encourage patrons toward exorbitantly priced super-Tuscans, decanted over a flirtatious comment or two then poured into large glasses.

Neither of the men is a wine snob but they do know their reds. Yet they're too exhausted to consider dinner a pleasure. After sitting down at a table on the outdoor patio, a quiet spot beneath the skyscrapers, they ignore the wine list, each ordering a Moosehead beer.

Their state of exhaustion is devoid of accomplishment, and they fight the temptation to whine about the mediation process, the indignity of being turned into bystanders. There's silence before the beers arrive. While they have worked closely for over a year now and know each other's business logic—and strengths and weaknesses—with a kind of molecular accuracy, this is the first time they've gone to dinner under the pretence of the event being mainly social.

The subject of grandchildren eases the conversation through appetizers, and the exchange leads into the past, family origins and career histories, which they relate back to the current predicament.

"I grew up in Windsor, a blue-collar town if there ever was one," Stephen says. "I grew up around all these union guys."

"Hap, we're not out there screwing the union. We're not even asking for concessions, for Christ's sake."

They both fall silent.

Pratt finally says, "When I took this job, on day three I got a call. A fatality in the mill. A guy with a family. Then you go to a funeral. Meet the family. Pay your respects. Not the first time I've done this in my career. Things like death, serious injuries, that's real, and that changes you, colours how you see things. And how you relate to these perception battles. And to whom you're accountable."

Stephen nods, a signal to keep it coming, but Pratt stares off into the distance, wondering why these terrible images are present right now.

Pratt continues, "At Noranda, you know, I ran a really big machine there. Mining, oil and gas, forestry. In a dozen countries or more. The survival of some communities depended on collaboration and trust between unions and management. As a manager, you did things—or didn't—realizing there could be human consequences. Here I don't see any appreciation for real consequence, no empathy for what matters most: the survival of the company. People are playing games. Including us. Necessary games, but it doesn't mean I have to like it."

Pratt, still preoccupied by a jumble of ghostly images and half-remembered moments from decades ago, doesn't yet seem alert to what may be skepticism in Stephen's gaze. "When I was younger," he says now, "a teenager, my early twenties—I spent time working in some rugged places. I spent one summer way up north in Ungava Bay, at an iron ore site, driving a bulldozer—serious manual labour—being eaten alive by mosquitoes, blackflies. Spent a couple of summers at a cement plant, a terrible place back then. I remember cleaning up a pit of black steaming goop . . . I don't know what it was. But it was poison. The mask I had was about as effective as a Kleenex. I was sick all night after that. I mean ill. It really makes you sit back and think. Health and safety policies? What health and safety? Nothing like it, then. It's not like we've solved all the problems in the industrial world, but you can't tell me we're not moving ahead in Canada—that we're not concerned about the welfare of our people. And yet this perception persists, Christ, that we're trying to screw them."

His voice trails off.

"Pratt, next you're gonna tell me you were raised by wolves," Stephen jokes, swirling the dregs of his beer, peering into the glass as if the next conversation topic is engraved at the bottom. "Manufacturing jobs, Canadian jobs," he says, with a grimace. "I believe they're worth saving. I've been through—how many restructurings? And each time, the same argument, whether Canada should get out of manufacturing—and do what, I don't know. Each time, people say, ah, shut the place down, move it offshore. Sell the plants to the Americans—to China, India. The highest bidder."

"And do what after? Design websites? Sell jewellery on eBay? Buy shares in Chinese steel companies with money you no longer have because you no longer have a job?"

"As if the past hundred and fifty years didn't occur here."

"As if, as if." Pratt is winding himself up again. "It's not like three thousand families in Hamilton are all gonna move on to Silicon Valley after this and start a dot-com or something."

"I wish I knew what the hell Adams was doing," Stephen says, shaking his head. "If this mediation goes south . . ."

Pratt lets that statement steep. "Want another beer?"

"No."

While Pratt signals for and then signs the bill, Stephen gets on the BlackBerry, on speed-dial. After the call he says, "Barrack. He's heard nothing from anybody, nothing. He's coming down."

TIME OUT

A hotel bar. Dim lighting. Three men. One TV.

The final thirty minutes of the basketball game take forever. Time outs, the cheering crowd, celebrities courtside, the coaches whiteboarding plays, the sweating nods in the huddle. It's play-by-play at feverish broadcast pitch, then, during a time out, there's a cutaway for sponsor identification: a car commercial with its computer-generated sheen, the sky and clouds reflected on the gleaming vehicle, the flawless pale skin of the supermodel at the wheel.

"Our steel goes into that car," Pratt volunteers. "High-strength, low-alloy steel, next-generation. Exceptionally formable. Steels that become harder, more dent-resistant during the stamping and painting process. There's a huge future for this."

"Pratt, the game is tied, ten seconds left," Barrack says.

"We're heading into a second overtime," Stephen says.

"People have this idea that the steel business is locked in the past," Pratt continues, eating peanuts by the handful.

"It really amazes me how long this is taking," Stephen says.

"There's got to be a law of physics that explains this phenomenon, how we experience time in different ways," the bartender says, a bespectacled guy in his mid-forties. He's in bar-polishing mode, needy for conversation. "The closer you get to zero, to the clock running out, the more time seems to slow down. Or stands still. A second takes a lifetime. It's something you don't experience, say, at the beginning of the first quarter. But in the final seconds of the game? Time sometimes reverses. As you'll notice, after every basket, now, they put the clock back a few hundredths of a second. Time is time—but is it really? And if it can move forward, can it also move backward?"

He's silently but only briefly contemplated by the three men.

The ball is inbounded across the half-court line. It's a one-on-one show now, eight seconds left, the Detroit guard against the San Antonio defender. The guard dribbles between his legs, then behind his back into a savage crossover, searching for a driving lane or an open man, in the event of the double team from the wings. Seconds pass.

"He used to play for Toronto," Barrack says, "and we let him go."

"Free agency," says the bartender. "You go where the money is."

"No loyalty any more," mutters Stephen.

The Detroit guard drives to the hoop. A spin dribble in the paint, then a fadeaway jumper over the outstretched arms of two defenders.

Swish.

"I don't believe I saw that," Barrack says.

"Three seconds left, plenty of time," the bartender says.

"No way," Barrack says. "Three seconds, still?"

Three point seven seconds left. Detroit up two.

Time out.

The same car commercial.

"Stelco's got good products for the auto sector," Stephen says. "It's more or less the upper end of the business. But it's also 'me too,' in some respects."

"Good products," Pratt replies. "But we're not competitive, not costwise. Not without serious changes. Changes we can't make right now."

"And if the car industry tanks?" Barrack says. "What then?"

"Detroit's in a tough spot right now, guys," Stephen says.

"They're up two points, Hap," Barrack replies.

"I'm talking the auto sector."

"It's a joke, Hap."

"There's always going to be markets for steel," Stephen adds. "Prices may vary, true, depending on where we are in the cycle."

"And where are we?" Pratt says. "A company in bankruptcy protection. And there isn't enough money to make everyone happy. There just isn't."

"I hear you," Stephen says.

"It's bizarre that the CEO of a nearly bankrupt company is of two minds about having good steel prices," Pratt says. "We'd be out of this restructuring if the pricing hadn't spiked and spooked everyone."

"Prices have fallen and they may fall further," Stephen says. "They always do. The cycle."

"Great—our salvation is falling prices," Pratt says. "An interesting situation for a company needing every last red cent."

A beer-sipping pause.

"Is it possible to make a car commercial without a woman in it?" the bartender wonders. "The issue being, if you buy this car, does the babe come with it?"

All three stare at the bartender.

San Antonio inbounds the ball at half-court. A high pick from the big man frees up the speedy guard for a layup, the ball released from his fingertips an instant before the buzzer. It seems to roll around the rim for an hour, as all three men cheer it down.

Tie game.

SINKING SHIP

After the basketball game, they take a stroll around the grounds of City Hall accompanied by a breeze off the lake—then they're back at the hotel and into corridor politics again, the non-action of mediation. Pratt and Stephen are still in the same clothes they started the day with. At different moments, they have each resentfully glanced over at Barrack, who went home for a shower and costume change, an option unavailable to them as they live in suburbs to the west of the city, with no way to get there and back in rush-hour traffic.

It's four in the morning and they're wandering the corridors. No one knows what to do, who to call, what to say.

They see one of the bondholders—a young guy—slumped on the floor, against a wall. He's dishevelled and it looks like he was trying to sleep, but his eyes balefully contemplate the opposite wall. A laptop is open beside him, along with a bag of chips.

"Hey, where are your guys?" Stephen says, good-naturedly.

"They're somewhere around here."

"So are we getting closer to a deal?" Pratt says, also genially, but he is quietly seething—not at the kid, just at having to pump for information when he's a so-called sponsor of this mediation.

"Things sort of went non-linear."

"How so?"

"It sort of just crawled out at us. Right along a beam. A hole in the ceiling. The construction work. It was a big fat fucker."

The story of the rat coming out of the ceiling, scattering the bondholders in mid-meeting, energizes everyone for the next hour or so. *So, was the rat running to—or from—you?* But soon even the rat has lost its entertainment value, and they have to accept that once again they're adrift, on the fringe of a mediation process going nowhere.

Around dawn, a five-minute meeting with Adams, the whiteboard cleansed of conflict but also of possibility.

INTERMISSION

Adams ordains a three-week break in the mediation. A time for reflection. A chance to create authentic conditions for negotiating a deal.

Now what?

Hundreds of hours of brainstorming back at the shop, boardroom arguments, whiteboard moments, blue-sky thinking, best-case and worst-case scenarios, bottom-line approaches, fallback positions, a million e-mails, bleary breakfast conversations with despairing spouses.

I won't be home until late, very late.

But we're having the so-and-so's over for dinner.

We'll have to reschedule.

Honey . . .

I'm sorry. It is what it is.

When is this going to be over?

Nobody's been voted off the island yet. Not even close.

People haven't forgotten the two days at the hotel by any means. There is some nursing of grudges, the water-cooler bravado, the woulda coulda shoulda, the bluster about the consequences of failure, some still bewildered that those on the other side, on the multiple other sides, can't come to their senses, do the right thing.

It's a fucking octopus of a problem, isn't it?

You think you've got all the arms, then you get smacked again.

Countless phone calls, media leaks, press releases, TV interviews; endless talk-radio blather, courtroom antics by all parties testing the patience of Justice Farley, who keeps reminding them that unless a deal is reached soon, Stelco may go *splat.*

Eighteen months and counting—

In these three weeks there's much grunt work, the exhausting non-drama of strategists rethinking positions and some deciding they were right in the first place and telling their colleagues, look, compromise is a dirty word when the others are playing dirty to begin with.

Fuck them and the boat they came in on. All of them.

Spreadsheet-conjuring. Updated forecasts. New estimates of cash flow, earnings, steel prices, pension obligations, workforce levels, capital investments. Number-crunching. Media-spinning.

Numbers don't lie, right?

Right. People do.

The birth and death of new financial-engineering strategies that few except the financial engineers understand.

Letters to the editor. Outrage from steelworkers, pensioners, the concerned citizens of Hamilton, demanding more invasive government intervention to clean up this mess, demanding the heads of Stelco executives and American bondholders. Reputations tarnished further.

Ongoing debates about the wisdom of Rolf Gerstenberger, the Hamilton union leader, who has refused to participate in the mediation because he considers the recourse to CCAA a transparent excuse to degrade proletarian dignity.

Brutal comparisons in the boardroom, cafeterias, living rooms.

Another Canadian steel company, Dofasco, which operates a mill next door to the Stelco facility in Hamilton, is now openly viewed as a takeover target by at least two global industrial conglomerates. Experts in the steel industry and within the Stelco negotiations expect Dofasco to be sold, absorbed into a multi-billion-dollar corporate structure, put under the control of managers and shareholders outside Canada. Dofasco is expected to fetch a price to warm the heart of any financial speculator or shareholder.

Some people hope for a similar destiny for Stelco but acknowledge that the company needs a serious makeover—these would be the financial speculators, the bondholders.

Some fear a similar destiny for Stelco but won't acknowledge the company's in bad shape. These would be the union leaders.

Some say it doesn't matter what people hope or fear, because at some point, Stelco—or whatever is left of Stelco after the bankruptcy proceeding—will be sold, absorbed into a multi-billion-dollar corporate structure, put under the control of managers outside Canada.

Some say, over my dead fucking body.

During the intermission, Pratt's life is a carnival of surreal imbalance, long hours, nights and weekends lost, a blur. As the time approaches to restart the mediation, it feels like only yesterday that he was in a downtown hotel, unable to productively affect the destiny of the company he was hired to protect.

DOWN THE AISLE

In the cavernous exhibition hall, a group of about eight corporate men, maybe ten at most, are riding up a long escalator to a walkway that offers views down to the trade-show floor. It's the Stelco team, Pratt and the CFO, the COO, along with an assortment of investment bankers, lawyers and other consultants. They're en route to the meeting rooms of a conference centre that sprawls over the rail yards near the CN Tower. The place looks like a new terminal at an international airport not yet up to projected traffic levels, but that's because it's early, the conventioneers still likely at the breakfast buffet table or updating their daily voice-mail messages.

Some of these restructuring men are lugging bulging briefcases up the escalator with sherpa resolve, an indication that there is serious business about to be conducted, requiring the security blanket of printouts, memos, spreadsheets and strategy documents. It isn't nearly comforting enough to have the information in digital form on the laptops that they're also lugging. No, the physical archive is also required.

Most of them are long-standing members of the corporate elite and know how to appear politically correct—a Canadian attribute if there ever was one. They've learned to stifle laughter at things that used to be funny but are not considered to be funny now. So, as they get off the escalator and stride along the convention hallway, girding themselves for the Adams mediation, part two, there's tension in the group over whether anyone will dare crack a joke about the trade show being set up below: a bridal convention for same-sex partners.

Finally, a brave soul leaps into the comic abyss, asking in a loud mincing voice, Sir, are you the bride or the groom?

There's wariness in the responding laughter—these men would prefer not to find this funny but heartily do.

SECOND HALF

In the conference room, the principle of "bigger is better" is evident, as if the failure of the first mediation were the result of striving for human intimacy among the negotiators. This error has been rectified. The horseshoe concept has been expanded. Many more people are involved. It depressingly reminds Pratt of a televised debate—say, politicians considering constitutional reform.

It's not long before Pratt and his team again find themselves in a windowless breakout room waiting for instructions.

"Have we achieved anything?" he says to no one in particular. "This is all risk, all downside, if we don't come out of here with a deal."

After a long while, Barrack peeks in the door. "Adams wants us in on something going on right now—a meeting between Bloom and Delman."

Gary Delman is a heavy hitter, a leader among the bondholders. He's been described to Pratt by one of the junior investment bankers on his own team as a major swinging dick—a compliment of the highest order. Pratt wonders when investment bankers started talking like rappers. He also wonders if he's getting too old for this.

"What's our role?" Pratt asks.

"Observer status. Although there's an expectation that Bloom or Delman will hurl abuse at us, allowing us to respond," Barrack says.

The meeting is under way when they arrive, twenty people in yet another breakout room. An investment banker is projecting a presentation on a wall screen from his laptop, plodding through the bondholder argument that everyone has seen so often that even the presenter is bored. He's frequently interrupted by Ron Bloom, who has the ability to absorb an enemy's point of view and turn it into a weapon. Bloom is demolishing the presenter—a brutally effective, foul-mouthed deconstruction that focuses on the elephant in the spreadsheets: there's no fucking solution to funding the pension deficit, the company will be burdened with too much fucking debt after paying the bondholders a hundred cents on the dollar, and when steel prices crater, as they will, the balance sheet won't weather it, sending Stelco back into bankruptcy protection within a year. Are you guys fucking blind or just stupid?

As this brutalization continues, Gary Delman, the major swinging dick from New York, wades into the shock-and-awe of the Bloom approach. Delman is in his early forties, French-cuffed and suspendered, and he exudes familiarity with big cigars at the closing party and trophy women at the mansion. He has the audacity to suggest aloud to the union guys that whatever happens here, hey, no problem, I'm still gonna make five or six million this year . . . and you guys, hey, good luck.

His message: Threaten all you want, Bloom, you're not going to squeeze blood from us, forcing the conversion of our bonds into equity, because there's too much risk in this company. We want our money—the money owed to us. And we have the final say over the plan that gets Stelco out of bankruptcy. You don't, and that's that. The law of the land.

You guys are whacked if you think this Tricap proposal will fly. Whacked.

Pratt thinks, when did financiers start talking like TV mobsters?

Bloom and Delman exchange bile for what seems to Pratt like an hour but is likely only fifteen minutes. It's a fight in which the middle ground is quickly defined as no man's land, a compromise-free zone occupied only by a thesaurus of profanities describing how each side feels about the other.

"This is what it comes down to," Pratt whispers to Stephen. "Two Americans deciding the fate of a Canadian company."

"What's wrong with this picture?"

All the while, George Adams, reputedly the most skilled and experienced mediator in the country, keeps impatient watch over Bloom and Delman, poking his nose in for clarification here, offering the occasional reminder there, guys, we're here for a reason, to move the ball forward, and if you can't do that, let's draw the curtain down, I've got better things to do than babysit you.

He's not ignored. He's tolerated.

FOOT IN MOUTH

Only blackness is visible through the glassed roof over the hallway—another lost night. With the trade-show crowds long gone, the convention has a mausoleum stillness. Only the Stelco mediation crowd, cleaning staff and security guards remain in the building as midnight comes and goes.

Pratt finds himself wandering around in possession of the strangely hopeful view that the mere act of barging in on people, randomly joining meetings in progress, will change the dynamic and lead to the breakthrough. He isn't alone in this desperate optimism. There's lawless information promiscuity by everyone, room-hopping, hallway gossiping, an orgy of perspective-sharing and speculative chit-chat. Everyone knows that something more brutal and improvisational has to happen soon. No one wants to sit around a whiteboard any more, pretending to give an inch when the request is ten yards.

Most would agree this isn't Adams's fault.

Pratt would later wonder why he hadn't seen it coming: the unstated desire for dramatic developments of equal stature to the psychological turbulence, the resentment building up after eighteen months of fruitless negotiation. All that frustration is looking for visible expression. For conflict.

For some, it's now beginning to make perfectly ethical sense to gang up on the weaker players. Pratt accepts that the malevolence beginning to surface isn't caused just by the usual suspects—the blinding zeal of ideology and greed, the venality of special interest striving for power over other special interests. There's darkness in his own biases, too.

What if treating everyone fairly delivers a deal less than the sum of its parts? What if we win and the company dies anyway? Is there a better way? Something we haven't thought of?

Just give me something that lets me sleep at night, he thinks. That lets me look a steelworker and pensioner in the eye and say I did my best for them and the company. That lets me answer to my board that we had the company's survival at heart. That keeps the lawyers and financial people happy—or at least restrained in their unhappiness.

In one room-hopping interlude, Pratt enters a lecture in progress. Gary Delman is addressing an assortment of investment bankers, his suit jacket off, shirtsleeves rolled, loafer-clad feet up on the table. Delman gives him a nod, but the lecture continues without interruption, the implication being that Pratt should be grateful for the educational value in being exposed so eloquently to the purity of hedge-fund wisdom.

Pratt is stunned by what Delman now appears to be doing: removing his loafers to walk around in his bare feet.

A barefoot man in a breakout room? Exposing his fucking feet?

Sweaty feet released from the luxurious trappings of butter-soft black leather. He's actually touching his feet now. Fingers between his toes. Massaging them. Toenails. Leg hair visible to the ankles.

And still talking.

Pratt considers himself reasonably adept at interpreting body language in executive situations. But corporate men exposing parts of the body below the waist? This isn't a pool party. This isn't someone's patio. This is a tense gathering of exhausted white-collar men in business suits who do not, as a tactic in asserting economic power over other men, expose their naked feet for lingering observation.

Delman is caressing one foot very intimately now, scratching at a calloused area under the heel, then rolling dead skin into a ball between his fingers, holding it up to the light as if admiring a priceless diamond.

In the midst of this display, Pratt thinks about female attire—or lack of it—as a language that can reveal much about the nature of corporate power relationships. It's a super-charged subject, he knows, evoking all sorts of diversity and equality issues—sexuality in the office, the meanings of skirt lengths, of high heels as compared to flats, of cleavage hidden or displayed. In bare legs crossing beneath the boardroom table while the chairman calls for a vote on the layoff strategy. In women crossdressing in business suits, in loafers and brogues rather than open-toed pumps, or in mules that unavoidably draw the eye to the naked heel. And so on. That language he more or less understands. But bare feet on a man in this situation? As Pratt sees it—and he's not sure why he knows this, but he knows this as much as he knows anything about power and men—when Delman slipped off his loafers, pausing in his speech on risk analysis to wiggle his toes, he might just as well have dropped his pants.

Major swinging dick, he thinks. Sure you are.

UNION STATION

In the middle of the night, the union requests a private meeting with Pratt.

Right on schedule, Pratt thinks.

"I thought we weren't doing this," Osborne says.

"I thought so too, but I thought wrong."

"In a duel, if you pick the time and place, the other guy picks the weapons. I've got golf clubs in my trunk. What about nine irons at dawn?"

"We've got to do it—let's go."

Having spent many years managing unionized employees, Pratt long ago grew tired of the predictable tactic of being invited by union leaders to late-night meetings for negotiations. It's standard operating procedure in the union handbook at collective agreement time, designed to wear the other side down and force errors in judgment. But as they walk over to the table in the big hall where Ron Bloom and Bill Ferguson, the Lake Erie union leader, are waiting, Pratt accepts that once again he's going to a meeting in the middle of the night, exhausted, frustrated and holding no real cards aside from his ability to attend this meeting.

Word reached him from people close to George Adams that the mediator is on the verge of calling it quits for lack of any meaningful effort at compromise by anyone.

"We'll do as bystanders do," Pratt says before they arrive. "Even if it's only writing down licence-plate numbers or putting a blanket over the guy who came through the windshield."

"I thought we *were* that guy," Osborne replies.

"No, that guy is six thousand Stelco employees and ten thousand pensioners if we don't get a deal."

When they sit down, Bloom launches himself at Pratt. There is no slouching act this time, but a full-frontal attack; Bloom is speaking as if there's venom inside his body that will kill him unless he ejects it right now. For the first few minutes of Bloom's tirade, Pratt's not listening in the sense of taking in verbal information and processing it—not that he has to, because the message is violently clear: management must make a choice right now and side with the union and tell these bondholder scumbags to fuck off. We'll deal with the bondholders together, Bloom says.

Pratt is still marvelling at the velocity and depth of the man's transformation from the cagiest of union diplomats into total gonzo street fighter, the guy handing out bats and brass knuckles in the alley, unwilling to entertain a strategic retreat when it really is time to bust heads or have yours busted. For Pratt, it's not any one manifestation of Bloom's personality that makes him such a difficult adversary—it's his ability to change his spots.

What Pratt hears the words "nuclear option," he interrupts the flow of anger directed at him and Osborne. "You know I can't do what you're asking," he says. "My board won't allow me to do that. We can't do the cram-down on the bond guys. We may not like them. But we have to respect who they are. They're legally entitled—"

Interruptions. Sputtering rebuttals, Bloom telling Pratt not to fuck this up, to deliver for once.

After the meeting ends, Pratt and Osborne are wordless for several long minutes as they walk back to neutral territory.

"Serious hardball," Osborne finally says.

"Playing is right—but it's not a game I like much."

TOUCHDOWN

Hut-hut-hut—hike.

Pratt accepts the snap from the invisible centre, steps back and fades to his right, eyes scanning the hallway, which is surely half as long as a real football field. He fakes this way and that, deciding against the buttonhook option to his COO, who is waving near the escalator, not deep enough for a first down. He doesn't give the securities lawyer near the soft-drink machine so much as a glance, because he's more or less standing out of bounds, but then he sees Stelco's chief legal officer downfield—dashing along a slant route—getting free of the kid who is apparently an investment banker but who mainly runs the computers and gets coffee.

Pratt lets it rip, the Nerf football spiralling in the air, a trajectory splitting the overhead lighting tracks.

For an instant he thinks the company's top lawyer, who is chasing the pass, is going to collide at full tilt with a concrete pillar.

One less lawyer won't hurt, Pratt thinks, but not this guy, please.

As Pratt's intended receiver gets within a second of brutal convergence with the pillar, he trips and falls. No collision.

Incomplete pass.

The Nerf ball zips back and forth among the men, patterns are run, elaborate evasions undertaken from invisible linebackers. It's the schoolyard again. Some are more at ease with the jock patter and being creative on this imaginary field of dreams, and Pratt is one of those.

The chief legal officer of Stelco is tireless, a man possessed. He mimics moves that look good on TV, spiking the ball in the mythical end zone and high-fiving the invisible fans on the sidelines.

After thirty minutes of this, everyone's sweating.

It's four-thirty in the morning.

TERRIFYING

As it becomes clear to everyone that Adams cannot bring the main parties together and create a deal, the exhaustion turns morose. Once again Pratt is marooned with his team in their breakout room. There are no more meetings to invade. No gossip to share.

"This company is going down, man. We're sinking."

"I heard the bondholders left the building."

"No, really?"

"Where's Delman?"

"Who the fuck cares?"

"Where's Adams?"

"Yes, where is he?"

"No one is totally certain."

"What about the government people?"

"Whatever."

"It's terrifying—I mean, this is all fucked up."

"Very sad and scary," Pratt says, softly. A conversation stopper.

Pratt knows that this isn't a time for speeches about the darkest moment being the last minute before the shining dawn, or that there's light at the end of the tunnel, or that this isn't the beginning of the end but only the end of the beginning. It's never a good time for those speeches, except at movie plot points.

"I'm having a nap," he says. "Fifteen minutes."

His bed is a row of four chairs. When he closes his eyes, he realizes sleep is impossible, but just closing his eyes—this is restful, necessary.

Terrifying, he thinks. I'll tell you what's terrifying.

He has a waking dream, a familiar nocturnal recollection:

He is sedated, lying on the operating table, the light in his face, feeling no pain, frightened by his inability to lift his arms or move his legs much, and then the surgeon walks by, prepped for the procedure, asking him, are you sure you want the metal valve, you'll be on blood thinners forever, why not go for the pig valve, it's organic, but it needs to be replaced in ten years. Are you sure you want to do metal?

Weeks of worry leading up to this terrifying moment—

Weeks coming to grips with the birth defect that none of his doctors had ever caught, the heart murmur, no symptoms, a very small problem that had gone undetected for decades while the aortic valve weakened, putting pressure on the cardiovascular system, a small problem that could become very big—and then you collapse on the squash court, at the office, boom, dead.

Pratt sits up.

There's something he could say about keeping things in perspective. Knowing what is genuinely terrifying and what is merely upsetting. What is life and death, what is not. What is posturing. Knowing the difference is essential to keeping your cool in weird situations.

He thinks of Alexa at home alone tonight. Her fight.

He stops thinking about Alexa. This isn't so easy to do.

Is this situation terrifying?

"We're getting a deal," Pratt says. "Even if it kills me."

"There's no deal, not a chance," Adams says.

Minutes after the mediator departs, while Pratt is packing up, his BlackBerry vibrates. He takes the call. There's a situation at the Lake Erie mill, though the details are sketchy. It appears that a strike at the nearby power plant is spreading, or wants to spread. Some striking power plant workers are preventing Stelco employees from entering the mill. Provincial police are on the scene and lawyers are being dispatched to get court injunctions.

As the day ended, so it is beginning: in conflict, confusion, fear. The possibility of failure is like a virus, mutating.

Rising from the lower level, they escape the scene by escalator. Dawn light pours in everywhere along the façade of plate glass on the long walkway that leads to the exhibition space and the parking lots. Pratt leads a glum group, half-listening to the commentary.

"You gotta believe the union is going to milk this in the media. I wouldn't be surprised if there's something in the morning papers. All our mugs. With a big fat bull's eye."

"The judge is going to massacre us when we go back to court."

"When are we in court again?"

"Honestly, when are we ever not in court?"

Pratt could contribute to the negativity, but enough is being said already. As CEO of a company in CCAA, he's paid to contemplate the implications of this colossal failure and to plot out the next move. But first he needs some sleep.

He has known all along that this mediation was a high-risk venture. But he thought that by holding firm at the middle ground, he had some negotiating authority. That belief has been shaken. In this particularly bleak moment, he realizes that he's the Canadian CEO of a Canadian company whose destiny, it now appears, is probably in the hands of American bondholders fighting with American union bosses.

Do we control anything?

He remembers he left his car at home and took the train into Toronto. He tells his people he's going home, that's it, the end of the normal week, Friday. As he walks toward the train station, he pauses at the street corner, even after the light turns green, to indulge in a moment of sweet, blinking awe at the sunlight glinting off everything, blossoming over the sidewalk as if, he thinks, the sun is searching for me and me alone. He wants to laugh out loud at this momentary delusion of self-importance but doesn't want to upset the elderly man standing next to him.

Silly moments like this—no, not silly moments, he thinks, irreverent ones—have come over him before, after working through the night and then instantly realizing when the sun comes up that life is worth living for so many reasons that have nothing to do with the seriousness of the preceding hours. He doesn't blame men for being—well, he doesn't blame them for being only human. For allowing stupidity to rule on occasion. Perhaps "stupidity" isn't the word—but there's a word, he knows, in some dictionary, to describe the complicated games of those who aspire to power in the name of people who are not around the table but who are always invoked as an excuse for getting on the highest of horses. No matter how exhausted he is from being trapped in windowless rooms for days with men who, in their collective enterprise, have failed to make good decisions, he's frankly happy to be going home. There he will get the latest news on the grandkids, maybe have a coffee, fall asleep on the couch, the newspaper flattened to his chest, intending to wake up north of noon to debate whether he should go to the office.

Home today.

He's too tired to think clearly, but also restless, wanting to sift through the experience right now.

Can anything positive can be taken away? Well, we really know who's who now. We've all been through something together. We've bonded.

If intensity of effort won't work—what will?

What I need, he thinks, I *have,* somewhere, inside. But what is it?

He has watched Adams carefully throughout the mediation: admired the nuances in his pose of neutrality, the professionalized objectivity. Adams is good, very good. The best there is. But ultimately, Pratt thinks, no one in this crowd respects objectivity purchased from a consultant. No one wants a balanced perspective if it has to be outsourced. They only respect the ability to put something on the line: to feel the risk—or suffer the consequence—of failure. No one here wants a referee, no matter how rough the game's getting.

In this mediation, Pratt and his team have been on the sidelines far too much. No more of that, he thinks. We're gonna be on field for every play from now on, no matter how much mud we get on ourselves.

RICHARD (RICO) ESPOSITO, HEDGE-FUND PARTNER

We're flying into La Guardia an hour late on a smoggy afternoon. It's likely blistering hot on the ground, the asphalt at the melting point.

I don't like airports where you descend toward the runway with a body of water on your flank. Logically, I'm not supposed to be concerned, but I'm pretty clenched until we bump and bounce down fully.

As the seatbelt signs go off, I hear noises and see gestures from my fellow passengers that indicate that they've turned their phones and BlackBerries on. An elderly lady in the next row decides not to wait for a flight attendant to help her off the flight but instead gets up on her own to hobble down the aisle at the speed of her walker. I hear curses, not quite under one guy's breath, about the temerity of that ugly old bag.

The flight was packed, the middle seats all taken, the air stale with sweat and other odours—potato chips, feet, salty peanuts. The guy next to me was just plain sour. Kept mopping his face between scotches.

We're all cranky, including me. I'm here to visit Rico Esposito to gain more insight into the psychology of our bondholders, a stakeholder group we're not exacting satisfying these days. I'm hoping I'll learn something to help us propose a fair compromise with these guys. Otherwise we'll never get out of CCAA.

When I got in touch with him, Rico unthinkingly assumed I would come to him, and maybe I'd feel that way too if I were sitting on three or four billion dollars.

The limo guy holds up a hand-scrawled sign in the arrivals area, with my first name misspelled as "Cortney." He wordlessly leads me out of the terminal into chaotic traffic, then through the maze of the parking garage. Soon we're heading toward the coast, to the town of Greenwich, Connecticut, an acknowledged mecca since the early 1990s for hedge-fund and financial service professionals who started migrating from Manhattan, a forty-minute train ride away. I've read reports, impossible to verify, that more that $120 billion in investment money now has a management home in this—for lack of a better term—hedge-fund Disneyland.

It's bumper-to-bumper on the interstate.

Two hours later, we pull off the highway and navigate small-town streets, soon turning up a leafy lane protected by a gate that looks capable of stopping a missile. Rico's offices are in a shingled country house, set back on a large property, surrounded not just by mature trees on all sides, but also by high fencing and many video cameras. On the inside, the house has been gutted of all rural pretence, the floors and walls done up in polished limestone detailed in bronze. Or maybe it's gold.

I'm shown into Rico's suite of offices—again, wordlessly—by a very tall, young, beautiful Japanese woman, dressed in black. A full-length dress, it seems, like some modern version of a kimono. She can barely move in it, but this doesn't detract from her silent elegance. After I sit down, Rico swivels around from his console of computer screens, his head framed by bold views of gardens that stretch on forever, the trees and shrubbery more like sculptures than anything horticulturally alive.

"Isn't Suki something?" he says as his assistant leaves. He's a jock, with a shit-eating grin. He might be forty, tops. As trim and fit as you can be.

"She sure is."

"She's like three inches taller than me. Legs that go on forever. Problem is, my mother calls crying every Sunday. 'Ricardo, get married, make babies.' Ma, I say, I'm gonna marry a nice Italian girl one day . . . that kind of crap I tell her. She's caught between wanting me to marry a girl from some village she came from in Sicily and wanting me to move up in the world with some blonde princess, theoretically from Venice. As if those chicks haven't all left for London or New York or LA."

"And you, Rico?"

"Dude, do I look like I live in this suburban shitbox? I have a loft in Tribeca. For weekends. And . . ."

"And what?"

"And there's Suki here. We met at a party. One of my parties, at my place. Legendary parties. Legendary. She puts in a few days here now and then, on retainer. But she's doing this degree at NYU. Some art thing with fashion."

I want to like something about this guy—his energy, his business brains. But he's one arrogant little prick.

He speaks into a speakerphone built into his massive desk. "Have the car brought around in ten." He looks at his watch. And then sees me looking at it too. It's impressive corporate bling.

"The Steve McQueen watch. From TAG Heuer. We gave them out at a closing party. I got a special one made. Worth more in diamonds than you assholes at Stelco have in debts. Dude, what are you guys thinking?"

I just sit there. He needs to explain the world to me.

"I gotta be honest," he says, a streetwise Boston accent barging in. "Irregardless of these fucking two-bit Canadian laws. The fucking unions. The fucking government. That judge. It's the bondholders who have the votes to get you out of CCAA. Without guys like us giving you the thumbs up, you guys are dead. Is this message not clear to you yet?"

The tough kid from Little Italy—a rabid Boston Bruins fan, judging from the sports memorabilia along one wall, some of it clearly very pricey to anyone who knows hockey history. A million bucks of stuff here. I've heard he uses private jets to attend playoff games.

"The message is loud and clear, Rico." I try to keep my own aggression in check, but I can't resist a dig. "Out of curiosity, seriously, where do they train guys like you?"

"Train?"

"The MBA schools teach you to read a balance sheet and write up a business case, if maybe not how to spend four grand on a bottle of wine when the bonus comes in. Then they must take you straight from graduation to some secret al-Qaeda–style camp. Teach you to swear like a man, and to have absolutely zero loyalty to anything but the almighty dollar."

"Yeah," he says, his eyes gleaming. I've angered him, obviously, but he speaks softly. "Like you've never swirled around a glass of the best when guys like me pick up the tab? As for al-Qaeda, that's a dirty word here."

"Rico, I didn't come here to insult you or your country."

"So what are we here to talk about? You want some strategic advice on how to cut yourself a better deal on the takeout, on the back end, how you can make change of control seriously work for you, personally?"

I get a grip on my temper. "Rico, there's a great Canadian icon on the operating table. And guys like you are digging in the guts, just as happy to harvest the organs if it'll make you an extra few bucks."

"You didn't come here to lecture me on capitalism, did you? A big-time CEO of a public company? That's the pot calling the kettle black."

I pause at that. "You just asked for your car to come around."

"Yeah. I gotta be in the city like very instantly."

I want to strangle him. "How much time do we have?"

"Drive in with me. We can talk. Then have yourself a meal at Harry's. On my tab. Seriously. The pork chop. Beyond excellent."

Strangle, then behead, draw and quarter, and burn the pieces.

He gets up and walks over to a walk-in closet to his left. I glimpse a phalanx of suits, all at crisp attention. He steps inside. It seems he's changing his clothes.

"As I see this situation, Courtney—and I have seen many situations like this, in many countries of the world—if you're not careful, if you don't respectfully cave in soon and start seeing who's in charge here, someone like me is going to have your head on a platter."

I pour myself a tall glass of designer water. "We're not idiots, Rico. Guys like you are at the table and will be, as we pull a deal together. We're not doing any cram-down on the bond guys—not because we can't, but because I think it's the wrong approach."

"You got that right," he says distractedly, then with real energy: "Hey, you're a hockey guy, too?"

"A Canadiens fan. The Habs."

"The fuckers—the Canadiens."

"If you're talking about the series when Guy Lafleur destroyed the Bruins, yes, I'm a big fan of those fuckers."

He pokes his head out of the closet. "I was a kid then. I think I cried."

"I was older. Lafleur coming down the right wing. A slap-shot about an inch off the ice. An inch inside the post. Poetry in motion."

He disappears again, laughing to himself. The sound comes from a distance, as if he's gone deeper into the closet.

"What's so funny?" I'm almost shouting.

He comes out in black tie.

"I'll tell you what's so funny," he says as he leads me out of the office, adjusting his cummerbund. "Money has become this different kind of game. Like almost a religion. Its own country. It's not us versus you, the Canadiens against the Bruins. There are a million Stelcos out there for guys like me. You have to compete for us. *Compete.* And why the fuck—yes, why the *fuck* should we hang around in Toronto while you guys pretend that the judge and the unions are in the game? We are the real game here, my friend."

"Because there's money there," I say. "And you know it."

"Don't I ever," he says, grinning at me.

"At least Ron Bloom cares about the workers, the pensioners. You guys, it's only the money. Only that."

"Bloom? I don't know what kind of crossdresser he turned into, going over to the other side. He's still one of us, you realize. A deal junkie. You think Bloom 'cares' about the workers? What does 'care' mean when you get paid to do it? A nanny isn't the same thing as a mother."

"You underestimate him."

"He lives in Pittsburgh. *Pittsburgh.*"

We get into the car and then he's on the phone for the next twenty minutes. Then we're driving past a golf course.

"See that?" he says. "I own half that operation."

"Impressive."

"I'll tell you what's impressive. It's playing at a club where you and only you determine who gets in. Where you can throw someone out if he's rude to the staff. I don't put up with that." This is his way of telling me he's a man of principle. He's trying to connect with me, it seems.

I let him go on.

"You think I'm arrogant," he says.

"You don't strike me as a character who worries too much about what guys like me think of you."

He's unsure whether to be offended. "How many years have I dealt with guys like you? You think you're better than I am. But we perform a social function. A community function. You think Silicon Valley would have gotten off the ground without us? The dot-com thing? We take risks. We make it happen. Without us, you have, well, communism. A dead economy. Russia before it got serious, and it's very serious right now."

"Putin's your kind of guy?"

"He pulls serious moves. He farts and the electricity goes off in France and the pumps runs dry in Germany. Major-league dude."

"Yes, and without the rule of law—boom, he'll take your investments away from you if he wants to. Just like that."

"Don't stay up nights worrying about my hedging strategy. We're so ahead of the curve that's it not a curve any more."

"You're a success, Rico. I'll say that much for you."

He ignores the sarcasm and launches into the nutshell version of his rise to financial glory. He went to college in Minnesota on a hockey scholarship. When he wasn't drafted for the pros, the backup plan was an MBA, followed by a few years in Boston doing grunt work on deals for a venture capital outfit that went bust in the meltdown of the high-tech sector. He graduated into a big job on Wall Street—mergers and acquisitions, specializing in turnarounds of tobacco companies. He made a nice chunk of change, but he realized he'd never get stupid rich without serious leverage. Today he's the second-in-command to a mysterious billionaire and corporate raider who lives on a yacht and appears to be resident nowhere but offshore.

"A couple more deals, Courtney, then I am personally gonna buy the Bruins. And then I'll put my little brother behind the bench to coach. And my father in a skybox with all his bricklayer friends where they can drink their own wine and roast a pig right there if they want to. And then I'll buy free agents and eat—I mean, like, aggressively consume—the Montreal Canadiens, for dinner, with a nice Chianti."

"Dream on, son."

He doesn't like me calling him "son" but lets it pass.

There are loose ends in the encounter, so I get back to work. "I appreciate what you call the social or community function. And how money works. Christ, I'm a CEO, as you say. But the hedge guys in the Stelco situation—there isn't any story here beyond a quick trade. They get in low then sell high. And sell fast. More power to them—if they succeed. But I won't feel sorry for these guys if they get burned on this. It's a risk they're taking for the chance at an obscene profit."

"They own the bonds, the creditor debt. They control this."

"How do you think the creditor debt got bought up. At what price?"

"The guys who bought it from all those mom-and-pops? You ask them that and they'll tell you to fuck off. It's none of your business."

"You guys think you rule the world."

"And?" He gives me a look. Outside the car, we're passing through more suburbia. I have no idea whether it'll take us another fifteen minutes or three hours to get to New York.

I say, "It's an awesome achievement, harnessing all that money and power. But there comes a point—or I think there should come a point—when money can't be divorced from an emotional context. Like the belief that the people of a country should have some say in how they manage their economy, their economic relations . . ."

"You're in the past, man. Worse than that. In my reading of history, that past never even existed. Money has always been money."

"At least admit this: you know nothing about us. The guys from your field, they fly into Toronto. They couldn't really place Hamilton or Lake Erie on a map. And if they could, you can be sure they wouldn't actually go there and get to know the people involved."

"I don't give a shit about any of that." When he realizes he's really offended me, his tone softens a little. Less posturing, definitely more informed. He gives me a rundown of his perspective on Stelco's strengths and weaknesses, the evolution of the global steel industry and its ongoing consolidation. He knows what he's talking about.

"You guys are like so low on the food chain," he says with some finality. "The company, Stelco, as we know it, as you know it—it's dead. Or certainly the life that's left will migrate to a new corporate body. It'll become part of something bigger. I can see why you're so worked up about jobs and pensions. You might be able to get money for the pension fund somewhere. But the jobs? How long can you control that agenda? I mean, consolidation, Courtney. It's gonna happen. *We* didn't cause that."

"But you profit from it."

"Absolutely—look, I gotta make a call."

He's talking to—screaming at, at times—someone who has apparently failed to update his holiday card mailing list. He's unhappy with the balance between Democrats and Republicans, although he doesn't say what the optimal balance should be.

The city in the distance. Always a daunting vision.

Soon we've crossed one of the bridges and are approaching the Upper East Side. The limo pulls over near the Plaza, next to Central Park.

"Courtney, it's been real."

"I don't know how real it's been. But thanks for your time."

"Don't mention it."

"Good luck buying the Bruins. We'll still kick your ass."

"You wish."

It's a good-natured way to close things off.

"Harry's is across the street. The pork chop. It's on me."

"Thanks, but I've got a flight home."

"I'd love to continue this conversation, you know. But there's a big dinner. A fundraiser. I have to be there."

"Always good to be doing that type of thing."

"Yeah," he says solemnly. I expected a boast. "It's something for the 9/11 kids. Kids of parents—dads, mainly—taken down in the towers. We put on a show. We go for serious coin."

"It sounds like this is important to you."

"You know how many friends I lost that day?"

CHAPTER FIVE

FORGING AHEAD

DIVING IN

It's embarrassing, Pratt thinks, as he stands next to the pool in his back yard, on a hot evening after work. It's like being a kid again, scolded for bad behaviour, told to leave the sandbox and go to your room right now, mister, and don't come out until you've thought about you've done. That's what the judge ordered for those involved in the mediation, a "cooling off" period of a week, during which active negotiations are forbidden.

No time to sulk, he thinks, ruefully admitting to himself that the worst part was having to send a letter to Stelco employees letting them know about the failed mediation and the judge's edict. And now what?

He dives in, eyes closed to the chlorine sting, pressure in his ears, the acoustics otherworldly. Rising to the surface, he floats face down, content in his ebbing forward momentum. Pratt isn't an inch-by-inch guy who wades in, arms crossed protectively across his shivering chest. The water isn't a vintage wine that invites analysis of the intriguing contrast between surface warmth and colder temperatures lower down—it's there to be immersed in. Anyway, he thinks, if it's cold, then it will be cold whether you dive or inch your way in. Why torture yourself?

He starts to crawl, lifting his head to get his bearings. The pool is vaguely kidney-shaped: two amorphous blobs, connected. Soon enough he's into the flow, his mind doing what it wants even as his body moves.

Forget hiding in breakout rooms, he thinks. No, go right up the middle of this mess. Do it out in the open. And do the right thing.

UP THE MIDDLE

Things heat up at Stelco even during the cooling-off period.

Immediately after the failed mediation, Pratt, the management team, their advisors and the board get to work on a restructuring plan they had talked about in generalities during the failed mediation. The plan involves going "up the middle" among the polarized stakeholder positions. They file the plan with the court while stepping up efforts to let everyone know that the company will fight to remain the "honest broker," through whom the restructuring stalemate will be broken. In a press release, Pratt explains the company's intent:

> Our plan outline is reasonable, realistic and responsible. It's reasonable because it treats stakeholders fairly and in accordance with their rights. It's realistic because we believe that it's financially achievable. And it's responsible because we're the only party with a legal obligation to balance the interests and competing demands of stakeholders . . . . This balance does not propose to expropriate one party's interest to satisfy the demands of another.

The plan hangs on the assumption that the company is worth $885 million, its enterprise value.[1] It has two objectives: to extend the company's debt maturities and to give something back to everyone, even shareholders, after secured creditors are paid in full. The plan would provide for the recapitalization of Stelco by arranging new loans, selling "non-core" assets and issuing new securities. The key features include:

- refinancing loans with secured lenders;
- retiring the pension deficit of $1.3 billion by 2015;
- providing unsecured creditors with full recovery on $665 million owed to them by conversion of part of their debts into equity, with the rest provided in refinanced debt, of which some would be secured; and

[1] The enterprise value is typically determined using financial valuation methodologies that attribute a value to a company's assets, its competitive position and its forecasted cash flows and profits. It also compares the valuation with other companies in its sector.

- offering existing shareholders up to 2 per cent of Stelco shares, the right to purchase new shares under a $100-million rights offering,[2] and warrants[3] to purchase up to 10 per cent of the company.

The plan is designed to be implemented in two phases. In the first phase, which would go into effect upon Stelco's exit from CCAA, the unsecured creditors will be issued $566 million in new debt, plus $100 million in new equity. The company will contribute $100 million to its pension plans in the form of secured debt, to be followed by up to another $100-million cash payment from the sale of non-core assets (Stelco subsidiaries operating in steel segments the company intends to exit).

In the second phase, which would go into effect once management negotiates a pension funding agreement with the Ontario government and new collective agreements with the unionized employees at the Lake Erie and Hamilton mills, the company would convert $200 million in debt to equity and complete its $100-million rights offering to raise capital.

Ultimately, the plan, as the board approves it, is intended to give Stelco the financial strength to exit CCAA with

[2] A rights offering is a capital-raising mechanism that reaches out to potential investors with an offer to buy shares in the company at a discount to the market price.

[3] A warrant enables you to buy a stock in the future at a price agreed upon today, the hope being that the actual price will be much higher than the one stipulated under the warrant.

- a lower pension deficit, and the company on track to eliminating it totally in ten years or so;
- sufficient funds, including new capital, to modernize the business and enable it to operate as competitively as possible; and
- a reasonable debt load.

The up-the-middle plan, as Pratt knows, is not the final product but a compromise to bring people to the negotiating table in a positive frame of mind. No one gets everything they want, but there's something in it for everyone. The next step is to meet stakeholders to discuss the plan, relying firmly on the principle that the company won't make changes to enrich one party at the expense of another. Pratt hopes everyone will react in the spirit of collaboration to get a deal done.

WANTED: CORPORATE DOULA

Driving home to Oakville in expressway traffic, squinting into the sunset, Pratt is still so angry that he can't remember with clarity the sequence of statements—or the actual words—between himself and Ron Bloom. The meeting made it disappointingly obvious to him that the union guys and the company still have irreconcilable views of the restructuring. He'd gone with his advisors to the court monitor's office in downtown Toronto to brief the union on the company plan, and he'd anticipated a heated but fair exchange. All he remembers now is Bloom's theatrically disinterested posture and sarcastic tone, offering only desultory remarks, which

Pratt interpreted to mean, you have nothing to say that I'm interested in because you're not serious about negotiating.

He remembers telling Bloom, in no uncertain terms, that he can't negotiate by taking something from one stakeholder and giving it to another. That's not on. That's just not on.

Then you're not serious, Bloom said.

After he parks in the driveway, Pratt steps out into the evening and a refreshing breeze. The rage inside him shifts into hopelessness, which he knows will pass if he waits it out right here. It's high summer now, the blue surface of the pool awaiting him, cold beer in the fridge and Alexa in high spirits, gaining strength every day, the prognosis as good as it can be, the doctors say. So here he waits for a long minute that soon becomes two minutes . . .

"Courtney?" Alexa is on the front steps.

He turns. Her eyes are full of life and in her hand is the phone, which she waves around as if it has delivered up good news.

"What is it now?" he says with a fake grimace.

"Lisa is feeling better. And the baby's kicking like a champ."

"Good," he says forcefully. "So they got the doula all signed up for round two? That's how you say it, right? *Doo-lah.* I'm still not clear on the difference between a doula and a midwife."

She frowns, a tiny scold.

"I know. No jokes. Well."

"Well what?"

"If their doula is looking for extra work, we can give it to her at Stelco. At the rate we're going, we're gonna run through more than a few midwives to pull this thing off."

After changing into shorts and a polo shirt, he joins her in the lawn chairs beside the pool. He tells her a little about the day.

"You've dealt with worse, Courtney."

He shrugs and lets his gaze flit across the patio. Nothing moving for the moment, the breeze suddenly gone. But something is moving, he realizes: the light. The changing shadows, the shift from daylight to dusk.

She tells him about her day.

He tries to empty his mind of everything but the sound of her voice and the feel in his hand of the beer bottle, cold, beaded with condensation. He wants nothing to change or move for ten seconds, but the day moves on, time passing even in this slow moment, passing too fast.

Dinner is grilled chicken, grilled organic vegetables.

The white wine is stingingly fresh, clean.

They talk of family matters during the meal—her next trip to Vancouver to be there for the baby's birth, another possible trip to Ottawa to see their other son, Brian, and his wife—and it's an effort for him to stop Stelco business from reasserting itself negatively in his mind.

Tonight he's thinking that if Stelco suddenly evaporated from the storyline of his life, that wouldn't be such a bad thing.

After dinner they go for a short walk through the neighbourhood. People are still out, sitting on porches, clipping hedges, dragging water sprinklers across long green lawns, throwing the ball around, shooting hoops even as night descends. It's a lovely place, he thinks as they saunter along. And it's home, or at least home for now. But they wouldn't be living out here if it weren't for Stelco. Where would they be?

"It's nice out here," he says, "isn't it?"

"It is nice."

The tone of the exchange is polite, the unspoken message being, where, and when, are we going to settle down—for good this time?

Alexa has expressed a stronger desire lately to relocate to Vancouver, where her parents came from and where she spent the summers of her youth on the Sunshine Coast. The pull is stronger now that one of their sons, Steve, is out there with his family. Pratt isn't sure where they should go or when; he's still in the throes of corporate career logic, the opportunity afforded over years of proximity to Toronto. And yet here they are, in family-friendly Oakville, a prosperous community filled with parents and kids, minivans and station wagons, the back-yard socials on hot summer nights and all the shopping you need just minutes away. This place has the look and feel of home, he realizes, but they know no one around them and their sons are dispersed in different cities, nearly a continent apart from one another.

As they come full circle back to their house, he realizes that there will be another move at some point. They have moved so many times.

But all by choice, he thinks, not necessity.

His parents had moved out of necessity, his mother having grown up on a farm in Saskatchewan during the Depression, when money was very tight and it was natural to migrate to the big city just to fill your stomach or put shoes on your feet. And both his parents, being World War II veterans, had the experience of making sacrifices for something other than a paycheque: his dad spent years in Europe, his mother at an army base in Ontario. He tries to imagine what his dad would make of the Stelco mess. There are still people who come up to Pratt to remark appreciatively on his father's willingness to take a risk, to lend money to start a practice or a business, buy a house or a car. Ted Pratt, a banker, often made bets from the gut, not always on the numbers.

Before bed he watches Alexa line up the medication she's taking, humming to herself, as if the task were no more upsetting than rearranging a spice rack. He thinks of his father in that final year, only three years older than Pratt is now, a brave man horrifically disfigured by surgeries that didn't stop his cancer. Pratt doesn't like to dwell on what would have happened if his father had had access to today's medicine, although, tonight, when he looks at his wife, getting healthy again, and as he thinks of the mechanical valve clicking away in his own heart, a sound he can hear very clearly at night when he's lying on his side in bed, he wants to fly back into the past, just this once, and bring his dad forward to meet some doctors of his acquaintance in downtown Toronto.

JULY 27

The Lake Erie union local serves a ninety-day strike notice, accusing the company of not having any intention of engaging in meaningful negotiations to restructure Stelco.

GIVING US THE HEISMAN

The bondholders aren't happy with the plan, either, a fact evident in meetings involving Pratt and his team, including this meeting.

The bondholder, a middle-aged man capable of uttering profanities with each breath, expresses disappointment by saying that Stelco—and Pratt in particular—is guilty of "giving us the Hice-min."

He thinks he's being funny. But no one understands him.

Hice-min?

The bondholder repeats himself, this time gesturing at Pratt, one arm shooting forward as if to stove in an invisible face within its range.

"The Heisman," Pratt says. "I gotcha."

The reference is to the famous bronze trophy awarded annually to the most outstanding US college football player. It depicts an athlete on the run, the ball in one arm while the other is straight-arming an invisible tackler. Here the victim in danger of decapitation is, the bondholder contends, himself, even though he's playing by the rules as he attempts to strip Stelco of what it's holding onto for dear life.

PRATT THE MUDWRESTLER

"This is getting very down and dirty," Pratt says.

"Maybe you're reading too much into this," Osborne replies.

"Did you read the union's last court submission? Bloom seems prepared to risk Stelco being broken up."

"He has, to a certain extent, been playing that card," Osborne admits.

"And what comes then, if that should happen?"

"What do you mean?"

"I am saying that if the USW is willing to entertain Stelco being declared bankrupt, willing to see the pieces sold . . . I am saying they're willing to cut Hamilton loose. To fend for itself."

"It doesn't help that the Hamilton union guys are not part of the process. Letting nature take its course like this."

"That's a Canadian Communist for you. Christ. Standing on principle when your union brothers and sisters are carving you up. The point is, who is going to buy that old Hamilton mill for much more than scrap metal, with all the pension obligations, the pay scales?"

Osborne has nothing to add.

"This is ugly, Colin. And dirty. Very down and dirty."

A TALE OF TWO MILLS

Late morning, sunshine, blue skies, the car at the speed limit on the two-lane blacktop winding through the flat farmland of southern Ontario.

It's a welcome respite for Pratt, a half day away from the restructuring madness. He's driving to the Lake Erie mill to review the local management's plans to invest in a new steel-rolling process and to make himself visible among the workforce, a CEO's duty.

Around noon he pulls into Port Dover, a resort town on the lake with a diversity of tourist amenities: motels, boardwalks, hot dog vendors, a large colony of artists, a vintage car rally, a perch-fishing derby, sailboats galore.

Because his meeting is still an hour away, he stops for lunch at a restaurant famous for its delicious fried perch.

When they bring him his plate, he's baffled. The fried perch are shaped like some complicated pasta shell, not fish as he knows fish to be, the filets only two or three inches long. This is the kind of fatty food he needs to avoid to get through the weeks ahead. But he cleans his plate anyway.

When he arrives for his meeting, he's still early and, feeling stuffed from the meal, he decides to take a short walk. Immediately he confronts a gaggle of Canadian geese, blocking the path. He doesn't know if they're squatting here en route to somewhere else or are part of some scheme orchestrated by a local nature group. There's goose shit everywhere, that much is obvious, so the walk isn't really a walk. He takes a few steps, stops, diverts around goose shit, moves on again, stops. Although he doesn't get much exercise, he at least has an opportunity to admire the facility and the grounds around it. From a distance beyond the clamour and heat of the mill, the place looks like it has the bones of a good golf course or some vast equestrian estate.

And then there's the facility itself: one of the most modern steelmaking operations in North America. He stares long and hard at it.

No matter what happens to Stelco, he thinks, no matter what happens in courtrooms in Toronto, in hedge funds in Connecticut, this mill is going to be making steel for a very long time. There will be jobs here and a future for this community. A future. It's a stark contrast to the aging mill in Hamilton, which is older than its oldest pensioners.

THE FORECAST

On August 4, the company releases second-quarter financial results. While Stelco is still making pretty good money, the forecast for the third quarter is less impressive. As Pratt has long feared, global steel prices are beginning to soften, meaning the outlook for the company is uncertain, likely worsening. Pratt and his advisors are now concerned that there may not be enough money to implement their plan, never mind sweeten it enough to satisfy the new demands coming from all the stakeholders who are unsatisfied with what's currently on offer.

UNHOLY ALLIANCE

The government officials are polite during the meeting at the court monitor's office on a hot August afternoon. That much Pratt respects. At least the pretences of communication and collaboration are there.

The government's steel industry advisor, Jim Arnett, reads from a script to start the meeting, evidently concerned that the message must be made crystal clear, nothing forgotten or distorted by improvisation. Pratt has the feeling that Arnett's script has been vetted at the highest levels of government. It sounds much like the letter he has just received from the minister of finance, which is the subject of this meeting:

> As you were previously informed, on Stelco's emergence from the Companies Creditors Arrangement Act protection, I will seek the approval of the Lieutenant-Governor-in-Council to amend the regulation under the Pension Benefits Act so that Stelco will no longer have the benefit of section 5.1 of the Regulation . . .

In the meeting, government officials say they are rejecting the company's plan because they believe it's designed to get bondholders to approve it at the expense of leaving Stelco financially unstable after exiting CCAA. They say the plan has too many contingencies, including a need to get collective agreements with the unions and a deal with the government on pension funding. What makes matters worse for Pratt and his team is that the government has gone public with its position, to the media, which means there's little room left for negotiation.

The government, having rejected the company's offer of paying up to $200 million into the pension plan, has set up an impossible situation for Stelco, as Pratt sees it: no longer having recourse to the 5.1 regulation, Stelco likely cannot emerge from CCAA under its plan without heading right back into CCAA, swamped as it will be by massive annual pension contributions. How, then, does Stelco get past this?

The government's answer: sit down with Tricap, even though the Tricap plan doesn't work for anyone but the union and the pensioners and has zero chance of gaining creditor approval.

This is the argument, as Pratt hears it. Stelco has a clear need for money. Tricap is interested, and has done due diligence. It's the logical party to work with. The government believes the Tricap plan can be modified. And then everybody wins—the company, pensioners, employees . . .

What about the unsecured creditors? The shareholders? And how did Tricap suddenly become the government's best friend?

The answer provided during the course of the meeting is a careful equivocation, a sidestepping of the issue: We don't care about Tricap per se, only the money coming in.

Pratt doesn't buy that. He believes the government has been swayed by Ron Bloom's lobbying to make Tricap the favoured financial saviour. But why would an Ontario government be swayed by an American labour negotiator? Pratt knows everyone involved here—the Tricap guys, the government, Bloom. And as he considers how this has come together, he knows that only Bloom is capable of pulling something like this off.

He also knows that what he's witnessing here, in this polite meeting, is the fusing of the government's power to intervene where and how it wants with Tricap's deep financial pockets and the union's arguments about protecting workers and pensioners first—as Pratt sees it, an unholy alliance with the power, potentially, to radically affect the CCAA process. He feels very much as if the events of recent days, especially the hardening of the government's position, undermine all Stelco's efforts to restructure its finances by fairly balancing stakeholder interests. And while he appreciates what the government wants to achieve in the public interest, he recognizes that its invisible hand in the marketplace can sometimes be, as it is here, heavy-handed, late to the table, fresh from the last crisis and in a rush to get to the next one, sensitive to a fault on how things might play out in the media and the electorate. It's happened before, he knows, and it'll happen again.

FEAR, LOATHING AND ALLEGATIONS

On August 10, the company files a court submission claiming that, given the negative reaction of various stakeholders to its plan and their inability to work toward a fair compromise, the company's survival and that of the Hamilton operations in particular are at immediate risk.

Front and centre in the submission is the conclusion that the USW International negotiators, led by Ron Bloom, are willing to accept the court-ordered breakup and sale of the company in the event of a failed CCAA process. In that case, the company argues, there would be a serious risk that the Hamilton operations would soon close: potential buyers would favour the much newer, more competitive Lake Erie facility.

A day later, the USW reacts furiously by issuing a press release claiming the "allegations made are preposterous" and that the company "appears to have been captured by financial speculators."

A day after that, Pratt sends a letter to all Stelco employees to underscore management's view of the seriousness of the situation and to correct what the company believes are unfounded allegations by the USW, namely, that management refuses to negotiate and that it is proposing a ten-year freeze on pension improvements. "As I've said before, a positive result for all Stelco employees is still possible," Pratt writes. "But only if people want it to happen and are willing to work together . . ."

COUNSEL FROM THE MONITOR

Another tense, late-night meeting in Toronto, attended by Pratt, the court monitor, Alex Morrison, and Morrison's legal counsel, Bob Thornton.

"There's nothing positive going on at all," Pratt complains as they finally dig into the submarine sandwiches that were brought in hours ago.

"What did you expect—a coronation?" Thornton says.

"I expected our plan to be taken seriously. I didn't expect the government to force us into an arranged marriage with Tricap. There's something unhealthy about courting the bride like that. It makes the negotiation a little suspect. Also, we're being pushed—really pushed—into a situation where we now have to sweeten the pot for one stakeholder by taking something away from another."

Morrison and Thornton exchange glances, unsure who should go first in wrestling Pratt's black mood to the mat.

"There was something in our plan for everybody," Pratt continues.

Morrison and Thornton jump in simultaneously, talking over one another, then both they go quiet again. Morrison thinks back to the afternoon he sat on the train leaving Toronto for Ottawa. It was supposed to be a few days away from the restructuring chaos. The train had barely left the station—the city still in view—when the nasty calls started to arrive on his BlackBerry from different stakeholders, everyone saying how much they hated the company plan. As the city receded from view, Morrison kept fielding the calls, imagining a mushroom cloud of rage above the downtown skyscrapers.

"If we don't start making meaningful progress soon, Farley's gonna kick us out of CCAA and leave us to the wolves," Pratt continues. "Or we can risk leaving ourselves, call the government's bluff on the pension and see if they're really serious about putting us into bankruptcy, and try to get the creditors onside. Just fight our way back to solvency, Christ. But leaving CCAA now? We could be crippled if creditors or the province stick it to us. Never mind the lawsuits that'll be piling up on my desk. And throwing up our hands and letting the court sell off the assets? Let's not contemplate that. That's the end of Hamilton. The end."

"Courtney," Morrison interjects quietly. "You're getting ahead of yourself here. There are alternatives.

"I am that pissed—"

Thornton interrupts him. "You're reacting to the fact that no one likes your plan. Understandable. But I'm not sure what else you're reacting to, except maybe the bleeding wounds up and down your back from the daily whipping you're taking in court, in the media, and with everyone, basically."

"I'm glad I can count on you for an inspirational perspective," Pratt says, giving in to Thornton's humour.

Morrison says, "There may be something in your plan for everybody. But in our considered opinion, it doesn't have much chance of success for getting past anybody."

"Okay, then, what do we do next?" Pratt says.

QUANTUM LEAP

En route to a meeting with the product management guys at the Hamilton mill, Pratt stops at Helen Reeves's office.

She's deep in a phone conversation with one of her message guys, trying to end the call, signalling to Pratt that she'll be off in a minute.

Then Pratt sees the scrawled handwriting on the whiteboard.

> The definition of insanity is doing the same thing over and over again and expecting different results.
>
> —Einstein

"Who put that there?" he asks after she puts the phone down.

"The writer, last month. I forget why. I'm sure he's forgotten, too."

RISK MANAGEMENT: PRATT AND STEPHEN TALK

Hap Stephen corners Pratt outside the courthouse after another fruitless day. "We need to go underground for a while," he says bluntly. "Get some talks going with these guys."

"Which guys?"

"Tricap. The Province. Bloom and his team."

"The lay of the land," Pratt says gloomily. "The known world, as dictated from on high by our good buddies at Queen's Park, on the advice of their new favourite son, Ron Bloom."

"If we don't take the initiative, it will be taken for us. This media tit-for-tat, and arguing through the courts, isn't going to get us there. Look, steel markets are going soft on us. Everyone's hardening their positions. At some point, if sanity doesn't prevail, we're dead here."

"What about the creditors, the bond guys?"

"Let's put them on hold for now. We know we're not getting out of CCAA without them, but we need someone to move first and put something concrete on the table that at least some parties agree to."

"Hap, the creditors will go crazy if we cut them out now."

"We're trying to build a plan they'll vote for."

"Hap, I can't negotiate like some gunslinger on the run. The board needs to be informed at each stage. I can't run too far ahead of them."

"I didn't say negotiate. I said explore new options. Explore. We need Alex and Bob to get us together with people. In a room. Small rooms. Just us and them. The different 'thems' we have."

"Very risky."

They go back and forth, saying the same thing in different ways.

"This thing is dying," Stephen concludes. "We need to move."

"We can only set the stage for negotiation. No negotiation. And that's a very fine line."

"If you don't shoot the puck, you don't score."

A long pause.

"Let's see if we can't get the game going again," Pratt says.

EXPLORATORY MEETINGS

What if?

What if I said this and you said that?

What if I said, that's that?

What if I said you were smoking something?

What if we left CCAA?

What if you thought about someone besides yourself?

What if you did that for me?

What if you fuck off and die for a minute?

What if—never mind.

What if we kicked in a loan to grease this along?

What if you gave us more time to pay the pension down?

What if you give us the real number it's gonna take to make you guys happy on the pension?

What if we said it begins with the letter F, as in four or five hundred million?

What if we said the letter T, as in two or three hundred million?

What if we stopped for coffee?

What if we stopped to hit the can?

What if you considered the consequences for once?

What if you stopped talking about the nuclear option?

What if you stopped this bullshit about fairly balancing everything?

What if you stopped denigrating the board's integrity for once?

What if you stopped saying this is only exploratory?

What if I asked you to stop asking me to do that?

What if we got down to business here?

What if you went to your board with this?

What if you got real?

What if I did, would you?

What if?

SHAREHOLDER REVOLT

On August 31, the activist shareholder Roland Keiper and his legal advisor, Michael Woollcombe, tender their resignations from the Stelco board, citing among their reasons the "unauthorized" meetings that Pratt and Stephen have had with stakeholders. In a resignation letter faxed to arrive at Stelco head office just before a scheduled board meeting, the twosome wrote, "At a meeting of the Board on August 22, Mr. Pratt assured the Board that the discussions that were ongoing with the stakeholders were limited to exploring possibilities of 'what ifs' and were not negotiations in any sense of the word, that the ability of the Board to accept or reject any possible changes to Stelco's plan had been fully reserved and that he would keep the Board fully apprised of the discussions." The letter alleges that Pratt overstepped his authority as the company CEO and violated board instructions by not ensuring that all financial advisors of the company be present at all negotiations with stakeholders.

FROM "WHAT IF" TO "WHAT NOW?"

"Complete and utter bullshit," Pratt says to Mike Barrack on the phone after the board meeting. "All we did was open up the channel of communication to see if there were any grounds to create a deal. Once we knew we were headed into real negotiations, the meetings stopped."

"We still have an issue here."

"Of what nature?"

"The allegations are serious enough. And we need—the board needs—to take them seriously. And investigate them."

"I am having trouble with the attack on my integrity here."

"We need to clear this up, Courtney."

"How should that be done?"

"Let me work on it."

A week later, as a result of discussions involving Barrack, the court monitor and Justice Farley, the court appoints the Honourable Coulter Osborne as a special officer of the court to assist a newly struck special committee of the Stelco board to investigate the broad set of allegations made by Keiper and Woollcombe against Pratt, Hap Stephen and the Stelco board itself.

Who is Coulter Osborne? He's the definition of integrity, according to Barrack and others who know the Toronto legal world. Osborne has been a judge in Ontario—an associate chief justice—since the seventies, and once served as the provincial "integrity commissioner." He will work with the special committee of the Stelco board to look into the allegations and either clear everyone of wrongdoing—or not—providing his own report, independent of what the special committee concludes. If he gives the seal of approval here, no one will question it, Pratt believes, except possibly Keiper and Woollcombe.

THE DEAL, PART I

On September 20, 2005, the company files a revised restructuring plan with the court. This happens after several days of negotiations with the government. After its bad cop routine—and its threat to revoke the 5.1 election—the government now steps forward as the good cop, offering a $100-million loan on favourable terms: a 1 per cent interest rate, with 75 per cent of the principal forgiven if the company's pension-solvency deficiency is fully funded in ten years. The idea is that Stelco would put that $100 million toward its pension deficit, plus throw in another $300 million, adding up to $400 million—thus doubling the amount it originally wanted to pay.

Additionally, they agree on a formula for Stelco to pay down its remaining pension deficit, based on $60-million annual payments in the next five years plus $70-million annual payments for the five years following that, with any deficit left at 2015 being paid off within another five years.

The company has now dealt with the government and the unions on the pension. But no other stakeholder has agreed to anything yet—certainly not to taking less money so that the pension deficit can be reduced. In a press release announcing the new plan, the company claims that:

> there is insufficient value to provide full recovery to unsecured creditors . . . The actual level of recovery to be realized by unsecured creditors cannot be determined at this time. It is conditional upon a number of complex factors which, themselves, cannot be determined at present.

Could any statement be more opaquely conditional?

In the company's original plan, the idea was to give creditors $566 million in debt, plus $100 million in new shares. That would have been full repayment, although some bondholders were likely to be unhappy with the terms of repayment. Here there is less to like. The new plan offers them $525 million in debt, plus all the shares in the company, and the right to subscribe to $75 million in convertible notes (debt that can be turned into equity). Frankly, it's all complex financial engineering, but the net of it is that the package offers less to unsecured creditors than the original plan.

The company also says, as a consequence of unsecured creditors not being paid back in full, that shareholders will now get nothing.

The existing Stelco shares will be cancelled. What's also new here is that Tricap has entered as a provider of $350 million in new loan financing.

To Pratt's regret, there is insufficient value to provide something to all stakeholders. While the cost of doubling the company's pension payment to $400 million is a factor in that shift in stakeholder value, Pratt and his team mainly blame the deteriorating market conditions that have weakened the company's forecast, which in turn lowers its enterprise value.

But there's also real progress here, the "first move" that Hap Stephen said was necessary to get the restructuring going in a positive direction. Everyone knows tougher negotiations are coming. Ron Bloom and his lieutenants are itching to negotiate on many other issues, aside from the pension, so that unionized employees will come out of CCAA financially better than when they went in. Those in the creditor group are calling anyone and everyone associated with Stelco to bitch in the foulest terms about a plan they'll never vote for. And the shareholders, now denied entirely, are also agitating. If that isn't enough, the deal with the government is conditional on two things falling into place.

One: Stelco needs to firm up a financing deal with Tricap.

Two: It needs to get collective agreements with the unions.

Oh, and by the way, you have three days to get those deals done, or no loan from us. Your deadline is Thursday, September 22, at 9:30 a.m.

THE DEAL, PART II

The Stelco team divides into two groups, each tasked with satisfying one of the two conditions in the new deal negotiated with the government.

One group is led by Hap Stephen, who takes Stelco's financial advisors with him to firm up the Tricap agreement. There's nothing routine about their task, given the tight deadline and the fact that they must come to terms with a financier blessed in advance by the government, which is sure to affect the give and take. But the worst that can happen is that the money people will disagree, and then there'll be no deal—or at least no deal until adjustments are made.

The other group is led by Pratt, who takes charge of the negotiations for the collective agreements with the unions. Here, a failure to agree could result—in what? More antics in the media and courtroom? Large rallies by outraged employees and pensioners? A strike that could kill the company.

After some twenty months in CCAA, there's still no shared language of collaboration between the participants who'll be across the negotiating table. Theoretically, there shouldn't be a problem, since the current restructuring plan doesn't call for any employee or pensioner concessions in wages, benefits or pensions. But nothing in collective bargaining is ever that straightforward. Achieving a new collective agreement usually involves a time-consuming adversarial process, acted out over months. Who's to say the unions will be satisfied by a plan that offers only "no concessions"?

Specifically, deals are required for the two union locals whose collective agreements expired during CCAA: the Lake Erie mill and the Alta Steel subsidiary in Alberta. In addition, the unions are looking for a separate agreement to give them a greater say in major corporate decisions, a demand that the company has so far rejected out of hand.

The truth is that since Stelco management and the Lake Erie union made a ceremony of exchanging their proposals for an agreement—almost a year ago now—there has been little progress toward a deal. Each side naturally blames the other. Also troubling is that neither side has even discussed money yet—the issue of wage increases. And now they have to come to agreement virtually overnight?

Alta Steel, a producer of steel bar, has been identified by the company as "non-core" and is thus on the block to be sold. Pratt and his team resisted the government's insistence that a deal with Alta Steel be among the conditions, its preference being to let any new owner handle that. To no avail. It's a victory for the union and its mantra: "Until everyone can go ashore, no one goes ashore." The company's response: What if the boat sinks before anyone gets to shore?

The Hamilton union, which represents well over half of Stelco's unionized workforce, remains absent from the negotiating table. Its leader, Rolf Gerstenberger, continues to refer to the restructuring as "legalized theft." As well, the Hamilton agreement doesn't expire for another year, which may be why Gerstenberger is electing to sit tight. No one is certain how Hamilton will react to a restructuring agreement constructed without its involvement. Some on the Stelco team are concerned that Hamilton is reserving the right to disagree later in the process, when the plan (if it survives) is paraded before creditors for approval.

All in all: no one knows what to expect.

Representatives from the union and the company, the court monitor, a professional mediator and other advisors all gather in the boardroom of Bob Thornton's law firm, Thornton Grout Finnigan, situated many floors above the financial district—yet another workplace in this restructuring process with otherworldly views of Lake Ontario.

For the Stelco team, it has been a brutal slog just to get here, an intense couple of days. They filed the new restructuring plan in the courtroom just that morning. All involved say they need just a little more time to prepare, even though the clock is now ticking to a tight deadline ordained by the government. The consensus is, let's get some rest, a fresh start tomorrow, then we'll go all night if need be . . .

The only topic remaining on the agenda is where to hold the negotiations. Everyone is fed up with hotels, with the hassle of trooping between ballrooms and breakout rooms, with calling room service to fix the Internet connection.

"Let's do it here," Alex Morrison says with a *bingo!* look in his eyes. "We have everything we need here. Admin support. Phones."

A chorus of "great idea," "fine by me," "good."

After the meeting, Thornton takes Morrison aside.

"What?" Morrison says, an imp visibly present in his smile.

"Speaking here on behalf of my partners," Thornton says, "we just spent the equivalent of the GDP of Iceland to renovate these offices. Said reno, completed last week, involved quality materials and finishings from lands far away. Many were sourced, I can tell you, at very unfair trade prices, and then inaugurated by a ceremony involving a sacrifice of virgins and prayers for profitability to the gods who make companies insolvent to end up on our doorstep. What am I gonna tell my partners, Alex, now that you've turned our temple of work into a frat house?"

"So let me get this straight, you're opposed to this?" A deadpan joke, which gets a hollow laugh in response.

"Alex, we're going to be knee-deep in lawyers, accountants, mediators, steelworkers."

It's Morrison's turn now to utter a hollow laugh.

The next morning Thornton watches them arrive in twos and threes and fours, dropping briefcases and knapsacks everywhere, firing up laptops while talking away on cellphones, rooting around for power and Internet outlets with the instincts of starving aardvarks on the hunt for ants. Before long they completely take over this triple-A office space, including the lobby, a serene gesture in the art of the corporate hello: sleek furniture, contemporary art, subtle designer lighting.

The union guys have adopted these offices as their base for the next couple of days. Twenty-five people or so, many tethered to handheld devices, creating a racket the office has never heard before. Meanwhile, Pratt's team, about half the size of the union's contingent, has made its base in the nearby offices of Steve Shamie, the company's labour lawyer, and managing partner at Hicks Morley.

At first Thornton tries to play the jovial host, introducing new arrivals to the receptionist and the photocopier, pointing out the route to the bathrooms and explaining how you can't get back into the office after hours if you forget to take a passcard. He soon realizes that the pretence of control here is futile. There's no way he can nanny the office with this crew around.

When he walks into the boardroom, one guy has his feet propped on the edge of the polished table. Another guy is trapped in a snake's nest of computer cabling. A third guy paces a windowed wall, on the phone, cursing someone's mother to high heaven.

Here's how the first day, Wednesday, starts off.

The mediator, Reg Pearson, known for his managerial calm, employs shuttle diplomacy, much like the process that failed during the Adams mediation in June. In the morning he meets with each group separately to hear their views and proposals, searching for the possibility of productive discussion worth bringing people together in the boardroom for.

After the company's first session with Pearson—a low-key interlude, almost a formality—Pratt leaves the building with Shamie. As they walk back to the Hicks Morley offices across the expanse of well-manicured urban green space that connects the maze of towers in the TD Centre complex, Shamie takes it upon himself to review some ground rules: "Above all else, Courtney, never, ever go into a meeting alone with these guys. It's a common trap. I don't care who you are—it's easy to find yourself boxed into positions you'd never take."

"I hear you, Steve, absolutely," Pratt says, thinking that getting caught in that situation is something he'd like to avoid at all costs.

Shamie is a wiry, intense character, with a face deeply tanned in a way that suggests outdoor activity, not the tanning booth. As a veteran of these situations, his counsel—usually offered in a measured, patient voice—is frequently sought by Pratt because it seems to emerge from hardcore experience in hand-to-hand negotiating combat. And with Shamie, there are no airs: he's a straight talker.

"We have to keep our cool," he says.

"You and me both," Pratt says, momentarily distracted. Right in front of them is a cow. A grouping of cows, cast in steel, some standing, mouths agape, lowing at the world, others lounging in their bulk. The men veer around them.

Pratt wants to make a joke about bullshit but restrains himself.

Between meetings, Pratt learns that Coulter Osborne has filed a report with the court after investigating the allegations made by Roland Keiper and Michael Woollcombe. The report clears Pratt of the alleged improprieties, with regard to the suggestion that he was violating board decisions by engaging in "exploratory meetings" with stakeholders.

This development gives Pratt a psychological boost; but this is short-lived, as it becomes obvious that, once more, the restructuring is bogged down in a two-party mediation process going nowhere.

Once again, Pratt and his team find themselves sitting around talking to one another and engaging with nobody on the other side. Everything is mediated, filtered, taking forever.

There's small progress on wages and benefits. But not enough, and not fast enough. In a normal bargaining process, the differences would be bridged over time. Here there's no time left—not for reflection, or allowing the hot air of posturing to deflate. No time for dignified concessions, after fighting the good fight, or at least satisfying your ego that you have. But it's worse than that: Bloom is still insisting, citing US industry experience, that the unions be given a formal role in Stelco's corporate governance—the right to provide input on and, ultimately, to approve or veto a major decision, like a merger, asset divestiture, an acquisition.

Pratt is adamant: he'll never take that to his board.

"Alexa, what's going on?" Pratt says into his BlackBerry, on a call to Vancouver.

"No baby yet."

"Is the doula on board?"

"On call."

"Keep me posted."

Pratt calls Stephen and learns that the teams negotiating the Tricap financing agreement have gone home for the night: they've reached a deal in principle. There'll be a few more battles before the thing is papered, but Pratt is now certain there will be a deal. It may not be optimal, he thinks, but with nothing else like it on his horizon, it's good news.

It's nearly two in the morning when the mediator produces a written report of his recommendations. Pratt and his team dissect it in the Hicks Morley boardroom. They see things they like: their own positions. And things they don't: the union's positions.

They spend time discussing how best to send a message to the mediator that some of the recommendations are absolutely non-starters. Shamie says he'll talk to Pearson. After he leaves, Pratt says, "I guess we can forget about sleep. I'll have to brief the board on this tomorrow. They need to know what we're faced with here."

"We're going to be crunching numbers all night, if we want to show the situation as it stands," Osborne says. "Show the financial gaps between us, the risks for the company depending on where we end up. But we're so far apart with the union, like an ocean."

As Pratt listens to the gloom, he wants to crawl under the table and pass out for a few hours. This he cannot afford to do. For over twenty months, deadlines have come and gone, with no consequence. He worries that people, including his own guys, now may be negotiating on the assumption that another extension of bankruptcy protection will be granted by the court. As it stands, the current stay expires midnight Friday, less than two days away.

As for the government deadline, seven hours from now—the message that has reached him from the minister's agents is that the plug won't be pulled on the deal, as long as there's progress in the talks.

Progress?

"These guys keep coming back to us with the governance issues," Pratt says. "It's one way to make sure there'll be no deal."

"So they do."

"Well, how many times do you have to tell them?"

"As many times as they come back."

"I don't know how we're going to get this done."

They crunch numbers through the night. They drink more coffee and bottled water than they should. They become indifferent to personal hygiene. Once the acceptance of an all-nighter has kicked in, a collective surge of macho energy infuses the group. They know they're players in a real drama. They know they can affect outcomes. They know they can take on the night, tonight, all night—take on fatigue and win, then come out on the other side, staring into a rising sun.

Their brains keep functioning—badly. They're doing the white-collar equivalent of operating heavy equipment on no sleep, or after swallowing a big dose of cough medicine. People are less diplomatic in all exchanges, quick-tempered, prone to propping up malnourished statements with expletives. Typos get introduced into memos, errors into cost estimates. A few have genius insights that, in the morning, someone else will tell them are complete bullshit.

Have you fucking lost it?

Some guys send their wives e-mail. Some don't.

Some eat stale pastries lying around just waiting to be eaten.

But there's no tendency now to engage in hijinks, pranks. No Nerf balls zip along the corridors. No giggling fits where the giggling hives off from its original inspiration to become just mad, all-nighter giggling.

Before dawn, people are snoring over furniture. Under desks. Muttering awake from long moments spent slumped.

When the sun does come, it isn't a beacon. It's not the juice they need. It just throws light on failure and fear.

How the hell are we going to do this deal?

Impossible.

It certainly looks that way.

When the regular daytime employees start to arrive at the office, it feels as if they're invading the team's privacy.

What are they doing here?

It's called "work." Normal work.

Keep them away from the boardroom.

Believe me, they don't want to be here.

This coffee tastes like shit.

I feel like I'm crawling in my skin.

Where are my shoes?
Over there, can't you smell them?
My laptop is acting up.
Did you save the file?
What file?

Thursday, mid-morning.

"Farley wants to see us in court," Thornton says.

"He's unhappy," Barrack adds. "He says that he doesn't have enough information and that he's very disturbed by the prospect of extending the stay of bankruptcy protection under these circumstances. He's enraged that, after months and months of this, with a government deal and a deadline, we still can't get this thing done."

"What about the Province?" Shamie asks Pratt.

"We're good as long as the talks are moving ahead. They're livid that we're not accepting Reg Pearson's report, but I reassured them that we'll get to the finish line."

"You did?"

Pratt shifts his gaze to say he's had enough interrogation for now.

"Regardless, we need to get a court extension of the stay until Monday," Barrack says to Thornton. "I don't see how we're going to get both deals fully done by midnight Friday."

"Agreed—but at least all the stakeholders now agree that, with some extra time, we could actually work toward a deal," Thornton replies. "It's the first time we've had anything like consensus on the way forward."

"You're absolutely right," Barrack says. "Let's hope Farley sees it that way."

"You and me both."

"I stink."

"What?"

"I mean, seriously. I physically stink."

In open court, Barrack and Thornton take turns explaining to the judge that there may be a deal soon but that there isn't one yet, even though everyone is working around the clock and will keep working until it's done. They try to give the impression that all this situation needs is time and patience. When Barrack formally requests an extension of the stay until Monday, Farley jumps in: "You say everyone's in agreement with this. Well, I'm not."

Farley's tirade goes on. And on.

Pratt, in the gallery, watches the verbal lashing unfold and feels creepy about it. He's not sure what's going on. The anger seems to him to be paternal in nature, intimate, as if Farley were dressing down his sons or trusted apprentices for failing to protect the legacy, the commercial court he's laboured so long to build. How many times has Farley seen Barrack and Thornton over the years? Farley, it seems, is disappointed in them for something bigger than one more missed deadline.

The request for a stay until Monday is denied. The Friday midnight deadline stands unchanged.

"You've all got a lot riding on this, gentlemen," says the judge.

So does Stelco. A Stelco going splat.

One more day, gentlemen.

A conference call with the board.

Pratt has Osborne, Barrack and the finance guys with him.

"To be honest," Pratt says solemnly, "we don't have a deal. And I can't see our way to a deal."

He details the areas of disagreement, which are on all fronts: money, benefits, the role of the union in corporate governance.

"What do you need from us?" the chairman says.

"I'm telling the union, look, I can't go to my board with any proposal that limits its powers to govern the company. I have your support on this, right?"

"We'd never accept that kind of proposal, Courtney."

Pratt turns to Barrack. "Mike, anything you want to add?"

"Today wasn't my finest day in court, this I can tell you."

"How do you see Farley working with us?"

"It's uncharted territory right now."

You become aware that you stink, and that others stink, too, maybe worse than you do. One choice is scatological humour. The other is to hold your nose and get back to work.

The mediator brings groups together at different times for what turn out to be perfunctory exchanges. And not much else is being achieved in the corridor chat that so often provides a safe opportunity to hint at compromises. Someone makes a crack about this being a Seinfeld episode: a negotiation about nothing, leading to nothing.

As Thursday night turns into Friday, there is less than a day left until the stay of bankruptcy protection expires.

Pratt understands fatigue and the need to conserve energy for the last push. But there's nothing to push against or toward because Bloom and Pearson have left for the night. If this negotiation is about something important, he thinks, how come we're acting like it's about nothing?

His guys want him to get a hotel room.

Pratt waves them off, suggesting they all go home, to their beds, to their spouses. There's a stubborn edge to him now. He doesn't want anyone's consoling: no, you guys go home. I'll sleep here, right on this couch, in this lobby, and that's that, see you here at six.

He waves them off, and this time they know for certain that it's useless to argue with a man intent on making a point here about his general irritation with the state of things, and with himself.

After removing his shoes, Pratt rearranges cushions, experimenting with combinations of fabric-covered sponge and bodily position in the hopes of lowering the risk of back pain. There's not going to be much sleep. His eyes will close and he'll be aware of his exhaustion, a buzzing sensation around his forehead. He'll be aware, as he is now, that he needs a shower. At least he knew enough to bring a change of clothes.

He lies on his back, clutching at nothing but cushion, arms folded over his chest, breathing in some kind of rhythm with the HVAC system. The lights are low enough, on night setting, not a distraction if he turns his head into the back of the couch. He realizes that it's three hours earlier in Vancouver but decides not to call. They know how to reach him. His last thought before sleep comes is that, any day now, maybe a few hours from now, he will be a grandfather again.

He sleeps for about an hour, then lies fretting for another forty-five minutes. It's nearly four-thirty when he decides that if he's going to last another day, he needs a shower. For an insane moment he wonders if he shouldn't just use the sink in the bathroom. Strip down right there. Feet, armpits, the works.

And if someone walks in?

He takes the elevator to the main lobby and walks out into the coolness of the pre-dawn. It could still be summer. Some people, financial trader types, are already striding into tall buildings.

His garment bag on his shoulder, he walks to his health club a few streets north. He kept the membership up even though he lives in Oakville now. It's a good place for a business lunch or the occasional squash game when he's downtown, and he's been downtown a lot lately.

The club is situated on the top floors of the hotel where the Adams mediation took place. When he gets to the elevators, they're not functioning, and won't be for another half hour—until the club opens.

He takes a seat in the hotel lobby amid a cluster of chairs and couches, and decides he won't be caught dead lying down. It's the kind of thing that gets you arrested in hotels.

His BlackBerry goes off.

A voice tries to sound spooky.

"Courtney Pratt, listen, and listen well, this is the ghost of mediations past . . ."

"Hi, Bob, what's up?"

Thornton makes a ghostly *wa-whooo* noise.

Wa-whooo. Wa-whooo.

"Bob?"

"Bloom wants to know if you'll meet him, alone, more or less."

Pratt lets the conversation with Steve Shamie scroll through his thoughts. *Don't go in there alone, Courtney.*

"Courtney?"

"Give me a minute, Bob."

He doesn't know why he's reconsidering Shamie's advice—the wisdom gained, no doubt, from having watched so many executive meltdowns at crunch time. Shamie is right. But right isn't doing the job. Is it? Well, maybe it would do the job if I let it. Just tell Bob, no way, I need my guys with me. He looks at his garment bag, which has slipped off an armchair to the floor. A clean shirt, now rumpled all to hell.

"Who else will be there?"

"Me and Alex. The government. Reg."

"Me and Bloom, okay."

"Together at last!"

Wa-whooo—

Pratt's shower doesn't happen. There's no time.

What defines a successful negotiation?

The outcome, the deal?

The lingering memory, after the fact, of the last seconds when you hope your practical reach will catch up to your theoretical grasp? Punting the issues you can't resolve into the future, to a date where conflict will resume, clearing the way for a cessation of hostilities today?

The handshake?

The sick feeling in your gut that doesn't go away for days?

The things you'll never be able to talk about outside the room?

All of the above?

All of the above.

The feeling in the boardroom at Thornton Grout Finnigan is that this is it. *It.*

Pratt wonders why it always comes down to "it" moments when the sun's coming up, everyone bleary, pale, red-eyed. It shouldn't be like this, but it *is* like this, a pinnacle moment in the ritual, the fifteenth round, the third overtime period, the last few hundred metres of the marathon inside the stadium, the runners on bleeding feet. The clock is still ticking. And more clocks are ticking in the distance, notably those of the creditors, who are not involved in these negotiations. But first, there's this deadline to get past.

He's conscious of forces around him closing in as he and Bloom settle across the table from one another in Thornton's boardroom.

On one flank, Morrison and Thornton, representing the court—the court monitor and his legal counsel, monitoring.

On the other, a government lawyer watching the clock, in a sense urging Bloom and Pratt to hear the ticking out of the same set of ears.

The mediator is in the mix, too, mediating but saying little.

Pratt is surprised by his own nervousness. He's been in a million meetings in his life, and there have been many crises to deal with. He's been across the table from Bloom on countless occasions now. But he doesn't know what to say, where to begin. This is still a negotiation—there are things you don't say, weaknesses you don't advertise. Yet there's a surreal intimacy among the group that suggests that everyone here, whether they like it or not, is in the same lifeboat. He looks at Bloom and sees fatigue, a glimmer of something he hasn't seen before. If it isn't vulnerability, it's apprehension. Maybe, he thinks, deal junkies get like this before a major fix? The chills? But though he understands why Bloom has that reputation, and cultivates it, too, Pratt doesn't see much of the deal junkie in him today.

Bloom is on edge, Pratt finally decides, in the same way he is: he sees in the man a desire to get out of this situation by doing the right thing. But what to say? For a dangerous instant he realizes that anything could pop out of his mouth, including a string of epithets. He's really sick of the Ron Bloom he's seen on display for all these months. But he concedes that the current version of Ron Bloom is different. This is someone he can work with, and he tells himself he doesn't give a hoot whether he's reading too much into Bloom's expression.

"Ron, I'm really going out on a limb here," Pratt says. "My guys would kill me knowing I'm here without them."

Bloom says he's in much the same position.

They acknowledge, in only few words, that the space in this restructuring for ranting and raving has evaporated. The judge has lost patience, and no one dares predict his next move. And keeping the government deal together requires success right now.

They start discussing their respective issues with acupunctural accuracy, closing the gaps in non-ideological leaps and bounds, doing what makes sense, all things considered. Some of this is horse-trading of the most banal kind, as in, okay, Ron, or, okay, Courtney, I'll meet you halfway if you'll just shut up about this. Or, if you give me this, I'll give you that. Or, let's agree to disagree for now, there's not enough time to crack that nut, we'll return to it later. And within the hour, they know they're almost there—almost to a deal in principle, except for a few grey areas, contentious subjects, tiny in the grand scheme.

This is when the verbal equivalent of the wink and nod starts to occur. There are hints around the table: if you scratch my back on this, I may not openly scratch your back on that, but I will make sure your back is scratched, one way or another. It's something we can't really talk about for reasons I can't talk about, like saving face, or pissing off my people and my people's people and their people's people, because it looks like—well, never mind.

We'll solve the issue one way or the other.

Agreed?

Agreed.

The union's bid to participate in corporate governance—one of Pratt's major concerns—is finally taken off the table. Bloom gets most of what he wants in terms of money and benefits for the union locals he's negotiating for, Lake Erie and Alta Steel.

So they have the basis of two collective agreements—yet to be codified by the lawyers, labour relations guys and other advisors who will have things to say and things to disagree with as the day progresses. But when Pratt stands to stretch his legs after the meeting ends, in a room emptied of the others, he savours the sun glinting off the vertical lattices of steel and glass outside, the horizon unencumbered by fog or clouds except for a faint herringbone pattern way off, long, wispy clouds at very high altitude, a mackerel sky, the promise of rain.

"I know you guys are angry and think I may have done the wrong thing," Pratt says to his team. He's so tense his voice conveys not even a whisper of apology. "But I did it. So let's talk about it. And move on."

And now Pratt goes for his shower at the health club.

After he's clean, Pratt sequesters himself and dials into a conference call with his board. He explains the monetary impact of the deal over the life of the agreement, then reports that the issue of union participation in board governance has been cleared away. The chairman, an experienced labour lawyer himself, reaffirms the board's support of the CEO.

The lawyers and negotiators are in the trenches of the drafting phase of the agreement, into clause-by-clause warfare.

A collective agreement is the bible used to mediate relations—and grievances—between the company and the unionized workforce. It tells people not just what they get paid, but how to conduct themselves in a hundred different on-the-job situations. Every clause in this agreement, as a lawyer would see it, could have prophetic ramifications unless bleached of any ambiguity that could result in their clients taking on unintended risks or responsibilities. As such, every clause has the potential to be written sixteen ways to Sunday, saying virtually the same thing, where plain English is sometimes not the vernacular of choice.

The placement of commas and semicolons—or their misplacement, depending on your viewpoint—becomes the source of a few arguments that probably go on longer than necessary.

There are concerns expressed that the deal can't be papered by the time the current stay of bankruptcy protection expires at midnight tonight, Friday, September 23.

"They're still fighting in there over nothing," Osborne reports.

"What do you mean?" Pratt replies.

"I don't know exactly. Which typeface to use. That kind of crap."

"Do you want me to go in there and read the riot act?"

"Dangle a carrot. Anything. Time's running out, Courtney."

"The carrot? What about a big stick? By the name of Farley."

"It's Farley."

Thornton takes the call in his office.

When he emerges ten minutes later—

"Bob, you look like you've seen a ghost," Pratt says.

"I've never heard him so furious."

"Isn't this par for the course?"

"No. He wants an update. Every hour, on the hour."

"It's time for the next call, Bob," Morrison says.

"Only if Mike comes with us on this one."

Barrack exhales gloomily. "You, too, Courtney."

"What did I do to deserve this?"

Another hour passes.

"Time to call Farley again."

The deal is done. Documents are ready to be signed. A crowd in the boardroom, the mood all back-slappy, sleep-deprived giddiness.

The media has been notified. Camera crews are on the way.

It appears that some are now eagerly inclined to chime in when Thornton makes the call to Farley, who decides he'll come down in person to provide an interim stay of bankruptcy protection to get them through the weekend. On Monday, a formal order will be issued in the courtroom.

"I could meet you downstairs at your car," Thornton says.

Thornton sees Farley pull up in a late-model sedan. The judge, dressed in a light blue suit, rolls down the driver's side window, apparently intent on handing Thornton the handwritten extension while the car is still in motion.

"Your Honour," Thornton says with a tentative smile, "would you like to come up for a minute?"

Farley says he's only too happy to come up.

Applause greets Farley as he enters the boardroom.

"Congratulations, everyone," he responds jovially.

The media moment is now in full swing. The formal signing. Handshakes. Exhaustion disguised under video lighting and in the usual statements made to reporters in the aftermath of these affairs.

Nearing midnight, the media are long gone, the judge and union too. Only the Stelco gang is left.

Thornton decides it's time to review the state of the office.

In the kitchen, a garbage bin is overflowing with napkins and empty containers featuring the logos of fast-food companies. He ruefully observes that the separation of items into the recyclable and landfill bins was not a priority for the negotiating teams.

A cigarette butt is encased in a swatch of waxy sandwich paper.

In the boardroom, Thornton bends to study the surface of the table from eye level. There are no visible gouges, but much of the surface is smudged from greasy fingers.

He sniffs the air and decides not to spend more than a nanosecond decoding the combination of aromatic elements—more a locker room than a corporate inner sanctum.

The couches in the lobby need repairs, maybe new coverings.

And there are people still around.

"All right, everybody," he announces. "Everybody get the fuck out of here. Out of my office. Now. I've had enough."

Laughter.

Thornton pushes people toward the elevators.

As the elevator doors close on him, Pratt can hear Thornton, still cursing people out, telling them all to go home, his manic laughter rising above the sound of the steel security gate that he's pulling firmly shut.

HEISMAN, PART II

Getting into his car, Pratt is elated. Three deals—if not on paper, then in principle. The government, the union, Tricap. All conditions met.

A smiling judge.

Then the elation fizzles when he thinks ahead to the round of negotitions—with the creditors. The bondholders, especially. Now they'll really feel they've been given the Heisman.

SATURDAY

Steve Shamie is more a basketball dad than a golfer, constantly ferrying his daughters to their tournaments. But occasionally he laces up his golf shoes and goes out for a round, and that's what he's doing this Saturday morning, a half day after the deal.

On the ninth tee, he discovers he can barely walk he's so tired. And his stroke? He's been in the woods or in the water on pretty much every hole. A complete duffer.

"What's up, Steve?" his partner asks as they walk to the tenth tee.

"I can't even begin to tell you."

When he swings, the ball launches from his club face, hopping along the smooth green fairway like a demented chipmunk, coming to a dismal stop only thirty yards away on a six-hundred-yard par five.

"At least it's straight," he says, jamming the club into his golf bag.

DAWSON PRATT ARRIVES

On Sunday morning the phone rings.

Reaching for it, Pratt is thinking bad thoughts. Bloom has done something—The government has changed its mind—The creditors—

It's a call from Vancouver.

It's a boy. Mom's doing well. And it's all on video, with Dad behind the camera.

"I cut the cord," Alexa says.

CONSCIENCE DIALOGUE

MARY WALKER, STELCO PENSIONER

In the shade of her back porch, Mary Walker is contemplating the small garden—mostly potted plants—between the bungalow and the garage, clad in silver sheet metal. It's a warm October afternoon in a quiet Hamilton neighbourhood that has seen better days. When I sit down next to her on the porch, she pours tea, handing me a cup in what I'll bet is her best china.

"I don't see myself as elderly, Mr. Pratt," she says in a voice that sounds younger than her eighty-one years. "When I look at this little garden—well, it's not really a garden, only a reminder of one—I feel like I'm back on the farm, a young girl again. I've lived in the city now for sixty years, and life on the farm wasn't always wonderful, but I often go back there, in my mind."

"Mary, it's kind of you to invite me here today. Please call me Courtney—everyone else does."

"It's kind of you to come. There is a lot I find confusing, and I'm sure you can clear all this up for me," she says, offering the sugar, which I decline.

"I know you're worried about your Stelco pension," I say. "And it's true we're not completely out of the woods yet—we still have to get an agreement with our bondholders, our major creditors, before I can say for certain that things will be getting back to normal. But I hope to have good news soon."

She gives me her best grandmotherly look, as if to say she intends to trust me despite the doubts all over my face. "So," she says, "a new child in the family—your second grandchild! How wonderful for you."

"I wish I could have been there."

"Oh, I'm sure you're a very good grandfather." Her gaze has gone back to the garden. "Gerry—my husband—was a good grandfather, before the cancer took him. We raised two boys in this house after we moved here in 1951 from the country near Ancaster. We had a pretty good life—oh, we surely did, lots of laughs, a few tears, some hard moments, too. But who doesn't have those . . ."

She trails off in a way that lets me know she's waiting for other memories to translate into words. I wait her out, sipping tea.

"We were happiest I suppose when there was money for the mortgage, a new car every few years, two weeks in the summer at a campground on Lake Erie. Hamilton was growing in the years after we moved here, with new folks arriving, tall buildings going up. And Stelco? Oh, it was a busy time. A good time. There was time for dreams, maybe even of buying a farm we could move back to one day. I remember many Sunday afternoons, rain or shine, when Gerry and I took the boys for a drive in the country."

Mary has a gentle indirectness that I really appreciate, a feeling for the courtesies that should come before any talk of difficult matters. She's not shouting at me across a boardroom table or from a TV screen. She's trying to put me at ease, and maybe herself, too. It has been a difficult time, but she doesn't come right out and say this. Rather, she talks about how some dreams in her life didn't pan out. They didn't buy a farm. Hamilton became rundown, the homeless on her street corner, frightening her from walking to the local grocer.

"It would be nice, Mr. Pratt," she says, "to be able to spend as many of my last years as I can in my own house. With Gerry's pension I have enough money to pay my bills, but my savings are small. A seniors' home has advantages for a woman in my position, but the longer I can hang on here the better. We still have family dinners here, you know."

"That's great," I say earnestly.

"I don't do all the cooking any more, mind you. Now and then, my older son, John, and his family, visit me here. His boys are teenagers now, and with everyone so busy, it's not like it used to be. But we still have moments, and I want to keep living in those moments."

I nod and sip my tea. I've been working on the Stelco restructuring for almost two years now, and I still feel like I'm swimming in quicksand. How could anyone with a semblance of moral awareness ever sit across from Mary and tell her that her pension might be slashed because Stelco's going broke after years of not facing up to its problems? That's not the situation today, but it has happened to people before, and it certainly has happened pretty recently south of the border.

Mary continues. "Have you ever met my son?"

"I'm afraid I don't know John personally."

"He works near the coke ovens, just like his father did."

There's the tiniest rebuke in her tone, and I feel her retreat. It's nothing rude, but a veil has gone up, as she silently fusses with the tea service. There's something she's trying either to reveal or conceal, which I don't feel right probing.

"I try not to watch the news," she finally says, "or listen to the radio. I do find it disturbing."

"Mary, I know it has been a difficult, uncertain time."

She glances at me. "You know, I'll always make out fine, Mr. Pratt. But my son has, oh, twenty-six years at the mill. And he has a mortgage, and money's very tight around their house. And the stress has been—well, I don't want to go on too much about all that."

I realize that Mary can get her point across with an economy as fierce in its own way as Mike Barrack's. Hers is a different language but no less persuasive or forceful. Since taking this job, I've been clocked more than once by tough-talking guys in good suits. But I'd argue that no one has knocked me down—except Mary.

"More tea?" she asks.

"Thank you, Mary. I've had plenty."

She scrutinizes me, waiting for me to say that her son's job is safe forever. That's a tough one—no one can make that promise today, in any industry. I certainly can't make it. But should Stelco emerge with financial stability from CCAA, as

I'm now pretty certain we will, John Walker will have seniority in any layoff. He might even elect to take a voluntary retirement package if one is offered, though no matter how he leaves, if that comes to pass, he won't be financially set for life unless he has plenty saved already. He'll have to retrain for a new career, which won't be easy after so many years on coke oven duty. I have my own hopes that, with a restructured Stelco, we'll be able to make Hamilton competitive again so that the jobs of people like Steve will be as secure as possible. But a turnaround could require a smaller workforce. In fact, it likely will.

"I guess what is still confusing to me is that Stelco's problems don't seem to be ending," she says, coming at me again. "It's hard to know what to believe. The folks in the union have been telling us all along that you and the company can't be trusted to do the right thing by us. My husband—God love him—he used to sit up late many nights, on this porch, talking union politics with some of the men from the mill." She turns to me with a mirthful expression. "Naturally, they found evil just about everywhere in the front office. But that's how some men talk, isn't that so, Mr. Pratt?"

I'm in the palm of her hand.

"There were some very dark days at Stelco for us," she says. "My husband wasn't a talkative man, but he was principled, and he kept his counsel carefully, knew his own mind. In quieter moments when we were alone, he would talk to me about the mill, and what upper management was doing. And he'd shake his head. If his responsibilities to me, to his family, hadn't weighed so heavily on him, I know he would have created a different life, far from the steel mill—that very hard place he went to every day in order to put food on our table."

"We're taking it day by day, Mary," I say. "It's difficult to know exactly what to say about your son and his future. But we are doing all we can to protect what you and your husband earned after all those hard years."

She takes that in, then says, "I want to show you something." She stands up and, touching my elbow, guides me to the garage. We walk slowly but she's sturdy on her feet.

Inside the garage is an art gallery of sorts. Whitewashed walls, track lighting, transom windows at ceiling height. Throughout the room are waist-high constructions of steel mesh and steel bar, shaped then welded into plantlike forms.

It's a garden of steel, and alive as any art I've ever seen.

"Gerry had something else in him," Mary says, as she watches me walk around the room, studying his creations. "He saved something for himself."

"They're beautiful."

"Some folks from an art gallery in Toronto came down here one afternoon. Somehow they found out about Gerry's garden. Oh, they wanted everything he had for their gallery, for a show, with the newspaper and television people coming in to talk to Gerry."

"Did your husband enjoy that experience?"

"Well, no. He didn't want to do any of that. So he said no. This was his private life, and it didn't feel right talking about it to the whole world."

She clicks on the track lights, illuminating the sculptures in colourful variations. They remind me of underwater plant life; I feel like I'm inside an aquarium. It really is amazing what goes on below the surface in people when they're trying to cope with life's challenges. It's easy to miss what's in front of you when you have to look to the big picture, and make decisions for people as a collective, as I must. That's the reality of power and responsibility. It's hard to see the individual for the crowd.

I may never visit Mary Walker again, but I'll never forget her, or Gerry's steel garden and what it says about appealing to something inside people that deserves as much protection as their salaries and pensions: their dreams. In these many brutal months of fighting, no one has paid much heed to dreams. It's all been dollars and cents, the endless ways in which it's possible to slice a dollar, or to pretend that a dollar isn't a dollar but two dollars, or fifty cents, all depending on what you want.

Before I know it, Mary and I are at the front door of her home.

"Mr. Pratt, I appreciate you coming out to visit me."

We shake hands, and then she closes her door behind me.

When I took the Stelco job, saving pensions was a top priority, even though I didn't know where the money would come to reduce the pension deficit. But the government—for all I disliked their approach—finally did step in with a big loan to help us out.

Canada is a civilized place where civilized things still happen as a matter of institutional course. Yet as a country, we're under intense pressure from within and beyond our borders to become, let's say, less civilized in the name of efficiency and competitiveness. I have nothing against keeping Canada prosperous—in fact, a lot more vigilance should be applied to that matter. But it's a question of approach, of understanding the practicalities of change and being mindful of the immorality of inflicting that change on people by resorting to ideologies divorced from a humane perspective. An idea is one thing, its implementation another.

I have many moments in my job when the voice of Mary and others like her recede in importance as I go about my daily business. I'm only human; I can only be in so many places at once as CEO. And while I have a responsibility to Mary, I'm not in control of many other levers that, in combination, create the safety net in Canada.

When I think of the situation in the United States—a country that always seems to arrive places before we do—I worry about what's coming for Canada. It's a real possibility now in the US, especially in the auto sector, that hundreds of billions of dollars in pension obligations may outlive the existence of the companies that assumed them. And as the logic and structures of economic globalization take deeper root on this continent, possibly divorcing wealth even further from nationality and civic responsibility, who will protect the pensioners if worse ever comes to worse? What happens when money decides that it needs to be "free"—beholden only to its owners?

There are days when I don't know whether we're on the right path in Canada. But as I consider Mary and her poised tenacity, and inside that poise, her vulnerability, I don't feel like the work I'm doing is futile. There are creative responses to a world where the cycles of change always bring about terrible uncertainties. There's Gerry's garden of steel.

CHAPTER SIX

OUT OF THE BLAST FURNACE

MEDIA MOMENT

Courtney Pratt adjusts his stance to accommodate the microphone thrust at his face. As he prepares to deliver a sound bite, the reporter prompts him: "I heard you guys went drinking with the union after the signing ceremony."

"You heard *what?*"

"Like, you all went for beers after you signed the deal."

"Is that what you heard?"

The reporter gives him a look. Pratt doesn't know if the guy is truly misinformed or trying to sucker-punch him into saying something stupid.

What would the bondholders make of that, he thinks—us drinking with the union?

"Yeah, that's what I heard."

"You heard wrong."

GREED MANAGEMENT

On Friday night, September 23, Pratt and his team take a brief moment to celebrate the deals negotiated with the government, Tricap and the union. What is about to unfold, at the twenty-month mark of this restructuring, will test everyone's endurance. This is now the battle of the bondholders, the speculators—the real players in the creditor group, who have the right to approve any plan to get the company out of CCAA. They make it plain very fast that they intend to use their leverage to get as much loot as possible out of Stelco. Their message all along has been: we're not taking the Heisman from anybody.

How to describe the task still facing the Stelco team? You run the marathon, cross the finish line, hug your mother, then someone says, do it again, now—actually, do it three times, on one leg.

These last six months are often just more of the same: a lot of legalistic manoeuvring, courtroom arguments and hotel meetings between well-compensated men and women who often complain to the media about the lofty principles at stake and the outrages being perpetrated against their financial dignity. The fact is, the creditors are still owed money in the plan now before the court, and they won't allow Stelco out of CCAA until that changes. In late September, creditors representing more than 50 per cent of the dollar value in claims indicate to Alex Morrison, the court monitor, that they will vote against the plan. Since Stelco needs the approval of two-thirds of all creditor votes to get out of CCAA, with each dollar in claims equalling one vote, it's time to go back to the drawing board. As October begins, Pratt and his advisors hold negotiations in person and on the phone with bondholder groups. They explore angles to find compromises without losing the support of the parties they have already appeased.

The restructuring has become even more complex. But does it become more interesting? Not really. It's now mostly a melodrama of greed management: if you have enough money to play the game in court for month after month, test the patience of judges and governments, then greed will have its legal due. The bondholders keep on calling the judge's bluff over whether the company will go splat if they keep asking for more. They just keep asking. And this provides the main source of the delays that require frequent extensions to Stelco's stay of bankruptcy protection, often granted with very grumpy reluctance by Justice Farley.

Greed can be entertaining drama when it's viewed through rose-coloured glasses, where the thief has the charm of George Clooney and the morals of Robin Hood. But that's not the situation here. In the Stelco story, greed is manifesting as a quasi-institutional force, a global effect as complex, omnipresent and impersonal as the weather. This is greed as the efficient outcome of financial speculators knowledgeably working the legal system to the breaking point, unshakable in their faith that their money can mutate into any form and control any situation. Of course, greed has been generally evident throughout the CCAA journey among the posse of stakeholders who wouldn't, given the option, leave crumbs on the table for anyone but themselves. That greed expanded as steel prices rose, and it hasn't shrunk again as those prices have fallen from their record highs.

Greed, as the saying goes, isn't personal—it's just business.

HURTING

In a small office adjacent to the main meeting room, Pratt steps away from Morrison and Thornton toward the doorway, to watch the crowd arriving. Upwards of three hundred people are attending the November 15 creditors meeting, held at a conference centre near the Toronto airport. He recognizes a few faces, mostly from Hamilton, mostly Stelco suppliers, including the guy who criticizes him whenever there's a reporter's microphone or tape recorder within shouting distance.

This isn't a gathering of high-finance guys in expensive suits, the types given to massaging their feet while lecturing on the globalization of money or scheduling the corporate jet for the ride home. Many are dressed casually, in windbreakers, jeans, sneakers. Many wear an awed or disoriented look, as if they're not sure what to do or what to expect. Some have come with their spouses. These are people who look like they're hurting, Pratt thinks. Hurting a lot. And they're here with the expectation of hurting less following the vote on the plan, which, if all goes well, will enable them, finally, to get paid a fair portion of what's owed them.

There's also a media contingent here, setting up laptops, doodling in notepads, yakking into cellphones. Newspapers, TV, radio. Pratt feels tense, anticipating the scrum afterward.

"I guess we have to face the music," he says, deciding it's time to get the meeting underway.

"There's no point in holding the vote," Morrison replies. Thornton shrugs in agreement.

"This is going to be very embarrassing," Pratt adds.

They've known for the past day or so that this creditors meeting will end without a vote, because the bondholders have made it very clear through their lawyers that they won't vote in favour of the current plan. Furthermore, they're not even in the room. The company has made it clear, in return, that it's not willing to make further concessions. Both sides have been playing negotiating-chicken for weeks now. But Pratt is the one who'll have to stand up before this crowd and tell them they came here for nothing.

As they wade into the crowd, Pratt is approached by an elderly man who has impaired hearing and who would like to know if a special system has been set up to accommodate him. Pratt invites the man to sit in the front row, saying they'll make arrangements for him at the next meeting.

Then he, Morrison and Thornton seat themselves behind a table on a small stage. Pratt starts to apologize into the microphone in front of him. He's aware of repeating himself, but he keeps going. He tells the crowd that the bondholders, none of whom are at the meeting, will not vote in favour of the plan as it stands. As he talks, there's a parallel stream of worry needling at him: what if this situation gets out of control?

He keeps talking, scanning the faces below him. He's still getting looks of awe and disorientation. And then it's over. He wonders how long he's been apologizing. Could be five minutes. Could be twenty.

Morrison and Thornton seem unphased, packing their briefcases. Pratt doesn't know how he feels as he walks off the stage. Numb? Exhausted? Disappointed? All of these.

Then he sees the media clustered around the guy who personalizes his attacks on Stelco, usually making reference to the CEO by name.

Add "angry" to the list of my emotions, he thinks.

CONSENSUAL?

A day later, Justice Farley tells those in court that unless a plan is approved at the next creditors meeting, scheduled for November 21, he will entertain motions for "alternative processes or proceedings." Which means what? Potentially, it means inviting other parties to submit plans to restructure Stelco. This is classic Farley brinksmanship, raising the stakes for everyone when the process slows down. The implication is that he'll entertain offers that might even extend to liquidating the company or forcing the piecemeal divestiture of Stelco's assets.

Would he actually do that? Pratt and his advisors have no idea. But before he left for a short holiday in Florida, Farley did warn them that if there was no significant progress toward a deal, he would interrupt his holiday and return home a very unpleasant person to deal with.

On November 21, however, yet another creditors meeting is adjourned without a vote: despite round-the-clock negotiating sessions, the company has yet to strike a deal with bondholder groups.

At the next creditors meeting, two days later at the same location, Farley conducts a conference call from Florida, seeking a progress report. Morrison, Thornton and the Stelco team are dialled in from a small office at the conference centre. The bondholder lawyers are calling in from offices downtown and wherever else they happen to be. In the ballroom, the ranks of creditors have thinned out. When Morrison reports to Farley that there is still no deal, the response is an unhappy judicial silence. Then the judge repeats his threat to come home early to entertain new motions for new restructuring plans, in court, on November 25.

Pratt looks at Thornton, who is rubbing his eyes, as if trying to wake from a nightmare. Farley says he'll call back in a few hours, expecting better news.

Hours more of negotiations.

Then the provincial government steps forward with more cash to sweeten the deal, and there is finally some real progress. The Province agrees to provide an additional $50-million loan to Stelco on top of its $100-million loan for the pension payment. At least now everyone agrees, more or less, on the amount of money required to keep the bondholders happy, if not the precise terms on which they'll get it. When Farley calls in for the second time, Morrison is able to say that a deal is very close, and that's there no reason the judge should come home early.

During the call, the judge seems to be having some trouble hearing, and often shouts, even when he's not mad. At one point, Thornton says, "Your Honour, may I ask where you're calling in from?"

The judge, it turns out, is standing at the payphone of a gas station on the highway, next to a restaurant where he's attending a family birthday party. No one on the call laughs or makes a joke. Pratt listens hard, and thinks he can hear vehicles whizzing past in the sonic background of the Florida phone connection.

After the call, Pratt turns to Thornton. "Does he own a cellphone?"

"I'm not sure."

Some fifteen minutes are then spent by lawyers and advisors on the question of whether Justice Farley owns or knows how to use a cellphone.

Late that evening, Stelco finally announces a "consensual" agreement with creditors on the "economic terms" of a deal.

Consensual? Economic terms?

The corporate jargon signals that the deal is woefully short on specifics at this stage and that all the negotiating parties will likely keep torturing one another for weeks on end in regard to finalizing the actual terms and conditions.

Consensual—but by no means final.

As the November 30 creditor vote approaches, the consensual agreement falls apart. On that day, the company requests that the court monitor delay the creditor vote until December 2. This request is soon amended to December 9, because new investors have suddenly surfaced—investors who change things dramatically. An entirely new deal now begins to take shape for the Stelco board to consider, featuring the equity participation of two more hedge funds, now joining the mix with Tricap: the Canadian-based Sunrise Partners and the US firm Appaloosa Management.

Where did these guys come from? And why didn't they surface earlier?

The simplest answer is that conditions are now right for these hedge funds to make a bet on Stelco. The government has stepped in to financially backstop the company and help reduce the pension deficit, and the threat of union strife has gone away. As an investment opportunity, Stelco now falls within the risk profile of many more funds. As a result—and suddenly—hundreds of millions of dollars are available. In this instance, two new investors agree to make an equal contribution of $137.5 million, to give them each 26.4 per cent ownership of the post-CCAA company, while Tricap would retain 35.2 per cent. The new cash will go to the bondholders.

The board approves the new plan, which should seal the deal—but doesn't.

A lawyer for a bondholder group announces to the media that the latest version of the deal lacks the flexibility that his clients require so that they can choose either stock or cash compensation: his clients will reject the deal and present an alternative.

There are more negotiations.

On December 8, the company announces yet another revised plan, amended to give bondholders the right to take new Stelco shares and cash in any combination they like. In this scenario, the triumvirate of Tricap, Sunrise and Appaloosa, will still maintain a strong ownership majority, the exact percentage depending on the subscription to the new shares by the bondholders. As part of the new deal, upon exit from CCAA, the current board will be replaced by one selected by the new owners.

The bondholders are still not satisfied—apparently crumbs remain on the table. On December 9, the day on which the creditor vote is now scheduled, negotiations, which ended late the previous evening, start again before the sun comes up. On that morning, Pratt leaves home for the airport conference centre knowing two things: the first is that there's still no deal; the second is that his team is committed—with the full support of the judge—to holding the vote today, come hell or high water.

By now, the lawyers for the bondholders have also made their base out at the conference centre. Negotiations continue all day. As close as they are to agreement, there are, somewhere, crumbs not accounted for. Finally, the Ontario government steps forward again, ceding to bondholders half the share warrants it had gained in the deal it negotiated with the company. The last crumbs are allocated.

The vote is taken in the early evening, and this last deal is approved.

The company can now proceed to the next stage: the sanction hearing, where the judge will pronounce on the fairness of the deals negotiated and determine whether the company is allowed to exit CCAA.

The next day, Pratt is quoted in the Hamilton newspaper: "We can all start thinking about the future . . . we have some very ambitious plans for Stelco."

When Pratt reads himself in print, he feels genuinely optimistic: we've held it together, he thinks, but can we keep it together?

THE COMING OF WINTER

A week or so after the restructuring plan is approved by creditors, Pratt gets a call from a managing partner at Tricap, asking for a private meeting. Pratt has worked closely with this man in recent months and respects him. They get together after work at a hotel bar in Oakville. Pratt is under the impression that the purpose of the meeting is to review a list of candidates being considered for the new Stelco board. It's not. He's being fired.

The Tricap guy is clearly troubled by the assignment of breaking the news. It's all handled respectfully. Pratt has been in this position himself, and knows the routine, but this knowledge doesn't make it any easier to be on the receiving end.

It turns out the new owners don't want to get rid of him entirely: they want him to stay on as CEO until the end of the CCAA process, and then to become chairman of the new board. The message the Tricap partner delivers is that Pratt will make an ideal chairman, if he wants the assignment. But the new owners definitely want someone else to lead the operational turnaround. This stings him, bad. He thinks he's done as good a job as possible in managing the company through a very turbulent period.

When he gets back in his car, he drives around for a while, merging carefully when he shifts lanes. He feels like the last kid cut from the hockey team, after the last tryout, just when he thinks he has made the team and his future career in the NHL is a sure thing.

He lets the rationalizations flow.

It's often the case that, following a restructuring or merger, the CEO is shown the door so the new owners can bring in their own guy. Why should I be an exception?

It's also true that there are different CEOs for different situations. When the board hired him, they needed someone who could manage the conflicts—the difficult "people" issues—of a CCAA process.

That's me.

So now you want a real operator? A turnaround guy?

Do you know who you're losing here?

When he gets home, he climbs out of the car into the December night, so crisp and Canadian, the coming of winter in the air.

He just stands there and breathes deeply, inhaling darkness and wondering where all the years have gone. Was it all just bad coffee in dawn meetings, rubber chicken at a thousand company dinners, weeks and months lost between airplane connections and operational reviews, a million memos hidden in the part of the brain that stores things we no longer need?

This isn't self-pity. It's genuine wonder. He feels like an amnesiac as he asks himself, what have I achieved in my career?

His thoughts turn irrational: I was fired, he thinks, for doing the right thing. How ironic. They fire the guy who gives a damn about people, who wants to treat people fairly no matter how much ugliness they shovel at him. As if being nice means I'm not tough or smart enough to turn Stelco around. Do they know who they're losing?

He poses that question to himself this time, and doesn't want the answer. Not tonight, anyway.

He feels useless. And used up. Exhausted.
Like we all feel, he thinks, some days.

NEW HORIZONS

"Oh, we're not going to buy anything, you know," Alexa says to her son Steve and daughter-in-law Lisa on the morning of New Year's Eve, as she and her husband put on their raincoats.

The Pratts are in the last days of their holiday visit to Vancouver, and the real estate agent is parked outside in the pouring rain.

"How many places are we seeing?" Pratt asks once they're outside.

"Four or five. Just to get a feel."

The second listing is a townhouse, a block up from Kitsilano Beach. When they go inside, Pratt leads the way upstairs and steps out onto the deck. Even in the heavy rain, there are magnificent views across English Bay all the way to the horizon.

As rain drips from his face, he thinks, why not?

Why not now?

DIVIDE AND CONQUER

On January 9, the company announces that the new major shareholders have decided to replace Pratt as CEO upon Stelco's exit from CCAA, and to appoint Pratt as the new chairman. The company also announces that the sanction hearing will be held January 17.

And things start to unravel again.

On January 13, the court monitor reports a weakening stitch in the financing deal with Tricap for a $375-million loan. Tricap is now insisting that Stelco, before exiting CCAA, be reorganized into nine separate companies. The strategy is to slot the company's remaining assets and operations into different corporate boxes, potentially making them all easier to sell should it ever come to that. The Hamilton and Lake Erie mills would become separate companies, despite their operational interdependence. There would be new companies for Stelco's real estate assets, its mining operations and its ventures in energy production—into cogeneration, which involves the recycling of steel-mill exhaust gases to create electrical power, and a wind-power startup to be situated on the shores of Lake Erie. This Tricap-proposed reorganization also has financial implications, potentially involving a reallocation of pension plan assets and liabilities.

Some voices in the union and the media see an ulterior motive here: the hiving off of the aging Hamilton mill from the modern Lake Erie mill. Company officials deny that this is, in itself, the intent.

As a consequence of this development, the sanction meeting is postponed until January 19. On that day, in court, the company's lawyers request that Justice Farley sanction the plan. He declines, expressing his disappointment at the extreme lawyering going on and over the lack of detailed financing agreements between the parties. He says he won't sanction a deal unless he's more certain it can actually be implemented.

A day later, Morrison reports to the court that Tricap and the company are still trying to formalize their terms of agreement on financing and on the proposed corporate reorganization. The court monitor states his optimism that the transactions contemplated can be implemented.

A day after that, January 21, Farley, after receiving the detailed financing agreements, finally sanctions the plan, even though negotiations between the company and Tricap on the corporate reorganization continue and remain to be approved by the court. A hearing on that issue is scheduled for February 14.

On February 14, Farley announces that he will retire from the bench, the announcement a Valentine's Day gift to his wife, who apparently hasn't seen enough of her husband in recent years, between the Stelco restructuring and the Air Canada proceeding before that. The retirement plan is intended to take effect once Stelco exits CCAA.

Farley also approves the corporate reorganization of Stelco into nine separate companies.

A BAD SMELL

From the February 15, 2006, edition of the *Globe and Mail:*

> There really weren't any skunks in Mr. Justice Farley's courtroom at the Stelco hearing last Friday. That's the truth, the whole truth, and nothing but the truth.

> The pungent odour wafting around the room didn't come from any counsel, either, although Judge Farley appeared to think some of the lawyers' arguments stank.
>
> There was, however, genuine eau de skunk, courtesy of one Stelco employee who was sprayed Friday morning and couldn't quite get rid of all the offending residue. The aroma sent one reporter scurrying off the spectator benches and to the back of the room.

ACTUARIAL ASSESSMENT

In March 2006, Farley orders those still at the negotiating table, or their lawyers, into his chambers because he's angry with their failure to get the restructuring deals finalized.

It's him against a crowd of twenty or so, and he glares at them all from behind his desk, his arms folded across his chest.

"Well," he says belligerently.

Lawyers cringe and slump.

One of them finally gets the ball rolling, and soon enough there are progress reports being made. Farley is sharp with everyone.

When someone mentions the need for an actuarial assessment on a pension matter, Farley cuts him off by saying that if another actuary is brought in right now, this actuary shall and will be thrown through the nearest window. Bob Thornton breaks the silence. "With all due respect, Your

Honour, don't you think that would be a waste of good glass?"

Farley tries not to laugh but soon joins in as the room goes nuts.

ENDGAME

In the final months of the restructuring, the Stelco board practically functions as a call centre in corporate governance, evaluating the deal through the perpetual changes arising from never-ending negotiations. Meanwhile, Stelco is finalizing asset sales to raise additional money, like a jetliner dumping fuel before an emergency landing. There are problems to the very end.

Even as Justice Farley is evaluating the final restructuring plan, lawyers for various shareholders are making courtroom arguments to prevent Stelco's exit from CCAA, saying that they're being treated unfairly and that other alternatives should be explored. Where have they been for two years? They argue as if the company hasn't explored alternatives, which have all failed except the plan the judge will eventually sanction in which shareholders lose everything. Shareholders get treated badly, yes. But unfairly? They're treated in accordance with their rights within CCAA, legally at the bottom of the list to be repaid in a court-supervised restructuring.

By the end of it, the bondholders, who at first moaned loud and long about accepting equity in Stelco, and demanding only cash, are jumping over one another to subscribe to a new pool of common shares.

THIS RESTRUCTURING IS "OVV-AH"

On March 13, Rodney Mott, an American steel industry turnaround veteran, is appointed CEO of Stelco, effective upon the company's emergence from CCAA on March 31, 2006. On March 22, the court monitor reports that the parties who still haven't struck a deal are working diligently toward one.

On March 24, Pratt advises his wife that the fat lady has not yet sung. Alexa Pratt, being familiar with sports lore, understands immediately that the Stelco deal really will not be done until the last possible minute, perhaps a second before the stroke of midnight on March 31, 2006.

On March 31, 2006, the company emerges from CCAA.

This is Courtney Pratt's last day as CEO of Stelco.

OUT OF THE BLAST FURNACE

In his final week on the job, Pratt started ferrying his personal effects home in legal-sized boxes. But on this, his last day at Stelco, he finds himself pausing to look at what's left in the office of the memos, newspaper clippings and photographs acquired during his stint as CEO. Memories of the past two years come and go. Sometimes he just stands there, looking out his office window toward the mill, the flames shooting into the sky that draw his gaze toward the blast furnace operation.

The door to his office remains open as the packing continues. Now and then a colleague drops in for goodbyes, which are hard on Pratt, the exchanges accompanied by handshakes and a few hugs, a joke or two if appropriate, a promise to stay in touch or get together for a round of golf when the weather really turns good.

Pratt gets the sense that for the people left behind, there will soon be a terrible letdown as the stress and excitement—and media attention, too—ebb away completely and the reality of turning Stelco around sets in. The new CEO has served notice even before officially starting that Stelco needs to become a lot more competitive, and needs to do it fast.

In his conversations of late with Colin Osborne, Pratt has heard things that make him wish the situation at Stelco had turned out differently for himself. He knows that if he'd stayed on as CEO, Osborne, who proved himself capable and loyal not just to Pratt but to making the company more successful, would have had a very good shot at running the company one day. But that's not likely to happen now. Stelco has been put on a turnaround trajectory by turnaround people, the basic idea being to get the company in good enough operational shape to flip it—at a profit—to a real steel company operator, not another interim steward, which is what the collection of new investors is. Osborne is showing every sign of wanting to get out now.

As Pratt thinks about Osborne's likely departure, he feels bad. It'll be a big loss for Stelco should he leave (which will happen, in fact, within a month), but this is what often happens today even in the most stable, profitable companies. Osborne, he knows, has a bright future but is learning the hard way that there's no guarantee of continuity as an executive, no matter how good you think you are or could be.

There's always a counter-argument in the wings, a perspective contrary to your own, and someone else to sit in your desk and manage your people when you walk out the door. This is a lesson Pratt himself has learned, and is still learning.

He leaves the office late in the afternoon, emerging into bright sunlight at four o'clock, and once he's loaded the car and starts driving away from the mill, he doesn't look back.

Alexa reaches him on the Blackberry and gently directs the conversation toward their upcoming trip to Vancouver, where she's looking forward to their first days in the new townhouse. They plan to divide their time between Vancouver and Toronto now that Pratt has left Stelco, his goal being to adopt a semi-retired lifestyle—sit on a few boards, help out a few non-profits, and stay away from hardcore CEO jobs.

"Just think, Courtney, how nice this is going to be—for once, we'll have time for ourselves, the kids. Their kids."

"Yeah, it'll be great," he says, conscious of reaching out to her through his glumness. "No Stelco on my back. For once."

She waits for him.

"I just feel a little empty, Alexa."

"Well, I don't," she says brightly. "Think about all the things we have to look forward to."

"Yes, and more grandkids on the way. How lucky we are!" A few weeks ago they got a call from their younger son, Brian, in Ottawa, to tell them that his wife, Kerri-Lynn, was pregnant.

"What time will you be home?" she asks now.

"Soon."

EPILOGUE

IN THE GARDEN

AUGUST 2007

"Hi."

I hear Cedar's little voice behind me, calling me away from the BlackBerry. We're on the deck of our rented cottage on Pender Island, one of the Gulf Islands off the coast of British Columbia. It's just the two of us awake, an hour past dawn, a cloudless day in the works.

Alexa and I are on vacation with Steve, Lisa, four-year-old Cedar and Dawson, who is nearly two now.

"Hello back to you, little one," I say, opening my arms. She wipes sleep from her eyes as she tiptoes toward me.

Cedar snuggles against me as we watch the tide going out, just like we watched it coming in last night after she was ready for bed. I could watch the tide all day, secure in the knowledge that the cycle will repeat for as long as I keep watching.

Stelco, too, is going through another cycle in its long corporate lifespan, after being reclaimed from near death. Its rebirth, however, isn't in a form that an economic nationalist would like much, given that eighteen months after leaving CCAA the company is about to be sold to interests outside the country.

It's tranquil on the Pacific shore, hardly a breeze, the air resonant with the bounty that draws everyone to the ocean: fresh air, the pleasingly acrid smell of sand and seaweed drying on the beach as the tide retreats. There are horizon views, and sea birds wheeling, and calm everywhere but in my head.

This has turned into a working vacation. As the chairman of Stelco, I sit on a board committee that has been reviewing the proposals we've solicited in recent months from buyers interested in acquiring Stelco. Our so-called auction process has narrowed to two bidders, and we've set a deadline, fast approaching, for receiving their final bids. In a few days from now, in fact, there will be an announcement that Stelco has been acquired by U. S. Steel, an American company that has emerged in recent years as a sizable international competitor, mainly through acquisitions.

"I want to go to the beach, now," Cedar says definitively.

"Okay." I look around for her sandals and don't find them.

What the heck—kids need to walk barefoot, don't they?

And so off we go, the two of us barefoot, Cedar running ahead, my eyes trained on her, but a fair portion of my mind already gearing up for the wave of e-mails and phone calls coming today.

No matter how far I get from Stelco, it keeps stalking me.

The glory of Pender Island is the sweet illusion it nurtures that living in nature is utopia. It's late afternoon, the sunlight streaming through the trees, the ocean rippling in a warm breeze. I'm following Alexa on a hike along a coastal trail—nothing strenuous, just some time for us to be alone after spending most of the day in the noisy embrace of our grandkids. I'm never happier than in these wordless moments when Alexa and I are together.

"You'll walk off a cliff using that thing," Alexa said as we were leaving the cottage and she saw me clipping the BlackBerry to my belt. So I left it behind, assuring myself that the integrity of corporate governance, at Stelco, could withstand a moment or two without the chairman on call.

We come out on a ledge, a natural resting point. It's hard to describe how I feel as we take in the views.

Stelco really is so far away now. Rodney Mott is leading the negotiations with the two remaining bidders. He's been down this road before, very successfully. I'm involved in an oversight role—evaluating the deals, not making them any more. This time the deal that wins must preserve what we laboured so hard to get during CCAA, including the pension agreement with the government that ensures Stelco pensioners are looked after no matter who owns the company.

"Look at that," Alexa says, pointing at sky around the bend.

I look up. Whatever it is is gone.

She gives me a look. "There's a BlackBerry in your head."

"What was it?"

"A bald eagle."
"Ah."

Although this book was written from a CEO's perspective, it wasn't written for CEOs, although I hope some will read it.

Our ideal reader is anyone who has struggled with the ethical challenges that are at the heart of so much organizational conflict. And that means just about anybody who's held down a job—in a company, the government, a volunteer group or, of course, the home.

My CCAA experience with Stelco was a test in conscience, the toughest I've endured in my career. Often enough, I felt caught in the viselike grip of irreconcilable differences. Sometimes doing the right thing felt wrong. Other times the complexity of the situation led us down paths we would come to question, like the point at which we elected activist shareholders to our board.

Could we have done things differently?

I believe I have a reasonably healthy capacity for self-criticism. One need not always weep long into the night over every little failure in life or on the job. But you don't forge a strong conscience without admitting your mistakes or questioning yourself hard. Did we underestimate the risks and the costs of stakeholder conflict at the beginning? Yes. Did we make other mistakes? Did I? Absolutely. This book details many of them. I'm sure some readers will have a long list of my omissions.

Truthfully, all too often during our CCAA journey I came

up against the limits of my capacity as a CEO and also as a human being.

At the beginning of my tenure as CEO, I was committed to developing a relationship with union leaders based on principles of mutual trust and cooperation. I wanted a partnership, and I considered this a priority. But, despite my extensive previous experience and indeed my successes in labour relations, I misjudged the situation. And so, when our board approved a decision to go into CCAA, I could not legally take the unions into our confidence in advance—because I had a fiduciary responsibility, a legal obligation, to disclose material changes happening in the business to all stakeholders at the same time. The unions felt blindsided and betrayed. I never heard the end of their complaints on that matter. And thus we got off on the wrong foot.

Could I have done otherwise? Not with respect to disclosure. But perhaps the error here was in creating the expectation for trust, or doing so prematurely, when the laws of disclosure would undermine my goal. Maybe I should have waited longer to offer the olive branch on behalf of the company, after letting the shock of CCAA settle in. Or perhaps, as the CEO who was leading the CCAA charge, I was always going to be the wrong guy to even mention the word "trust" to Stelco's unions. Regardless, I don't savour the conclusion that thousands of Stelco employees and pensioners have been ill served over a generation or more by a complete lack of trust between them and management.

Let me immodestly suggest that some of my limitations were actually strengths. All too often there was an explicit invitation—often tempting—to "mudwrestle" with my "opponents" in the media spotlight. I was viewed as "too nice" to get down and dirty in the public sphere. My commitment to avoid ruining reputations and making attacks personal may have cost us points in some battles of perception in the media. But now? After the fact? I find nothing to regret. We got to the finish line, the deals were done, end of story. I don't hide in the shadows when approached by anyone who was involved in our CCAA battles. And that's a meaningful result for me, given what we went through.

Potentially, a CCAA restructuring can go on forever, like a hockey game in sudden-death overtime. If the opposing team refuses to concede a goal, you can play forever. On many days, that's what it felt like—a battle with no end in sight, no one ready to concede, no matter how late in the game. If there's one hero in my Stelco CCAA story, it's the determined judge who was at the centre of the maelstrom from start to finish. As I understand it, Justice Farley used every technique in his judicial book, and probably invented others, to bring our CCAA process to closure with Stelco intact. I'm grateful for his skill and determination in keeping us alive.

As I share these reflections, I'm anchored by the belief that protecting your moral imagination—the ability to empathize with the people whose lives you affect by your decisions—begins with knowing yourself. You can't have a productive conversation with a real Mary Walker or a real Rico Esposito—two extremes in outlook—if you lack a strong sense of who you are. Otherwise, you'll never find an ethical route to decisions that affect them both. It's far too easy to empathize with Mary's plight in isolation. That's a no-brainer. It's a lot tougher when you have to balance your empathy for her with the reality of Rico's influence in ponying up the cash for Mary's pension. The money has to come from somewhere, and sometimes that somewhere is an ugly place. Conversely, it is relatively easy to fall for Rico's logic and reduce Mary to a variable in an actuarial statement, a blip in the expense line, something less than human.

As I see it, we all stand somewhere on an ethical ladder. We can climb higher or fall lower on that ladder, sometimes without knowing it, which is a scary proposition to me. But if you can describe your own ethical ladder, I believe you can make a proper deal with yourself on where to stand. Somehow, those who know where they stand end up standing ethically higher.

My Stelco experience also opened up perspectives on the interdependency of—the porous border between—family and work life. Why do we, as a culture, still largely act as if these are separate ethical domains? Many of us know someone who's a generous soul on the job but a ruthless bastard at home, and vice versa. I don't understand that personality split. Somewhere along the way, a lie is being played out at someone's expense. This strain of ethical selectivity is compromising, a marker for untrustworthiness. Boundaries should be respected between family and the workplace, but our actions in both spheres need to be consistent. We can't turn off our integrity the minute we leave the house in the morning. Neither should we turn it on the minute we walk into the embrace of our spouses or children. We can't live by shoving our values into silos, although in corporate life this often happens. If you've ever seen an organization chart, you know that managers love to sequester their people in functional boxes and label them as finance people, lawyers, spin doctors, engineers, human resource experts. And then we're surprised when people act like they live in boxes.

Don't misunderstand me: Stelco's ability to emerge from CCAA depended on the application of specialized skills to difficult problems. As the CEO of Stelco, I was expected to make sure our boxes functioned as more than the sum of their parts. But during the darkest hours of the restructuring, all too often I was asked to check my morality at the door by folks who didn't give a damn how many people we fired as long as the numbers added up to a more profitable company. The pressure was intense to visualize the Stelco workforce as a massing of numbers on a spreadsheet, not individuals connected to families, connected to communities.

As we near the end of my Stelco story, let me come back to what Larry Gaudet and I have implied throughout this book: in a world of globalizing economies and exceptionally mobile money, which has abetted the consolidation of the steel industry into planet-striding conglomerates, the Stelcos of the world are destined to be acquired—unless there's a meaningful shift in our industrial strategy as a country.

Should our governments intervene with new restrictions on foreign ownership? Or create economic development strategies that define a more patriotic linkage between Canadian corporate ownership and national prosperity? In theory, I'm all for that. But let's not be naive: while every country has—or should have—strategies to support the home team, the forces of globalization put an enormous strain on us, especially to open up our economy to foreign investors. Arguably, Canada has not stood up for the home team as much as some of our trading partners have, including our neighbours to the south.

I would also say that in Canada we're often guilty of affixing blame for the loss of Canadian control in any sensitive industrial sector as a consequence of an evil "them" from outside our borders. We have lost opportunities for made-in-Canada solutions when some of our leading companies have been sold to foreign buyers, especially in the resource sector. But let's forget about them for a minute and focus on "us" here. As Canadian businesses and governments, but also as Canadian consumers, we involve ourselves daily in changing the balance of power in economic affairs between nations and corporations, usually in favour of the latter, which, as we've all seen, are a force capable of acting much more flexibly and invasively across borders than ever before.

Canada, which has long been a trading nation dependent economically on exports, has thrived on internationalizing its commercial influence, particularly in the US. We have done so as the proverbial hewers of wood, and still we fester in national debates about why we can't invest more in research to create innovative products with our resources, instead of selling them as commodities. Leaving that significant challenge aside, let's admit that our companies clamour for more open markets, fairer competition and new growth opportunities in countries much larger than our own.

As consumers, too, we have come to enjoy the lower prices gained from global manufacturers with factories situated in developing countries where wages are so much lower than Canadian standards. Are we prepared to give up the luxury of some of those lower prices, in a sense, to subsidize our own economic security and invest more strategically in Canadian companies, Canadian workers, Canadian products?

That remains to be seen, but I don't think we're ready to make that sacrifice.

As our companies large and small keep going global—expanding outside Canada or buying their way into new markets—let's remember that it's a world of reciprocity and interdependence. If we restrict access to our markets, don't be surprised if this is done to us in retaliation. Let's also recognize, more importantly, that Canada is a small player in the global scheme, our economy vulnerable in a way that of the US, for example, is not. But is that really true? Talk to American leaders concerned about the trade deficit with China, which is still growing by billions of dollars every year: they would say that size has nothing to do with vulnerability, not in the world we live in today.

I'm not an economist. I'm neither pro- nor anti-globalization as a matter of ideological principle or because of a sabbatical taken in a think tank or policy institute. I've spent much of my career on the corporate front lines and have seen first-hand the benefits for everyone when businesses large and small flourish in the mainstream of civilized societies. My experience at Stelco leads me to believe that before we go running off at the mouth about foreign invaders and our government's failure to protect our companies from them, we should get our domestic act together in the companies we still own—if we still want to own them.

This book isn't offered as a primer for Corporate Competitiveness 101. But Stelco is an unfortunate case study in the failure of corporate managers, governments and unionized labour to work together to respond to the warning signs that led the company into CCAA in the first place. How could it happen—in a progressive, successful country like Canada—that a steel company with such a proud tradition, and with responsibilities to thousands of employees and pensioners, was allowed to run up a $1.3-billion pension deficit while also managing to become so uncompetitive that its survival was on the line?

No one in this story walks away from that question blameless.

The big boat opens its belly, an industrial whale of a thing, welcoming us into its gloomy depths. We're in the lead car, Alexa and I, with Steve and Lisa and the kids in the van behind us, boarding the ferry to Vancouver after our holiday.

As we rumble off the ramp onto the lower deck and into diesel fumes and the sound of roaring engines, there are guys walking around in orange safety vests and hard hats. I feel right at home. I love this stuff, the big boat, the steel of a massive hull carrying tonnes more steel across deep water, a full boat of trucks and cars. I miss being at the helm of an industrial enterprise. Will I ever do it again?

"Let's go upstairs, on deck," Alexa says, opening the car door, suspiciously eyeing the BlackBerry in my hands.

"I just need to get a few e-mails in. The deal's getting close."

She cuts me some slack.

The Stelco story, for us, is nearly over—really over, this time.

In the days that followed my firing, the anger and disappointment often leapt into my thoughts. But I took a curious pleasure in denying the hurt. I held my head up around my family and friends, my colleagues at work. I didn't pretend that nothing had happened. Neither did I take perverse pride in appearing brave, no matter how many arrows in my side. Sometimes, when you're hurt, you need to lie low, and focus on what truly gives meaning to life.

The BlackBerry isn't working below deck. No big deal.

I leave the car and walk up a stairwell to the passenger deck, then into the lounge, looking for my family, and when I see them, I enter a garden of my own—not of steel, but nonetheless made of something very strong, constructed by the people I love.

ACKNOWLEDGEMENTS

This book is the result of a collaboration between the co-authors that has proven to be a very rewarding experience for us both. In writing this book together, we built a friendship.

We would like to acknowledge:

At Random House Canada, Anne Collins encouraged us and elevated the manuscript at every turn with her uncanny editorial wisdom and collaborative genius. Brad Martin seized the moment and made it obvious to us where the book should be published. Kylie Barker provided high-energy coordination. Thanks also to Scott Richardson, the designer, and Pamela Murray, RHC's estimable managing editor. Stephanie Fysh did a superb job on the copyedit.

At Westwood Creative Artists (WCA), Bruce Westwood provided his invaluable perspective and enthusiastic support, qualities that make it such a pleasure to work with him and his agency. Thanks also to Ashton Westwood and Carolyn Forde for their assistance. Larry would also like to thank Natasha Daneman at WCA and Lesley Horlick at Random House Canada for their ongoing support and counsel.

Helen Reeves, a long-time collaborator and close friend of both co-authors, deserves special thanks for her support. Special thanks as well to Anna Porter, who was very helpful during this project's incubation.

We'd like to thank those we interviewed for the book and who agreed to be characters in the text, including Mike Barrack, Alex Morrison, Colin Osborne, Helen Reeves, Bob Thornton and Steve Shamie.

Finally, we'd like to acknowledge the Stelco employees and pensioners whose dedication and endurance provided the inspiration to write this book in the way that we did.